Inspiring Generational Leadership

Inspiring Generational Leadership takes the reader on a journey that reveals how simple it is for an organization, regardless of size, to embody the indispensable values of the conscious capitalism movement. DeLinda's writing style and interviews with fellow conscious leaders makes the journey even more enjoyable. She reminds us of the value of dreams; maybe none of us can make the world better, but all of us doing our part can make a significant impact for future generations.

—**John Mackey,** Co-CEO, Whole Foods Market
& author of *Conscious Capitalism*

DeLinda Forsythe is a leader who appreciates the value of people. I love how she utilized the book *Raving Fans* to transform ICE into an employee-centric organization that serves both customers and community. As more leaders share their success stories of leading with compassion and abundance, we'll see a shift toward application of the tenets of conscious capitalism as well as the philosophies of servant leadership, which we teach and live by at The Ken Blanchard Companies.

—**Ken Blanchard,** coauthor of *The One Minute Manager,*
Servant Leadership in Action, and *Raving Fans*

Deliberately setting out to change and lift up our future leaders is the platform for DeLinda's new book, *Inspiring Generational Leadership: Your Guide to Design a Conscious Culture.* This compilation of truly rare insights provides the roadmap to accomplish sustainable change. As the CEO of Innovative Commercial Environments (ICE), DeLinda has consistently shattered every glass ceiling for both women and men and is generously sharing her many years of expertise to transform business and encourage a positive and inclusive capitalism construct in America. This book will benefit generations to come and serve as a map to uncover pragmatic techniques to achieve success.

—**Saundra Pelletier,** CEO & President, Evofem Biosciences

I am pleased to write an endorsement for DeLinda's book, *Inspiring Generational Leadership: Your Guide to Design a Conscious Culture*. I have known DeLinda for many years through our mutual involvement in the San Diego business community. She has always exemplified leadership that encourages unity and involvement. When she reached out to interview me for her book, I did not hesitate. I knew DeLinda would represent my story as well as San Diego's story with integrity and would properly interpret San Diego's spirit of connectedness. I thoroughly enjoyed being part of the message in DeLinda's book that a "raising tide lifts all boats" through the free enterprise system. This is an attainable and important mission that soundly resonated with me.

—**Stath Karras,** Executive Director Burnham Moores Center for Real Estate University of San Diego

Collaborating with DeLinda for the last several years, I've come to know her and her heart well. She has a passion to elevate and advocate for those who our society has marginalized and for millennials—our next gen leaders. DeLinda's heart—and her fierce commitment to being a catalyst for change, opportunity maker and mentor—is why she is such an effective leader. *Inspiring Generational Leadership* is a compelling compendium of her story as ICE (Innovative Commercial Environments) CEO. Also compelling are the stories she's included of other conscious capitalists, and of the research that backs up the wisdom she shares.

—**Patricia Zigarmi,** Founder and Author, The Ken Blanchard Companies

As the CEO for CCI, I've gotten to know DeLinda quite well; she is a joyful, purpose-driven leader on an uncompromising mission to expand the perspectives of leaders today and into the future. I think you will be inspired by the story of ICE and the interviews with other conscious leaders sprinkled throughout her book, *Inspiring Generational Leadership: Your Guide to Design a Conscious Culture*. Perhaps her positive story of hope will encourage you to join us in our noble quest to elevate humanity through business!

—**Alexander McCobin,** CEO, Conscious Capitalism, Inc.

As a leader myself in the conscious capitalism movement and the author of a children's book teaching the fundamentals of conscious capitalism, it's been my pleasure to get to know and to collaborate with DeLinda. She is a catalyst for inspiration in the San Diego business community because of her passion for people and her unyielding desire to make the world a little brighter. You are going to love her book *Inspiring Generational Leadership: Your Guide to Design a Conscious Culture*, and I hope it fires you up to join us in this awe-inspiring and achievable mission to be beacons of light, change, and joy!

—**Laura Hall,** author of *The ABCs of Conscious Capitalism for KIDs* and Co-Founder of WHYZ Partners

Serving as CEO since 1997 of WD-40 Company has fundamentally enlightened my leadership style. My efforts seeking continuous self-improvement encourages others to seek to reach their potential, their aspirations. This desire to elevate each other is woven throughout the core fibers of WD-40 Company, creating positive lasting memories! The number one responsibility of WD-40's tribal leaders is to be a learner and a teacher. DeLinda is in complete alignment with our leadership principles; she has captured the inimitable potential mentorship offers in her book *Inspiring Generational Leadership*. When leaders generously share their learning, time and patience, it can propel any size company into a best-in-class organization.

—**Garry Ridge,** CEO & Chairman WD-40 Company and Co-Author *Helping People Win at Work*

Why would an office furniture company invest in regional economic development? Because DeLinda Forsythe *walks the talk* she shares in *Inspiring Generational Leadership*. As CEO of ICE, DeLinda has been highly engaged in the implementation of our inclusive economic development strategy, recognizing that adopting DEI principles mitigates skilled talent shortages. As a champion of Advancing San Diego, a program designed to develop local talent via paid internships, DeLinda embodies EDC's core values of collaboration, inclusion, and integrity. By framing constructive criticism as *coaching*, she bridges the gap in engaging millennial talent.

—**Lauree Sahba,** COO, San Diego Regional Economic Development Corporation

INSPIRING
GENERATIONAL
LEADERSHIP

YOUR
GUIDE
TO DESIGN A
CONSCIOUS CULTURE

DeLinda Forsythe

NEW YORK

LONDON • NASHVILLE • MELBOURNE • VANCOUVER

INSPIRING **GENERATIONAL** LEADERSHIP

Your Guide to Design a Conscious Culture

Published in New York, New York, by Morgan James Publishing. Morgan James is a trademark of Morgan James, LLC. www.MorganJamesPublishing.com

Proudly distributed by Ingram Publisher Services.

Every attempt has been made to source all quotes properly.

A **FREE** ebook edition is available for you or a friend with the purchase of this print book.

_____

CLEARLY SIGN YOUR NAME ABOVE

Instructions to claim your free ebook edition:
1. Visit MorganJamesBOGO.com
2. Sign your name CLEARLY in the space above
3. Complete the form and submit a photo of this entire page
4. You or your friend can download the ebook to your preferred device

ISBN 9781631956218 paperback
ISBN 9781631956225 ebook
Library of Congress Control Number:
2021937373

Cover and Interior Design by:
Chris Treccani
www.3dogcreative.net

Edited by:
Tyler Tichelaar
Superior Book Productions

Writing/Publishing Coach:
Christine Gail
www.ChristineGail.com

Logo Design by:
Jeannie Ma, Pilcro Studio

Author Photo by:
Brooke Preece

Morgan James is a proud partner of Habitat for Humanity Peninsula and Greater Williamsburg. Partners in building since 2006.

Get involved today! Visit MorganJamesPublishing.com/giving-back

To my husband Tom Forsythe, for believing in me when I did not.
You are the most trustworthy person I've ever known, and
I am a better, more patient person because of you.

To my children and grandchildren—you are the future and
the reason I write and teach.

CONTENTS

Acknowledgments   xiii

Foreword   xv

Introduction   xix

Chapter 1   Conscious Capitalism, Millennials, and an
             Evolving Perspective   1

Chapter 2   Begin with the End in Mind: Mentorship   23

Chapter 3   A Culture of Gratitude Bonds Our Humanity   65

Chapter 4   Embrace Workplace Family   83

Chapter 5   Staff Meetings Build a Collective Mindset   105

Chapter 6   Deliver Excellence: We Are What We Repeatedly Do!   133

Chapter 7   The Higher Purpose Journey   151

Chapter 8   Create Raving Fans   171

Chapter 9   Vulnerability in the Workplace   185

Chapter 10   Doing Well and Doing Good
             Need Not and Should Not Be Mutually Exclusive   201

Chapter 11   Become an Authentically Magnetic Leader!   225

Chapter 12   Fostering Community   237

Chapter 13   Begin with the End in Mind: Succession Planning   247

Conclusion   265

A Final Note   267

Additional Resources   271

About the Author   273

Endnotes   275

ACKNOWLEDGMENTS

Thank you, Alysse Cooper, for being the person you are and inspiring portions of this book. Thank you to my coworkers—it's been a privilege leading you. And thank you to the readers of this book—if this book inspires even one person to become a more inspirational and empathetic leader, it was worth the effort.

**Thank you to my writing and publishing coach, Christine Gail;
without your guidance, this book would have been
a wholly different challenge!**

**Thank you to the business associates who allowed me to interview
them for this book:**
Greg Horowitt
Saundra Pelletier
Dan Ryan
Tiffany English
Stath Karras
Steve Rosetta
Ron Hill
Shane Jackson
Maria Martinico

Thank you to the leaders in business who came before me and informed my work:
John Mackey, CEO Whole Foods and
Co-Founder of Conscious Capitalism
Raj Sisodia, Co-Founder of Conscious Capitalism
Garry Ridge
Stephen Covey
Riane Eisler
Alan Murray
Deloitte Consulting
Simon Sinek
Ken Blanchard
Malin Burnham
Joel Osteen
Sir Richard Branson
Brené Brown
Margie Warrell
Rebecca Henderson
Rick Warren
Jim and Don Clifton, Gallup
Yitzi Weiner, Authority Magazine
Forbes
Inc. Magazine

Thank you to the friends who encouraged me and were part of this journey:
Pat Zigarmi
Lee Wills
Rashmi Char
Laura Hall

FOREWORD

I've known and collaborated with DeLinda since 2017, serving on the board of the non-profit transcenDANCE, a nationally-recognized creative youth development organization that works with teens in underserved San Diego communities through dance, theater, and the spoken word. transcenDANCE instills confidence, inspires creativity and exposes middle and high-school students to life-changing skills in leadership, collaboration, and community engagement. We both understand how a foundation in the arts prepares young people for a more meaningful, creative and resilient life. DeLinda consistently and graciously opened her stunning showroom to host board meetings and holiday celebrations that made us feel like family. She has a gift for hospitality which is also evident in each chapter of this book.

As a founder and author at The Ken Blanchard Companies, I am as passionately committed to leadership development as DeLinda. I appreciate her commitment to developing next generation leaders. The content of this book is totally in synch with the books I have co-authored: *Leading at a Higher Level* (Pearson), *Leadership and the One Minute Manager* (Morrow) and *Who Killed Change* (Harper Collins) and with the content of the training products I've created: *Situational Leadership II, Leading People through Change, Crafting My Leadership Point of View, Building Trust* and *Adapting to Change.* Those products are used by tens of thousands of leaders globally to develop skills in creating inclusive, high-involvement, employee-centered work environments. When I attended my first Board meeting at ICE, I was immediately drawn to the company's life-size commitment to

Creating Raving Fans (Blanchard's product on legendary customer service) on the wall. I instantly knew we were a values match.

Reading the early drafts of *Inspiring Generational Leadership*, I was intrigued by the leadership principles DeLinda has embraced in her role as Founder and CEO of ICE and shared in her first of what I hope will be many books. We both recognize the importance of:

- **Shared purpose and values** –organizations that are focused on doing good and being good places to work.
- **Passion for the work you do** – workplaces that energize and encourage creativity, agility and change.
- **Authentic leadership** – leaders who have a clear leadership point of view and are willing to teach it to others; leaders who can admit to flaws and mistakes
- **Conversation** – leaders who are committed to increasing the quality and quantity of conversations they have with their team members; leaders who are committed to dialogue
- **Collaboration and community building** – leaders are interested in building consensus, involving others, and hearing everyone's voices
- **Intentional mentoring** – leaders who see it as their responsibility and privilege to teach, coach, support and inspire others
- **An abundance mindset** – organizations and leaders who are committed to all stakeholders' success, to the collective good, to personal **and** organizational well-being
- **A conscious culture of trust, gratitude and kindness**

Competition for talent is fierce these days. Intentional leadership at all levels of the organization is what attracts and helps organizations find, develop and retain talent.

DeLinda and her company are role models for these principles. DeLinda has thirty-four years of experience in her industry and has led her organization ICE (Innovative Commercial Environments) since 2006. ICE has consistently exceeded every benchmark for success in the furniture industry. When no one was coming to the office or buying furniture in 2020, ICE continued to thrive despite the COVID-19 pandemic, growing revenues by 6 percent and avoiding layoffs which ICE management defined as their primary 2020 goal because DeLinda knows *it's the employees* as much as the products that build and maintain an organizations' praiseworthy brand.

ICE has always focused on the development of people, specifically millennials. It has been in essence a corporate laboratory for conscious capitalism and millennial engagement. *Inspiring Generational Leadership* has been written to engage readers in a robust dialogue regarding both of these organizational commitments. In the book, DeLinda shares how ICE successfully implemented the tenets of conscious capitalism and millennial engagement in her organization. *Inspiring Generational Leadership* details the methodology they used to promote what she calls "ingrained engagement."

ICE's intergenerational journey as a conscious business enterprise offers us insight into what does and does not resonate with younger generations in the workforce. The payoff has been the long-term operational stability and resiliency ICE has enjoyed. An equally powerful aspect of her story is the personal joy she and her coworkers at ICE have derived through generational mentorship. In reading the book we realize how they've not only improved the lives of employees but have positively impacted the lives of their coworkers' children, America's future workforce.

Running a profitable business while creating opportunity and "abundance" for everyone are two aspirations that can and have been adopted by some of the world's most successful big and small businesses. Data reinforces that organizations that embrace, promote, and adhere to conscious business ethics are dramatically more profitable, more resilient, and more stable if they embrace the tenet that the most *authentic, truest purpose of business is to elevate humanity and create value for the benefit of everyone.* As DeLinda writes in her introduction to this book: *Doing well and doing good need not and should not be mutually exclusive.*

Inspiring Generational Leadership is a compendium of practical wisdom that captures not only the story of ICE and DeLinda's commitment to servant leadership but also learnings from interviews with other conscious companies. It is full of stories, exercises and tools that describe **how to** create a work environment that reflects millennial values and is committed to making a difference in the world. It has become clear that for capitalism to prosper in America, it must continue to change and lift *everyone* up. *Inspiring Generational Leadership*: *Your Guide to Design a Conscious Culture* teaches readers just how to make this shift. Enjoy!

Patricia Zigarmi

Founder/Author
The Ken Blanchard Companies
San Diego – June, 2021

INTRODUCTION

Doing well and doing good need not and should not be mutually exclusive.

Welcome, Conscious Reader,

Ever since the phrase above came to me, it has been dancing around in my head like a catchy tune you can't stop humming. Why is this phrase so sticky? It summarizes the essence of our company and what we stand for. This book is the story of Innovative Commercial Environments (ICE), a business I started from a spare bedroom in 2006. It is a simple story of joyful ups and painful downs, missed and seized opportunities. What makes our story unique is how we unconsciously and intuitively adopted certain principles that resonate with our mostly Millennial staff.

The inspiration for ICE was born from my desire to help my son achieve his educational goals. As a single mother I knew that would be impossible unless I took a leap of faith to become an entrepreneur. That leap proved fortuitous. Not only has ICE been a force for good in my son's life, but it has also positively influenced the lives of others as we've remained focused on the mission embodied in these words.

> *Doing well and doing good need not and should not be mutually exclusive.*

This phrase became my higher purpose years before I even knew what a higher purpose was! Today, after fifteen years, ICE is considered San Diego's most creative office and hospitality furniture dealership. We weathered the Great Recession just after launching ICE, which at the time seemed immense, but it paled in comparison to the 2020 pandemic and its resulting tsunami of repercussions. Still a few bright spots emerged in 2020, such as the opportunity to test our blossoming Millennial leadership capabilities during the most extreme business climate ever experienced in the modern history of the United States. We also were recognized as one of the 5000 fastest growing companies in America—for *the seventh time*!

This perplexing accomplishment sent me deep down into a rabbit hole, searching for "why" we had achieved this industry-defying revenue growth. That search led me on an aspirational eighteen-month journey of curiosity that resulted in the crafting of this book.

At ICE, we provide functional, beautiful, and creatively designed furniture along with an exceptional customer service experience for our business community. Our company creates physical spaces that are anything but ordinary, but we also create emotional space for our employee team members to thrive. Initially, we did not intentionally design our robust corporate culture; it developed quite naturally through a parental-inspired leadership style. As we grew, we began to invest heavily in our culture and team member development with a laser focus on advancing not only business skills, but more significantly, investing in life-enhancing skills. We view our teammates as young parents, community leaders, and developing adults who need to become better communicators, influencers, parents, and advocates for societal improvement. We hope they will gain a sense of accomplishment and pride in their livelihoods. Ultimately, we believe business needs to embrace societal needs.

Many of our employees came to ICE with little to no industry or work experience. Many are under forty and have been with us for quite a while. Many have purchased their first homes while employed by ICE, which is an accomplishment in itself, considering San Diego homes are nearly three times the national home average price.[1]

Our business enables us to contribute in countless meaningful ways to our local community. We take extraordinary efforts to enable our team members to personally thrive while our equally thriving company does beneficial work and good deeds.

We believe work should not hijack your soul; rather, business can be a force for good in the world, a source of inspiration. Until I started ICE, I only dreamed of this kind of work environment; I'd never experienced a workplace being a wellspring of happiness. My experience prior to ICE was an unkind and unforgiving corporate world. I realize that is the norm in the business world, so I hope this book offers a glimpse into our workplace family life that encourages the archaic and ineffective leadership style from the past to shift.

This book chronicles a journey we *unconsciously* traveled in discovery of our purpose and "secret sauce." The intention in sharing our story is that if others *consciously* embrace similar ICE methodology, they too might have the tools and perspective needed not only to build a profitable, successful business, but to find great joy by improving the lives of others along the way. My life purpose continues to expand the more I communicate the advantages of being an ambassador for ethical entrepreneurism.

In 2020, I connected virtually with other conscious leaders in a Mastermind group that led into a Senior Leadership Network pilot program, both facilitated through the national Conscious Capitalism Inc. organization. Through these conversations, I've come to realize that while many might consider a conscious capitalist approach a new way to lead, it is currently being widely implemented with tremendous organizational and financial success. I also learned that companies that do not adopt to the needs of Millennial and Gen Z employees will struggle to attract and retain talent, but more significantly, their existence and relevance as an organization will be compromised.

As you strive to reach your potential, both individually and then as a company, the potential to positively influence the community and future generations exponentially increases.

No doubt that is a lofty ambition, but every journey begins with a single step: a vision seemingly impossible. The American Revolution? Capitalism? Ending slavery? Women's rights? Civil rights? They all seemed impossible, but they all started with a hope and a dream to advance our lives and improve the lives of others for generations to come.

> *Everything that is done in this world is done in hope.*
> — **Martin Luther King, Jr.**

The seed for *Inspiring Generational Leadership* was harvested from the book *Conscious Capitalism*, written in 2013 by Whole Foods Co-Founder and CEO John Mackey and Professor and Conscious Capitalism, Inc. Co-Founder Raj Sisodia. They espouse that capitalism in its purest form offers us the brightest hope for the future of business in America and that:

> *The authentic truest purpose of business is to elevate humanity and create value for all stakeholders.*

No longer is business' sole purpose to generate profit for shareholders or owners—success must be equally shared with all.

The Power of Story

I often say, "This is *our* company," "*We* created this business," and "It's all about *the team*." I don't say this because I'm trying to portray a generous spirit. I say it because it's 100 percent true. Often, I didn't agree with the ideas or direction in which my leadership team wanted to take the company. I had never experienced these leadership directives in my career, so they felt very uncomfortable and perhaps even like a mistake that once you offer them and set the precedence, you can't take back.

I knew the outcome I wanted—to create an employee-centric workplace—but I didn't know how. I often say, "You don't know what you don't know," and I didn't know if the principles we were incorporating were a mistake; I had to suspend my disbelief even to entertain them, much less adopt them. As I let go of my past perceptions and we integrated these new leadership ideas, I came to realize that the results were not only successful, but they defined our brand, creating the company we're known for—a very human-focused organization.

Business in America is changing—it has for years—but in 2020, the gas pedal was flat against the floor. The acceleration is unlike anything we've ever seen or even imagined. My friend Greg Horowitt lectures at Stanford and the University of California San Diego on conscious behavioral leadership. Greg is also a renowned San Diego and Silicon Valley venture capitalist, serial entrepreneur, and public-private international developmental consultant. Greg notes that innovation—how we've defined capitalism, our reality as we imagine it to be—is "happening at the speed of thought." Business leaders no longer have the indulgent shortcoming of leading within their personal limited and limiting belief systems. Leaders must engage all perspectives and entertain other belief systems to find innovative problem-solving solutions. Not only do you "not know what you don't know," but you also don't understand how it can negatively affect your ability to be an effective leader and the resulting domino effect.

The sooner we become comfortable with that discomfort, the sooner we'll find solutions within our new capitalism construct that engage and excite peoples' "human operating systems." As technology such as Artificial Intelligence continues to siphon away our humanity, smart leaders will fight to keep people first and to establish a sense of personal belonging and identity within an organization.

I equate leading with parenting, which is the most significant "job" anyone will ever have because you are shaping a new person, the next generation. How you shape that generation is how you shift a paradigm and change the world. More than ever, we all ought to be figuring out our part. How we show up every day as the best version of ourselves is a small way to improve the world around us. When we simply show up with a perspective of abundance and a goal to make the world a kinder place for others, everyone benefits, including ourselves.

ICE's story brings to life practices that can be consciously implemented in your business and it edifies for everyone the benefits derived from doing so. *When we make our work a call to action to espouse a higher purpose—that purpose being the reason we're in business—and we bring this approach to the forefront of our daily decisions, all will benefit.*

Millennials' Values Reflect the Values of Conscious Capitalism

Capitalism, as initially envisioned, was not based on greed or exploitation of consumers and workers or the environment for the goal of maximizing profits. It was never intended to be a "someone must lose to allow someone to win" proposition. This perception is based on a false narrative that kidnapped the true character of capitalism. In reality, capitalism is based on cooperation and voluntary exchange; competition keeps everyone honest and in check with a mandated focus on the customer to provide the best value. Since employees have more options than ever before to work anywhere, competition forces management to provide higher wages, benefits, and a safe workplace.

The overlap of conscious capitalism values with the espoused values and perspectives of the Millennial and Gen Z generations is a major factor in the escalation of conscious social enterprises. These values were initially identified in the books *Conscious Capitalism* and *Firms of Endearment.* Business owners not only have the responsibility to positively influence change, but it is in their best interest to do so to attract the highest caliber of talent and create organizational resiliency during economic downturns. This responsibility became crystal clear during the 2020 COVID-19 crisis.

ICE has always been a company that employs mostly Millennials, and we have learned much about what motivates that generation. We have certainly benefited from this generational shift in harmony with business' synchronous and evolving purpose. I believe we have an enormous opportunity, perhaps a duty, to understand how we can positively influence future generations and affect significant transformation.

Markets depend on more than just businesses to function. They need the buy-in and support of people. Mentoring our next generation of leaders through an enhanced dialogue of conscious capitalism buttresses free markets against the counter-winds of bad economic ideologies and seeks inclusion on issues of gender and racial parity, sexual orientation, and social justice.

Childbirth and birthing a business have much in common, with all the pain, exhilaration, joy, and complications associated with each. I've had some of the most joyful moments of my entire life while forming and nurturing my small business. And yes, I did just compare starting a business to birthing a child; sit with that for a moment. Take a second to visualize and understand the commitment being made on behalf of another human being. Realize it's not about you.

The Importance of Small Business

You might not think the feeling of accomplishment when a child is born can be attained through business, but I assure you it can. Perhaps I would not believe it if I hadn't personally felt these emotions and been the recipient of hundreds of conversations, meetings, and emails from my coworkers, clients, and vendor partners who have elevated my awareness of their appreciation of our values and corporate culture, which is based on *valuing the family unit*. I'm going to unpack this concept thoroughly throughout this book.

Consider these 2019 statistics. According to the US Small Business Administration Office of Advocacy:

- There were 30.7 million small businesses in 2019.
- Small businesses represented 99.7 percent of companies in America.
- These small businesses employed 59.9 million workers.
- Those workers represented 47.3 percent of all US employees.

Small business, along with capitalism, is alive but struggling in the United States, especially after the challenges of 2020. With its expansive reach and influence, small business has the ability to affect significant, constructive, and generational transformation. I believe America's mature small business owners have a marvelous opportunity to welcome these changes and realize it is in our best interest to celebrate and embrace the tenets of conscious capitalism. We undervalue ourselves when we don't realize the influence small business can have in our communities.

We need not limit these concepts to small business; plenty of opportunity exists for all corporations to implement these changes. Many other books have captured that big business narrative, most recently Rebecca Henderson's *Reimagining Capitalism in a World on Fire*, published in April 2020 when the world, indeed, was a hot COVID-19 mess!

By reading *Inspiring Generational Leadership*, you will learn:

1. Love is the most powerful emotion on the planet; if you can foster sensitivities and empathy within your company, you will have achieved the greatest success possible.

2. What leadership tools and skills are needed to motivate and inspire Millennials and the emerging Gen Z cohort.

3. Mentoring future generations is more of a gift you give to yourself than to another; if you've selected the right person/people to share your wisdom with, you will be shocked at how gratifying it is to see them succeed.

4. Experiencing your mentee successfully mentor others and accomplish it with more grace and wisdom than you offered reinforces the value and joy of mentoring.

5. It is not possible to discern if a leader was successful while they are still leading; the most accurate measurement is discovered when you evaluate the subsequent success of the leader's followers. It's never about the leader; it's always about those who follow.

6. How to continue your business' legacy by selling to it to your mentee. It's never too late to start thinking of the potential you have to continue your legacy, which will benefit all stakeholders as well as you.

7. How to consciously develop a business and personal brand based on excellence, best business practices, and values that resound

equally with all stakeholders, and then understand how to reinforce and cultivate this brand awareness within your company and
the community.

8. How to inject your gift of intuition—your transcendent guide—
into your business to validate in practice what you might already
intuitively know.

As you positively influence your work teammates' lives, you also affect
the well-being of their children and family members, and ultimately, create an opportunity to make an imprint on your entire community by
initiating a ripple effect, potentially influencing future generations and
other businesses by modeling this "doing good—doing well" perspective.

This concept brought ICE uncommon success and inspired this book.
I suggest you experience our company's simple journey through the lens of
"what if"—what would the world of business in America look like if our
narrative were the norm?

I invite you to join me on this journey that just might lead our
society to a brighter place. Thank you for sharing your precious time to
explore our rather nascent but vibrant and blossoming mission to improve
capitalism. Our path is offering an optimistic spark—one that just might
have the potential to change hearts and minds. I hope to spark the innate,
innovative imagination that lives in you and in all of us.

I look forward to meeting you on this joyful journey!

DeLinda Forsythe

CHAPTER 1

Conscious Capitalism, Millennials, and an Evolving Perspective

I n 2006, I started my company, Innovative Commercial Environments (dba ICE), from a spare bedroom. The impetus for ICE was my son's acceptance into Georgetown University. As a single mother with few financial options to help him achieve his educational goals, I was forced to try entrepreneurship. It was a leap of faith that has proven most fortuitous.

Exceeding Every Industry Standard—for Seven Consecutive Years

For thirty-five years, I've thrived in the highly competitive contract furniture industry because of my focus on ethics, service, and excellence. The office furniture industry is not renowned for adhering to the ideals I strive for; it is a compromised and unregulated industry, as I'll cover in more detail later.

By far the most rewarding portion of my years of service has been opening ICE and contributing to it as CEO and founder. While the company has been successful, I've become increasingly curious about why we've experienced such unprecedented success.

ICE has consistently been named in the Top 100 Fastest Growing Companies in San Diego, but more astonishing has been our ability to rank as one of the 5000 fastest-growing companies in America, landing us on the Inc. 5000 Fastest Growing Companies list 2014–2020—a feat accomplished by only 1.5 percent of US companies. No other furniture dealership in America has been able to claim this accomplishment.

Some of our growth is attributable to our decision in 2013 to add hospitality and custom-designed, locally made furnishings to our scope of services, allowing us to expand our ability to furnish restaurants, hotels, nightclubs, etc. As the demarcation between work and personal life erodes, our office spaces have incorporated more personality and more residential sentiments, earning us several design awards and a developing reputation as "San Diego's most creative office furniture dealership."

In an industry that averages single digit growth, ICE has averaged 32 percent, and in 2019, we grew an astonishing 56 percent! We have experienced tremendous local brand recognition in addition to our explosive growth, which led me, in 2019, to ask, "Why?"

In 2017, ICE became an "aligned" Teknion furniture dealership. "Aligned" dealerships have far more success because they partner with major furniture brands; a partnership offers a substantially increased opportunity for stability and revenue generation than a "non-aligned" dealership. We were non-aligned for eleven out of fourteen years. Not to discount our company, but being non-aligned made our success even more unusual.

I had to wait patiently for the publication of *Conscious Capitalism* by John Mackey and Raj Sisodia, and *Firms of Endearment* by Raj Sisodia, Jag Sheth, and David B. Wolfe before I had something like an answer for our success. In these books, I discovered an explanation for why the ICE formula has proven so effective: We engage all of the principles and the philosophy of conscious capitalism.

The conscious capitalism movement brings a set of demands that are productive in reimagining enterprise as a constructive social vehicle and free markets as a social good in-themselves. The overlap of Millennial values and the tenets of conscious capitalism are remarkable when considered through *Conscious Capitalism*'s definition of business' purpose:

> *The authentic truest purpose of business is to elevate humanity and create value for all stakeholders.*

The four principles of conscious capitalism are:
1. Core values are the heart of an engaging higher purpose.
2. Fully integrated equal stakeholders are critical to the company's success; consequently, equitable achievement is realized for all stakeholders.
3. All leaders and managers must embrace conscious leadership.
4. The company has an active conscious culture.

The majority of the ICE workforce is in the Millennial age group. Millennials are projected to continue being a substantial majority of the world's workforce. Understanding their beliefs is critical for business leaders who want to motivate and manage this segment of the workforce. Millennials profess to enthusiastically embrace the tenets of conscious capitalism, and this alignment offers more potential for the movement to succeed. Millennial engagement is as much a factor in the emergence of conscious social enterprises as those identified in *Firms of Endearment* or *Conscious Capitalism*. The aging Boomer demographic in America has also been influential in this shift. Boomers, either retired or seeking legacy and purpose, appear to want to modernize the purpose of business, desiring and resulting in a more humanistic vision of capitalism, a seismic swing in consciousness that is shifting the basis of American society.

In 2020, COVID-19, followed by civil unrest seeking racial equity and societal change, further catapulted the desire for a much-needed evolution of capitalism. In the context of this change, I have reflected upon my own experiences, and I offer them in this book in my desire to share information and advance conscious capitalism, which I believe may be the most universally preferred way forward for the free-market system and businesses in America.

One of the most compelling reasons to adopt the concepts noted in *Firms of Endearment* and other books that promote conscious capitalism is that they are more resilient during times of crisis and turbulence and, surprisingly, they are far more profitable! The following chart clearly confirms that the organizations documented in *Firms of Endearment* are **actually fourteen times more profitable than the S&P 500!** Organizations only focused on profit have much to gain from adopting the tenets of conscious capitalism.

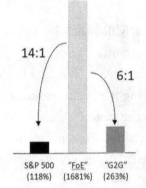

PERFOMANCE OF
FIRMS OF ENDEARMENT

14:1

6:1

S&P 500   "FoE"   "G2G"
(118%)   (1681%)   (263%)

Cumulative Returns (1998-2013)

Firms of endearment featured in this book have out-performed the S&P 500 by 14 times and Good to Great Companies by 6 times over a period of 15 years.

Cumulative Performance	15 Years	10 Years	5Years	3 Years
US FoEs	**1681%**	**410%**	**410%**	**410%**
International FoE's	1180%	512%	512%	512%
Good to Great Companies	263%	176%	176%	176%
S&P 500	118%	107%	107%	107%

Source: *Firms of Endearment: How World-Class Companies Profit from Passion and Purpose* 2nd Edition by Raj Sisodia, Jag Sheth, David Wolfe, Published 2014 by Pearson Education

The year 2020 proved to be unrelenting, with persistent, irrepressible outside forces that felt intent on destroying not only the free market system, but the fabric of what America considers to be American—the worth of the individual. It was the worst financial year not only for ICE but in US history; it was ICE's only negative growth year in fourteen years. By April, we realized we had to recalibrate how we defined success and elevate our organization's purpose. Our main goal was to avoid layoffs, which we were able to do despite more than a 50 percent loss in revenue. We place an enormous value on human capital, so our definition for success in 2020 became: Lose as few people as possible!

We have devoted extraordinary time, thought, and care to embedding into our corporate culture values that resonate with Millennials: equal opportunity, workplace family, ethical business practices, and the immeasurable value of an individual. Years of developing our passionately engaged culture reaped enormous positive consequence and an aura of resilience, despite the business turmoil of 2020. We indelibly proved that a culture built on trust and the value of human dignity and fairness can far better withstand massive outside forces.

According to the Small Business and Entrepreneurship Council, businesses with less than 500 employees employ 46.8 percent of the labor force. In total, 99.7 percent of US companies have less than 500 employees and are considered small businesses. The year 2020 revealed the fragility of minority-owned businesses as more than 40 percent of Black-owned businesses shut their doors due to the COVID-19 pandemic.[2]

Small businesses not only have the responsibility to positively influence change, but it is in their best interest to do so if they want to attract the highest caliber of talent and create organizational resiliency during economic downturns. Business' purpose has evolved, and we have the opportunity to understand how we can positively influence future generations and affect significant transformation.

Conscious Capitalism 2.0

The 2019 Deloitte Global Millennial Survey noted that both Gen Z and Millennials feel "government has the most responsibility for improving social mobility." The unfortunate truth is that government has never been able to provide income equality without substantial cost to long-term economic growth, innovation, and most significantly, human freedom because socialist and communist influenced governments value the "collective," not the individual.[3] Consider the loss of constitutional rights and the lack of caring for the individual reflected in decisions government made in 2020. As the data continues to emerge, the loss of life due to drug overdoses and suicide, especially teenagers and even those under fifteen, was unprecedented. Is this reflective of our government making sound decisions?

Our advanced and imperfect American economy developed as a result of our free market system, which has reduced poverty and expanded opportunity more effectively than any previous economic system. Alternatively, non-capitalistic government systems have failed dramatically; thus, it is concerning that so many in the current generation may be laying their hopes on such *proven* failed strategies.

Our Founding Fathers sought to lay the foundation of a governmental structure from which a more perfect union could evolve. Like all humans, the Founding Fathers were flawed, but in many ways, they were extraordinary visionaries. They envisioned a government and country that improved through generational wisdom in understanding and learning from our internal failures as well as the failures of other countries and governments. Our guiding American political philosophy is based on liberty, inalienable individual rights, and the sovereignty of the people as the source of all authority in law. The Founding Fathers rejected aristocracy. They expected their citizens to be virtuous and to disallow corruption. Integrity is needed for the free-market system to optimally function. What they created was more than a form of government; it was a way of life, a core ideology, and an uncompromising commitment to liberty.[4]

In many ways, capitalism has failed our Founding Fathers' expectations, but that should be expected as we continue to evolve and learn from our mistakes, always seeking opportunities to improve and progress. As the ancient Greek philosopher Heraclitus noted, "The only constant in life is change." If *anything* good has emerged from 2020, it's an extraordinary opportunity for much-needed structural change to happen so we can better realize the original vision of our country's founders.

Markets depend on more than just businesses to function. They need the buy-in and support of people. We can and should mentor our next generation of leaders through an enhanced dialogue about a reimagined capitalism that embraces the tenets of conscious/social/stakeholder capitalism, reinforces free markets against the counter winds of bad economic ideologies, and seeks more inclusion on issues of gender and racial parity, sexual orientation, and social justice.

The growing conscious capitalism movement offers the brightest hope for America's future. Free and fair markets are good, very good—*they reflect capitalism as originally imagined by our forefathers!* We have indeed strayed from our Founding Fathers' intent; it's time to reembrace these fundamental principles and reclaim what is rightly our American heritage.

Creating Space That Transcends Ordinary

The driving thread woven throughout this book is the unlimited and focused efforts ICE has put into creating safe emotional space. It has been the company's foundation and driving mission from day one. We've done this intuitively, but data consistently confirms the veracity of an emotionally safe workplace. Shelley Mika, as discussed in her article "The Four Drivers of Innovation," published on Gallup's website, studied why leading executives and management thinkers believe an empowered, participatory work environment produces increased innovation. Innovation is fostered by creativity and has become "the most important driver of macroeconomics today."[5]

Jim Clifton, Gallup Chairman and CEO, provides an overview of what drives innovation today, as well as what differentiates creativity (ideas) and innovation (action). Clifton notes that "*Better* doesn't work anymore. *Different* does." For organizations to thrive in today's highly competitive workplace, they must truly stand out.

ICE's well-established brand of an ethical company supported within a trusting culture thrives because of the four drivers Mika identifies:

1. **Finding and fostering talent:** This happens when people are relaxed and energized by the creativity of their colleagues and the subsequent friendships that develop.
2. **Managers matter:** Managers who are not just inspirational but "super mentors" play a key role in inspiring mentees and connect-

ing them with others who can activate their ideas and foster their growth. This is critical to organizational success.

3. **Relationships matter too:** Internal relationships among managers and coworkers are power drivers of innovation, so finding ways to build these internal relationships is as critical as building tenacious relationships with customers. Powerful internal relationships and friendships are what make a company "different."

4. **Keeping the right leaders:** Effective, highly engaged CEOs who are identified as the company's unique driving success are not easy to replace. When they leave, especially due to retirement, it can be highly disruptive and lead to the displacement of key employees.

The charts that follow clearly illustrate the magnitude of these metrics. They reflect workers' responses to statements about their work experiences.

INNOVATION AND CREATIVITY AT WORK

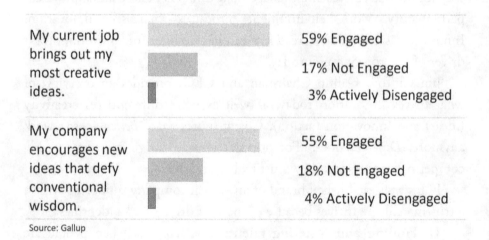

My current job brings out my most creative ideas.	59% Engaged
	17% Not Engaged
	3% Actively Disengaged

My company encourages new ideas that defy conventional wisdom.	55% Engaged
	18% Not Engaged
	4% Actively Disengaged

Source: Gallup

WORKPLACE FRIENDSHIPS ENCOURAGE CREATIVITY

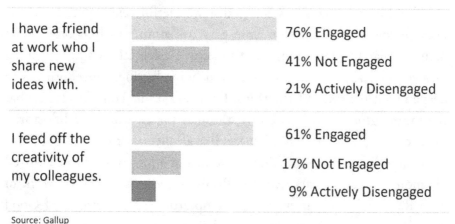

I have a friend at work who I share new ideas with.

76% Engaged

41% Not Engaged

21% Actively Disengaged

I feed off the creativity of my colleagues.

61% Engaged

17% Not Engaged

9% Actively Disengaged

Source: Gallup

Personal Relationships Within the Workplace

When ICE was first created, we had a tough time finding industry-skilled hires; we were too much of a gamble for them to want to work with us. My second hire in 2008 was Alysse McCree (now Cooper), the daughter of my former fitness instructor and current bookkeeper, Marylyn McCree. This book is as much about Alysse's journey, perhaps even more so, as it is about mine.

Alysse was twenty when she started working for me and attending California State University San Marcos (CSUSM). She needed full-time, flexible hours so she could attend school daily and I needed a receptionist/office manager/sales assistant. Alysse worked odd hours, coming in and leaving when it was still dark outside, working weekends—anything to get in her hours. Early on, it was clear she had a phenomenal work ethic.

Over the years, Alysse has hired family, friends, and industry colleagues who have helped create our workplace family culture, which will be discussed in Chapter 4. Many of our employees were personal referrals of current employees; it's a very common thing at ICE for friends to recruit friends. When you love where you work, you feel obliged to tell the world! You want to share with others the same opportunity to thrive that you have.

This hiring process has fostered a wonderful sense of camaraderie because coworkers who were close prior to coming to ICE often share many similar life happenings and milestone celebrations such as falling in love, marriage, career ambition, and home-buying; this continues to deepen their personal relationships. I've heard it said countless times that the meaningful friendships grown through shared work and life stories make coming into the ICE office feel like a collegial experience!

Gallup has been researching the results of a life considered well-lived for more than fifty years. Jennifer Robison notes the extensive work of Tom Rath and Jim Harter in her Gallup article "The Business of Good Friends: socializing is good for well-being—your employees' and your company's."[6] Two of the five barometers of living a positive life are social well-being and career well-being. Robison notes, "[T]o have a thriving sense of daily well-being, people need up to six hours a day of social interaction." This is a startling finding that sheds light on ICE's successful culture. Rath and Harter document the strong link between deep-seated workplace engagement and when an employee has a close friend at work because it checks both the social and career well-being boxes.

Sixty percent of the Gallup research participants indicated that strong personal relationships within the workplace resulted in a feeling of personal well-being. "Companies with thriving employees not only benefit from a greater likelihood of engagement, they reap the reward of healthy and productive workers. Career well-being is an essential element of overall well-being."

During the pandemic, we were forced to work from home. Because we had implemented work from home capabilities years ago, it was a seamless pivot for us. When asked, "What was the biggest challenge in not being able to come into the office and only have the option to work from home?", all indicated how much they missed their friends and colleagues and the social interaction from working in the office!

We decided not to mandate working from the office for the entire year. When restrictions were lifted, many employees continued to come to the office, not just because our offices are beautiful, but because they missed each other! That's the power of having a friend at work and a highly engaged workplace, and it is the number-one reason people stay with an organization!

The Gift of Thinking Less of Yourself

ICE has been cultivating tomorrow's leaders from its beginning. We did not do it intentionally. Now that we realize this cultivation is core to our company ethos, we do it purposefully, and our goal is to educate business leaders about the profound and innumerable advantages that reveal themselves when you focus less on you and more on others.

As ICE's founder and sole owner, I managed the organization independently until 2015. That is until my husband, Tom Forsythe—we married in 2009—retired from a thirty-seven-year career with MetLife to support operations and become my business partner. Marketing, sales, and brand development are my strengths—not operations. By 2015, the company had entered into an explosive growth stage and I lacked the skills to lead during this emerging period. One of my greatest strengths is my ability to acknowledge my weaknesses, which I'll cover in Chapter 9: Vulnerability in the Workplace.

At ICE, we recognize and address our professional shortcomings. We don't view mistakes as simply a negative; we share them openly in staff meetings so others can learn from our personal setbacks. There is no reason others always have to learn through personal experience—the "hard way." This sharing of mistakes provides an opportunity to learn from others' experiences and encourages communication, which leads to a very trusting culture. This ethos of accepted imperfection is one we've worked very hard to develop and maintain. I am quite comfortable acknowledging the gifts I do not have and ICE management also adheres to the perspective that perfection is a false idol.

Humility is a gift, and it continues to gain traction today as a highly desirable leadership trait. It is actively being promoted by many leadership coaches and books, but it can be traced back to 300 BC to Greece's Stoic philosophy. Stoicism is a philosophy of personal ethics informed by a system of logic, collectivism, and individual equality.

Many Stoic philosophers honored humility, but Socrates may have embraced it most determinedly. Socrates was an inherently humble man; when an oracle claimed Socrates was the wisest man in Athens, Socrates developed the Socratic system of conversational questioning and made it his life's work to prove the oracle wrong. The Socratic Method uses a simple system of asking questions and engaging in conversation that addresses the wisdom and "facts" of the day. Socrates believed in the value of thoughtful dialogue, and by appearing unlearned, he employed questions to engage discourse and, thus, unearth the fullest possible knowledge about the topic.

He is quoted as saying:

> I must tell you the truth—the result of my mission was just this: I found that the men most in repute were all but the most foolish; and that others less esteemed were really wiser and better.[7]

Dose of Stoism's website further addresses the gift of humility and captures how we can all deeply engage this virtue with very long-term vision:

> Humility is a tricky subject, if only because it's impossible not to sound laughably pompous when recommending it. *Look here, you: Be humble!* But that's not it. We're not talking about personal humility of the kind that can be so treacherous if pursued head-on, the sort that easily warps into conspicuous, Uriah Heepish self-abasement that's the opposite of what it pretends to be.

No, we're after a broader, more foundational humility, a mindset that grasps our status as utterly dependent beings and that has absorbed, fully, the fact of our mortality. We want a humility not of groveling self-negation, but a clear-eyed recognition that every moment of our existence, as well as everything we have and are, is a gift.

This book is as much about the foundational values Tom and I strive for as it is about the Millennial leaders now managing ICE and how they have embraced these ethics. These are values that resoundingly resonate with Millennial principles with extraordinary success and much of our story captures their perspective.

Our Past Defines Our Future

I planned for 2020 to be my final year as head of the company. Alysse would complete the transition of ICE President started in late 2018 in preparation for her role as CEO in 2021, and Elyse Stephens would continue to mature into her role as Vice President of Operations. We had planned for them to move fully into their roles as independent leaders in 2020, while Tom and I remained at ICE, offering guidance behind the scenes. Tom mentored Elyse for seven years. I have "super-mentored" Alysse for thirteen years, including preparing her to purchase ICE and succeed me as owner. As I shifted my mindset away from day-to-day operations, I became focused on understanding the root of our success, which led to capturing our story. My effort started out almost as an internal document, but as I did more research, it progressed into this book.

History is important. I needed to understand our story and detail it so that current and future employees would appreciate who we are, how we started, and what we stand for.

In preparation for the succession plan we started in 2015, we adopted a complete hands-off approach to prepare the organization for this much anticipated 2021 succession transition, agreeing that a slow process would be the healthiest approach, not just for the market and our vendor partners and clients, but especially for our staff because jolts and shocks do not lead to a seamless and drama-free transition.

A thoughtful ownership-transfer process not only leads to the most harmonious transition, but it also enables a thoroughly mindful "enhanced mentorship phase," honoring the gift of each other in a way one cannot appreciate when caught in the minutiae of day-to-day operations and distracting annoyances. Just knowing this was our last year together forged a genuine, no-holds-barred, peer-to-peer relationship.

Though our past does not limit our future, it certainly influences our future, so it became my quest to document our history as an organization grounded by values of mutuality, trust, respect, and ethical business practices. We started as a company that offered unlimited opportunity for young women with little to no business experience. That became the foundation we built on that ultimately benefited everyone.

As we implemented this critical transference of power, we granted our executive leadership team full authority to implement their ideas and hone their leadership skills. They confidently stepped up and took ownership of the company. Much of this book's content is reflective of their leadership experiences.

2020—A Leadership Year Unlike Any Other in American History

Thoroughly compelling is that this leadership transition happened during a year never before experienced by any business leader in America: 2020. It was the year every single life, and our basic and presumed sense of reality, was fundamentally changed—the year every sacrosanct belief, how we define American values and life, was stripped naked to its core.

I don't believe the universe gives us accidental thunderbolts; I see intentional and heedful fingerprints touching everything we do, every experience we have in life. Just as being marginalized for most of my career led me to creating a business that purposely lifts women up, this pandemic hit in a year that threatened and rattled our ability to exist and yet offered an enormous opportunity for our budding leaders to spread their wings and learn invaluable lessons through a traumatic workplace experience, which is far more educational than any academic institution.

I was especially grateful that these challenges hit when Tom and I still owned the organization because we had the financial stability to weather the storm. We had built strong relationships with our trusted advisors, City National Bank; Thor Eakes, CPA; and Mark Pearcy, CFP. By doing so, we felt confident we were equipped to finance the terrible trials of 2020.

Many a night, I lay awake wondering if we needed a "Plan Z" that entailed layoffs of irreplaceable coworkers. It took years to gather and grow our workplace family, and we were determined to hold the family together.

What Does the Millennial Generation Stand For?

Why is it so important to understand what motivates the Millennial age group? In 2020, Millennials comprised 35 percent of adult Americans, but by 2025, some studies project they will be 75 percent of the workforce.[8] Born in the widely agreed-upon range of 1981–1996, they are the largest demographic in US history.

The most influential and effective business strategies are needed to engage this cohort for long-term, sustainable success. I've interspersed my personal observations with consistently noted characteristics below:

1. Millennials have also been called digital natives because of their early exposure to computers, video games, and the internet. This has been a main driver of how they think, what values they hold, and what drives their behavior. They are more comfortable with technology than any previous generation and they are more inclined to embrace emerging technological tools.

2. Millennials are far more thoughtful about long-term decision-making, delaying marriage, having children, and choosing lifetime careers because they've lived through or seen the consequences of poor decision-making. This more thoughtful approach can lead to better critical decision-making.

3. Millennials are the most highly conscious generation of all time in regards to health, societal, economic, and environmental issues.

4. Due to this heightened awareness of global conditions and responsibilities, Millennials are quickly becoming aware of the potential of conscious capitalism, which focuses less on profitability and more on the interests of all stakeholders, including not just the customers and investors, but the community, the environment, employees, and suppliers.

5. Millennials are not as nationalist centric or patriotic as past generations but rather consider themselves global citizens with a responsibility to improve the world.

6. As global citizens, Millennials are more aware of their carbon footprint and the effect they are having, so they have developed an appreciation and reverence for the environment.

7. Flexible work hours and remote working even before COVID-19 have been drivers of Millennials' employment options, but 2020's mandatory work-from-home policies mean they will continue to rise in importance. Organizations should continue providing this option if they hope to attract and retain the best talent.

8. Millennials are considered to have the most entrepreneurial mindset of any previous generation, starting businesses at a higher rate. They also have the highest business failure rate compared to past generations. For the best alignment with this value, organizations need to encourage "intrapreneurial," as well as entrepreneurial, ways of engagement—to celebrate the individual while employing a collaborative, team-building culture that appeals to their independent spirits.

9. Millennials are highly social beings who feel most alive when working on and solving problems, crafting policies and procedures together. They are street-smart as well as technologically savvy; you cannot fool them with performative statements. They see right through inauthentic people and policies.

10. Because Millennials are authentic and pragmatic idealists, they want to work for transparent organizations that reveal their soft underbelly, their flaws and mistakes. They want to be able to voice their opinions on policies being made that they are to implement; it's critical to empower and engage every "level" and encourage their natural entrepreneurial tendency.

11. Millennials embrace progressive social beliefs and policies such as same-sex marriage, marijuana legalization, liberal political ideologies, co-parenting, interracial marriage, immigration, etc. They are less religious but more spiritual.

12. Millennials want to be change agents—they want to make the world a better place.

13. Millennials are socially responsible consumers; many are actually willing to pay more for an item if the organization producing it is actively engaged in social justice issues or pursues an environmental sustainability mission—it's not all hat and no cowboy; they will use their wallets to influence the world. Because of their comfort level with technology, they'll research how products are made, consciously choosing products that align with their values.

14. Studies reveal that only 35 percent of Millennials think it's important to keep abreast of political affairs; however, I believe this trend is changing daily. In 2020, politics came to them whether they liked it or not, so it will be interesting to see future polling results for this statistic.

15. Data suggests and experience confirms that Millennials prefer an equalized work-life balance compared to their work-centric parents.

In the 2014 article "How Millennials Could Upend Wall Street and Corporate America," published in the *Governance Studies at Brookings* newsletter, authors Morley Winograd and Dr. Michael Hais note:

> "Just as Millennials create communities built around
> shared interests not geographical proximity, causes will

create compatibility between otherwise disparate groups. The desire of Millennials for pragmatic action that brings results will overtake today's emphasis on ideology and polarization as Boomers finally fade from the scene. This cultural shift will be felt in all aspects of the American economy from its marketplaces to its workforce and from its board rooms to the daily decisions of its CEOs. The distinctive and widely shared attitudes and beliefs of this generation will slowly, but surely, reshape corporations in its image and end the confrontational and bottom-line oriented world that Boomers and Gen-X'ers have created."[9]

Alan Murray summarized this well with this overview in his November 2, 2020 *Fortune* newsletter:

"Why does this matter to business? Because we live at a moment when work and life are converging. Much is made of the role that the millennial generation plays in business, but here are some facts: millennials are less likely to be married than previous generations, less likely to join an organized religion, and less likely to join civic and social clubs. That means outside of social media—which can aggravate alienation as much as alleviate it—*millennials depend on employers as their main formal connection to society*. And the pandemic has only increased that dependence."

Deloitte Millennial Global Surveys

Deloitte Consulting is the world's largest accounting firm, specializing in the areas of human capital, strategy, financial advisory, and analytical consulting. It conducted its first Millennial Global Survey in 2012, anticipating how influential this generation would be. Deloitte has been tracking the sentiments of millions in this emerging cohort, adding in Gen Z's perception in 2018. This survey consistently provides thoughtful insights designed to lead to more intelligent business outcomes. It is, by far, the most comprehensive and complete study of Millennials I have seen.

In 2017, the survey uncovered that Millennials were seeking ways to be more influential in their communities and the organizations they served in; they were interested in creating a "ripple effect." They wanted to be involved in initiatives that resulted in improving social issues and good causes that empowered them. Although they felt they had little control in society at large, they wanted their jobs to result in meaningful outcomes that made a difference in society. Millennials are more loyal and more committed to working for organizations that have a genuine purpose, and they authentically care about social equality and the environment.[10]

The 2018 Deloitte survey conveyed that these young workers believe business leaders need to be more proactive in actualizing a positive effect on society.

> "Millennials want leaders to more aggressively commit to making a tangible impact on the world while preparing their organizations and employees for the changes that Industry 4.0 is affecting.
>
> One silver lining is that far more millennials believe that business leaders are making a positive impact on the world than government or religious leaders. Even so, four in 10 respondents see business leaders having a negative impact. Therefore, the timing is ideal for business leaders to step up and take actions that benefit all of their stakeholders."[11]

Deloitte's insightful methodology reveals that Millennials understand the influence business can have in positively improving society and individuality. By the 2019 survey, Millennials' optimism was eroding:

"Economic and social/political optimism is at record lows. Respondents express a strong lack of faith in traditional societal institutions, including mass media, and are pessimistic about social progress. They're not particularly satisfied with their lives, their financial situations, their jobs, government and business leaders, social media, or the way their data is used. Millennials are skeptical of business's motives. Respondents do not think highly of leaders' impact on society, their commitment to improving the world, or their trustworthiness."[12]

Below is the 2020 Executive Summary:

"The Deloitte Global Millennial Survey 2020 explores the views of more than 27.5K millennials and Gen Zs, both before and after the start of the COVID-19 pandemic, to understand their perspectives on business, government, climate, and the pandemic, among other issues.

The survey reveals that despite the individual challenges and personal sources of anxiety that millennials and Gen Zs are facing, they have remained focused on larger societal issues, both before and after the onset of the pandemic. If anything, *the pandemic has reinforced their desire to help drive positive change in their communities and around the world. And they continue to push for a world in which businesses and governments mirror that same commitment to society, putting people ahead of profits and prioritizing environmental sustainability.* [Emphasis mine.]

The world that follows the COVID-19 pandemic surely will be different and likely more aligned with the ideals that millennials and Gen Zs have expressed in this and previous Millennial Surveys."[13]

The Fallout of Chaos

This book captures ICE's personal Millennial case study sojourn as well as what conscious capitalism feels and looks like day-to-day when an organization incorporates the fundamentals of conscious capitalism. Though aware of capitalism's failures, I remain its most ardent fan. The Conscious Capitalism credo encapsulates my appreciation:

> "We believe that business is good because it creates value, it is ethical because it is based on voluntary exchange, it is noble because it can elevate our existence, and it is heroic because it lifts people out of poverty and creates prosperity. Free enterprise capitalism is the most powerful system for social cooperation and human progress ever conceived. It is one of the most compelling ideas we humans have ever had. But we can aspire to even more."[14]

The pandemic proved just how destructive government intervention can be when the government shut down our entire economy. The YouGov October 2019 poll indicates that 70 percent of Millennials are likely or somewhat likely to vote for politicians who offer socialist political solutions, and only 57 percent believe *The Declaration of Independence* better "guarantees freedom and equality" over *The Communist Manifesto*. This issue is not something we'll tackle in this book, but it is important to note that this same poll states that 36 percent of Millennials hold a positive view of communism.[15] Is this because 72 percent of Americans are unaware that more than 100 million people were killed because of communism and its policies?[16] How did we get here?

The idea that socialist policies improve job prospects or standards of living is a highly discredited myth.[17] Not only do the reasons for it being discredited need to be understood, but we also need to realize that discrediting it offers business owners, leaders, and corporations' opportunities to reinforce the positive role business has in elevating living standards.

Our Post-Pandemic Society

We are emerging into a new, post-pandemic COVID-19 society that demands alignment with this younger generation's values to improve lives, provide opportunity and livelihoods, and benefit all stakeholders equally. The Deloitte 2020 survey emphatically reveals the critical importance of Millennials and incoming Gen Zs. To lead these generations, it is not only advantageous to understand what inspires and motivates them but *how to* effectively engage them.

Corporate strategy for the first time in history must rise to acknowledge and meet social needs. Far too many performative stances have been issued by inauthentic CEOs and marketing departments about inclusion, diversity, equality, and environmental sustainability. Substantive leadership that addresses societal issues is in demand—business leaders now need to serve as agents for positive community change.

Employers who offer "super mentorship" opportunities (discussed in Chapter 2) will enable people to reach their potential and aspirations and better prepare them for the future by providing advanced training programs and employee development. Corporate cultures that empower individuality, creativity, and lifelong learning will continue to attract and retain elite team members.

Millennials' personal values as employees and their purchasing power as customers cannot be minimized. Millennials will emerge from this crisis cautious and aware of the fragility of life and employment. Gaining their commitment and loyalty requires a consistent and highly educated awareness, but business leaders who boldly lead with purpose and meaningful action as agents for equitable change will not only reap the benefits of a resilient business, but will make the world a better place.

CHAPTER 2

Begin with the End in Mind: Mentorship

The year 1986 fundamentally changed my life when my son Alex was born. I discovered my passion for the office furniture industry which would one day give birth to the productive work environment we created at ICE. I had just emerged from a six-year career in dance and the dramatic arts. After I earned my dance degree from UC Irvine, I had devoted my life to dance before discovering the office furniture trade. I was thrilled to find an outlet that continued to feed my creative side while allowing me to earn a consistent income, especially as a single mother with a newborn in tow.

I've long enjoyed the consultative nature of the industry and working closely with clients. I pleasantly realized my affinity to create beauty, my nurturing attributes, and my desire to seek harmony in my relationships offered an invaluable skill set in a sector that takes Murphy's Law to a whole new dimension. In the furniture world, what can go wrong will go wrong!

Eventually, I realized I was successful not because I was an effective salesperson, but because I was a creative partner and trusted advisor for clients.

My twenty years as a disciplined dancer produced an abundance of grit and tenacity. It is my nature to always seek self-mastery—dancers are always a "work-in-progress," never arriving, always on this journey to continuously strive for increased excellence. I was determined to work as hard as necessary to expand my industry knowledge and sales strategies to become a highly respected industry expert.

After putting Alex to bed at night, it was normal for me to create proposals and design layouts and station specifications well until midnight. We didn't use computers then and I never had an assistant or any meaningful guidance. Our industry didn't offer formal training, mentorship, or programs to ensure our success. It was clear I had to teach myself every aspect of the industry from sales to design to execution. The very idea of anyone investing in growing my talents, in encouraging or even training me, much less mentoring me, was unheard of. That was the way it was—I figured it out. With a young child at home, I had little choice.

I learned fast, succeeding almost immediately. Substantial financial success followed within five years at a family-owned furniture dealership in San Diego. For the first time, I believed I could support my family. For seven years, I thrived there and learned how a successful dealership should be structured. I was exposed to thought leadership and encouraged to read business books and define "my legacy." Thought seeds were planted, though life demands did not allow me to fertilize or grow them for years. My son was emerging as an intellectual, requiring a more advanced and nuanced education; fortunately, I was able to provide a private education for him during this time. We both were prospering.

Although I excelled at that dealership, I was not content. That was when I first realized the importance of corporate culture. Intuitively, I realized something did not resonate with me. For the first time in my career, I had tremendous financial security, but I made the decision to seek employment elsewhere. I can't explain why I had to leave beyond my strong instinct that it wasn't the right fit. I resigned, despite earning more money than I had ever imagined possible.

That courageous business decision laid a foundation to never waver from my convictions. I left for the chance to be a managing partner in a new venture with multiple locations. Although I took more than a 50 percent pay cut, it allowed me to manage the start-up San Diego division. I personally knew the owners and felt aligned with them.

The Ethics Equation

I went from the frying pan into the fire; the owners turned out to be the most unethical people I'd ever encountered in the industry. The furniture industry is entirely unregulated, so some owners realize they can behave as they wish, without regard for their employees, reputation, or clients.

Today, those dealerships have ceased to exist; only one dealership I worked for is still in business. In the fourteen years I've operated Innovative Commercial Environments, twelve San Diego dealerships that I know of, have opened and closed their doors or had ownership changes. This industry is not prone to stable growth. Nefarious players and unethical practices remain a consistent habit, at times taking deposit money from clients, not delivering goods, and not paying their factories. One dealer opened multiple dealerships over many years under various names with equally disreputable "partners" and filed multiple bankruptcies. He used this method as a recurring business strategy.

I struggled to find a dealership that shared my values, respected me beyond my sales numbers, and offered a "workplace home"—it was a challenging and disheartening eight years of my career.

In 2004, my son received a scholarship from a local university and left home. A few months later, I met and started dating my future husband. Right from the beginning, Tom became my biggest cheerleader and always encouraged me to start my own dealership; however, I lacked the courage. A year later, my son was accepted to Georgetown University, advising me that a degree from such a prestigious university was critical for his career. I realized I needed to take a leap of faith into entrepreneurship if not for my own future financial stability, then for Alex. For him to attend Georgetown and give up his scholarship at the local university would result in severe financial challenges since I couldn't cover the costs for a Georgetown education.

Accessing Your Personal Power

I believe the greatest source of the world's unhappiness is living with a sense of failure in pursuing your potential. Individual potential is completely relative, but we all know when we've fallen short. This sense of personal failure can breed anger and resentment toward others as well as toward ourselves, robbing our joy. Helping my son reach his potential had been my life's driving force for eighteen years, enabling me to reach my potential, and resulting in more joy than I could have imagined. I'll talk more deeply about this later because I firmly believe achieving our potential is the very foundation of happiness.

None of this made sense to me at the time; I just knew I had to find my buried courage. I had to dismantle my limiting belief system. Having the courage to take that first step, to make the decision to trust in my abilities wholeheartedly, was my first step toward transforming our lives, but more significantly to inspire others to transform theirs. Now, a week rarely goes by that someone doesn't acknowledge the effect I've had on their ability to implement personal change. In the beginning, I never did it consciously, but now it's the single biggest reason I get out of bed every day. Nothing provides greater joy. It's a gift I give myself.

Writing this book throughout 2020 was also an enormous gift to myself. It is one of my more courageous and galvanizing undertakings. I didn't have a clue what it took to create and publish a book, but I knew I would figure it out. Many women let me know they were watching me and learning from me. Of course, there will always be people who want you to fail, perhaps for the same reason we can't divert our eyes from a horrific freeway accident. It's just human nature.

This fear of failure, fear to live up to our potential and be bold, may partly be why we often choose to play smaller than we are. But Alex was never like that. He knew his potential would never be reached unless he pushed himself and attended the more prestigious universities; academia was his gift and his passion. He's always had wisdom beyond his years and a sharp intellect that inspired me to be more than I was. If he believed Georgetown was what he needed to reach his potential, then that opportunity was what I was going to provide, so whatever I had to learn or do or become to help him reach his potential, I was willing to do.

By refocusing my fear away from myself, Innovative Commercial Environments (ICE) was born. In creating ICE, I far exceeded my limiting beliefs.

Align with Those Who Believe in You

I often wonder if I would have had the courage to launch ICE without my husband's influence. Soon after Tom and I met, my life dramatically improved. Tom believed in me. He also saw how my clients appreciated my creativity and trusted me. Tom consistently encouraged me to start my own business.

Another supporter was my client, Steve Rosetta. Before I left my employer, he called me to help him with the furniture needs of a small real estate development company he was starting. Somehow, I found the courage to ask him, "If I start my own furniture dealership, would you give me this project?" Steve replied, "If you quit this week, yes!" That was all I needed. Despite not having a business plan, I resigned that Friday and launched ICE.

Steve and Tom were the advocates I needed. Tom even offered to pay my mortgage if I couldn't! Luckily, I never had to take him up on his offer. We rarely understand the power of our words to lift up others, but believe me, their words of encouragement were all I needed to believe in myself. They believed in me far more than I ever could have.

> *I started ICE from a spare bedroom, earning more income my first month as an entrepreneur than I had made the entire previous year.*
> **My only regret is I didn't do it sooner!**

The Millennials

Today, I rarely think about the unhappiness and despair of my past. However, my experiences with how unprincipled the industry can be and its blatant undervaluing of employees are why I cherish this generation coming behind me. Millennials do not want to tolerate such practices and they are vocal in sharing their opinions. Business today must be different to appeal to their inclinations.

The talent I initially attracted at ICE were younger females willing to take a chance with a start-up. Attracting talented industry professionals wasn't initially an option, but that fact ultimately created our successful hiring strategy. Our initial employees lacked prior furniture dealership experience, but we soon realized that was a bonus; we didn't have to unteach bad habits! I hired the daughters of friends and friends of friends. I was willing to give anyone a chance, perhaps because of the lack of support I had received.

Alysse Cooper—My First Mentee

I mentioned Alysse Cooper, one of my first hires, in Chapter 1. I didn't consciously decide to mentor Alysse; it merely evolved as we worked closely together. After being exposed in a business or accounting class at California State University San Marcos (CSUSM) to a particular skill or belief I held, Alysse questioned why I took a particular approach. I replied, "That's just what I believe; it's instinctual."

For at least a year, Alysse would comment that what she was formally learning at school was what I instinctively knew. She would press me with "why?" and I would brush it off like a parent who says, "Because I said so. Just do it as I've advised, please." I had little time to analyze anything; we were so understaffed and working so hard. My intuition never seemed important to me, but looking back, I now understand the value of intuition. I always took it for granted, as most people I imagine do, but what is intuition? Where does it come from? I've learned to deeply analyze this gift, and I have thoughtful convictions about its nature and foundation. I've also developed a profound reverence for it because the outcomes created when I've followed my intuition have never disappointed me.

Alysse is the most successful and respected sales executive I've encountered in the furniture industry. Due to her accounting degree, she approaches sales through a financial lens, respecting both the client's fiscal needs and our organization's requirement to remain profitable for financial stability. She models my client-centric, strategic, and creative sales philosophies while seamlessly incorporating monetary requirements, tailoring solutions that maintain alignment for all parties. She never compromises in pursuit of a "sale," which is short-term thinking. She understands the intrinsic value of personal relationships built with long-term solutions. She saw me lose lots of early projects because I refused to make those compromises that in the long run would not work for a client. As I mentioned before, many of my competitors that engaged in this approach have ceased to exist.

Consider these mentorship narratives:

- It is well-known that Socrates, credited with laying the foundation of modern-day Western philosophy, mentored Plato. Plato has often been deemed history's most important and influential philosopher as the father of idealism.
- Plato mentored scientist and philosopher Aristotle, who made vast contributions to biology, chemistry, psychology, history, and ethics, and is considered the founder of formal logic.
- Aristotle was a paid mentor to Alexander the Great, hired by his father, King Philip II of Macedonia. When Philip II was assassinated, Alexander the Great became King of Macedonia at age twenty. Though Alexander the Great died at the tender age of thirty-two, he created the largest empire in the ancient world and is

widely regarded as one of the greatest military commanders in history because he never lost a battle.

This rich history confirms the veracity of mentorship. Mentoring has stood the test of time as one of the most effective leadership strategies adopted by iconic people throughout history to achieve their destiny.

Super-Mentorship

When Tom joined ICE in 2014 as our Chief Operating Officer, he initially supervised our project managers, accounting staff, and all operational and financial functions. Having worked at a Fortune 100 organization for thirty-six years, many of them in a supervisory position, he brought in advanced Fortune 100 management procedures, providing solid structure for our growing company. He daily mentored Millennial Elyse, helping her achieve her ascendancy to Vice President of Operations. Just as Alysse flourished with my super-mentorship efforts, Elyse thrived under Tom's thoughtful, methodical, and intentional management style.

Initially, we didn't deliberately prepare Alysse and Elyse to manage the organization, but that is exactly what we accomplished, and by 2019, they governed almost every sales and operational aspect of ICE. By 2020, we were fully committed to having them lead the organization without us. Their depth of industry and company knowledge and their ability to effectively create and nurture our corporate culture runs deep. Although it takes years and close guidance to cultivate this type of employee, it has been repeated several times with extreme success in our other departments as well.

Of particular significance is how our "peer-to-peer" mentorship has evolved. It has proven to be even more effective than the "younger-older" mentorship model. Staff members see the opportunity and potential our organization has realized through their peers' success; they find it highly motivating. In a world where too many leaders are all talk and no action, ICE's leaders are just the opposite. We not only espouse and promote our values consistently and intentionally, but we live our values in very physical ways.

Millennials and the Significance of Social Contracts

In social and political theory, "social contracts" have been used to describe a fundamental agreement in a society about the basics of life and coexistence. Recently, commentator and comedian Trevor Noah used the notion of social contracts to frame the George Floyd killing and the resulting Minneapolis protests. On his podcast, *The Daily Social*, Noah asks, "What is society?" Then he goes on to explain that society is a "contract" that is neither written nor spoken, yet we collectively agree to "sign the contract" and adhere to a set of common rules, ideas, and practices that define us as a group. However, for Noah, our societal "contract" is only as robust as our leaders. Noah sees a major disconnect with this implicit contract held by all Americans but perhaps, in his opinion, not held equally. He asks us to consider "if our leaders don't abide by the contract, if the contract isn't working for everyone fairly and equally, when society doesn't hold up its end of the contract, isn't the breakdown of our shared societal contract to be expected?"

In this case, Noah is referencing the contract breakdown in regards to how law enforcement interacted with George Floyd. We all know it's the job of the police to protect and serve; that's in the "contract." When that contract was broken even the most ardent supporters of our police condemned this act as a very visible breakdown of one of our social norms. This casual loss of life reinforces the belief for many that a class system still exists in America, that a police officer can think they can take the life of another without any real punishment.

We have such an enormous need for healthy, robust social contracts because it is where the meaning that leads to societal connection is created. This apparent breach of contract is as much a reason for the social injustice protests as the individual death of Floyd. It certainly illustrates the evident absence of strong, insightful, and empathetic leadership.

In the introduction, I mentioned my friend Greg Horowitt. Besides being a university lecturer, Greg is a venture capitalist. Greg has recently become laser-focused on mentorship and the values of conscious capitalism, specifically, conscious leadership. Greg and I agree that Millennials and Gen Z tend to say the right things, using the proper language to express themselves regarding social injustice, gender equality, environmental concerns, and poverty elimination. However, they don't always actively support these concerns. While they strive to create an image of how they *want* to see themselves and how they *want* the world to see them, they are not always willing to actualize those values. Greg describes this situation in these terms:

> "I call this orthodoxy versus orthopraxy. Orthodoxy is your belief system, what you proclaim out loud and orthopraxy is how you conduct yourself, your actions. There is a major disconnect with some of our most visible business leaders in their orthodoxy versus their orthopraxy; they talk a great game but do not practice what they preach and thus there they break a known, yet unwritten social contract. This huge disconnect with acclaimed leaders and role models does not go unnoticed with this generational cohort. That is why my course is gaining in significance; we need to shine a light on this division and provide tools for the next generation to attain their portended aspirational values. In the future, though they have the awareness and skill set for alignment to occur, they too might not embody these values, but it will be a conscious choice not to."

Greg noted the Laine Hanson quote from the film *The Contender*: "principles only mean something if you stick by them when they are inconvenient." Most people don't want to risk their social, economic, or reputational capital in support of their values. However, the only time we're tested is when living those values is inconvenient. The year 2020 really brought this lesson home. We saw many of our leaders saying one thing—telling us to isolate—and then doing the opposite. They broke the social contract.

At ICE, our staff sees us living our values on a consistent basis even when it's inconvenient and difficult. We work very hard for consistency in our daily words, our orthodoxy, and our actions, our orthopraxy. Are we perfect in making our words match our actions? Of course not, but as you'll learn from this book and from Greg's course and upcoming book *The Concept of Social Contracts*, our aspirations are as vital to building our brand and healthy robust corporate culture as are our accomplishments. Too many Americans focus so strongly on outcomes that they don't see or appreciate all the effort being expended to achieve success. Accomplishments happen because of aspirations. Our aspirations create and support our corporate belief system of the importance of the individual, their work, the concept of equality, etc. Whether we achieve perfection or even our stated goals, we still applaud and encourage the effort. We unconsciously endeavor to match our words and our actions, valuing equally aspirations and accomplishments, and over the years, this has created an inherent social contract of unconditional trust. And, of course, trust is the foundation for every relationship; without trust, social contracts are meaningless.

> *Aspirations are vital to building a robust corporate culture and lead to accomplishments. Value aspirations—effort—equally as they form the building blocks to accomplishments—success—and ultimately to a culture built on the bedrock of trust.*

In a recent LinkedIn article, Deloitte Global CEO Punit Renjen said:

> "There is really no secret (to success) and there surely are no shortcuts. In my case, it was a pretty simple

equation: hard work + some lucky breaks + great mentors. The last of these, the positive impact of the mentor, is clearly highlighted by our 2016 Deloitte Millennial Survey findings. Among those who have somebody acting as their mentor, more than nine in ten describe the quality of advice (94 percent) and the level of interest shown in their development (91 percent) as 'good.' Among those with mentors, 83 percent are satisfied with this aspect of their working lives. Where it exists, mentoring is having a positive impact and six in ten (61 percent) Millennials are currently benefiting from having somebody to turn to for advice, or who helps develop their leadership skills."[18]

Results of Super-Mentorship

Alysse is now the President of ICE and is inspiring and leading our respected furniture dealership. Alysse understands the value and immense impact of cultivating personal relationships, maintaining the highest ethics, being involved in volunteer efforts, and giving back to the community. She understands this because she saw me model it. Although I did not, in the beginning, actively or consciously mentor Alysse, she was always watching and learning from me—it was "mentorship by example," the same way a child learns to become an adult from their parent.

Alysse's best hires have been young women with little or no furniture experience whom she consciously and carefully mentors. In 2018 she hired then twenty-four-year-old Cheyenne Burrows who not only lacked furniture knowledge, she also did not have a college degree and had not worked in an office. Cheyenne is one of the most creative, curious and hard-working Account Executives I've ever experienced. She spent enormous amounts of time learning our industry after hours, organizing the library, supporting Alysse in highly imaginative ways as her Sales Assistant. Her mind is so quick even Alysse was astonished. Cheyenne was quickly promoted into sales and has a devoted client based to include one of San Diego's most respected and commanding commercial real estate developers. As our team members work with her on her projects, not only have our abilities as an organization to deliver increasingly unique products and proficiencies increased, our level of creativity as an entire organization has evolved.

Part of Cheyenne's success can be attributed to Alysse because Alysse didn't mentor Cheyenne in the same way she was mentored; she did it more thoughtfully, more strategically.

> *That is one of the many benefits of being mentored—you have the advantage of a panoramic landscape to observe another's performance and do it better!*

Alysse manages, trains, and supports all sales efforts and salespeople while somehow processing 78 percent of our sales revenues due to her extensive personal client relationships. She developed our sales hiring and training process from our experience; it's one ingredient in our secret sauce!

It's been a gift to invest in Alysse's leadership development. It hasn't always been easy and, of course, we've had our disagreements. Alysse is always incredibly respectful, even if her personal beliefs do not coincide with mine. Mutual respect, not blind allegiance, is the key to a successful mentor/mentee relationship. The ability to respectfully disagree and debate leads to better solutions and is core to our corporate culture's robust success.

A Rigid Perspective Doesn't Yield Flexible Results

When I decided to become an author, my son encouraged me to read the publication *Medium*, where independent thinkers can publish their views alongside experts. I went online and clicked on all the topics that interested me. I was surprised to encounter some of the most unreasonable content I had ever read, along with perspectives that resonated with me. To be a successful business owner, parent, or community leader, it's imperative to understand others' opinions and beliefs and to let those beliefs help you formulate and develop your own beliefs. *This process is relevant in every area of your life.*

It is challenging to process new input unless you are able to approach information without a personal agenda and with a willingness to be wrong. Having an open mind and a respectful perspective is critical as you take in new information because that's all it is, even if you disagree with it. I steer clear of absolute statements because with an influx of new information, a stance I held to be without question often shifts.

Becoming open to new information is a process, so if you expect your mentee to embrace every kernel of wisdom that comes from your mouth without questioning it, you're going to be disappointed. A gifted analytical person will listen to your advice and then figure out what works and what doesn't for them. They will analyze the content and look for holes in your perspective—and you'll want them to because it provides an opportunity for you both to evolve and gain new perspective. Here's the biggest surprise of all in this relationship:

> *The mentor learns as much as the mentee!*

I hadn't anticipated this encouraging outcome but that's exactly what transpired. Alysse and I both evolved, almost equally! She helped me become a more tolerant and perceptive leader who actively searched to understand before understanding. She became my closest advisor, and soon I found it uncomfortable to move forward with complex decisions without first discussing them with her. Her wise counsel and Millennial peer insight became indispensable not only to me but to our company's health and stability. It is imperative to have an open mind with complex, multi-generational interactions.

One of this book's most important points is that business can and should be an enjoyable journey for all parties involved. It need not be a slug fest, a soul-sucking debilitating experience; it can and should be so much more. Having an open mind allows ideas and creativity to naturally flow and organically leads to the development of more gratifying and more authentic relationships.

The Humility Equation

As a dancer, I learned that feedback is critical; any athlete will understand this. Athletes not only accept feedback, but they crave it, understanding it is the only way to improve performance. The process becomes far more enjoyable if feedback is received with a humility mindset.

One reason I hesitated to become an entrepreneur was my lack of leadership experience, but perhaps that was why I was so open to receiving input, even from someone who was half my age and reported to me. Early on at ICE, we developed this mindset of continuous improvement and communication flow, always seeking to find more effective administrative procedures and marketing strategies. We had fun doing it! The hunger to seek continuous improvement is baked into our culture, and it began with Alysse and me modeling this behavior.

When I hired Alysse in January 2007, she lacked office experience, so I was constantly giving her feedback; I could tell she wasn't happy with this. I realized her frustration could become a major issue since she had so much to learn. I knew she had been a competitive figure skater. To avoid defensiveness, I asked her a series of questions regarding her past relationship with her coach, specifically, "How much attention did your coach give you?" She replied, "A lot, probably more than most of the other skaters." "Why," I asked, "do you think he didn't give the other skaters as much feedback?" She replied, "They weren't as talented as I am; they weren't as competitive." My response was "Exactly! The one with the most potential received the most feedback and direction, and the only way to improve your skating skills was to get this constant stream of feedback." When Alysse viewed my direction through those goggles, she more readily accepted it, though not completely or wholeheartedly. It was a process and lesson she's never forgotten as she mentors' others.

Parenting and Management Skills Are Quite Similar

I'm a far better person for having raised Alex because he prepared me to understand Millennial characteristics and a generation that has technology ingrained in their DNA.

I feel as connected to my staff as I do to my son. My parenting style is reflective of my management style. In evaluating several highly respected business leaders, I learned that many incorporate a parental leadership style. Simon Sinek specifically addresses this in his interview "Millennials in the Workplace."[19] I highly recommend you watch this video more than once to let it sink in, but let me capture the essence of this interview.

Sinek notes the failed parenting strategies of some Baby Boomers has led to challenges for their Millennial children in dealing with failure. Children who received participation medals, even for last place, knew they were being given medals they didn't deserve and this only decreased their confidence. I've witnessed in the work environment that many of our young people either have an over-inflated sense of self-worth or very low self-esteem. Sinek notes that this *lack of self-awareness*, partnered with our phone obsession and "instant gratification addiction," has created a lethal mix in our society. This constant incitement stimulates our brains to release dopamine, a chemical fueled through an addiction to social media, our phones, the internet—technology. Many Millennials struggle with managing stress and creating meaningful human relationships. Past social coping mechanisms may not be relevant, perhaps not even taught. We see the outcome with the alarming increase in suicide—now the second leading cause of death in ages 10-34. It's a horrific statistic.

Sinek argues that it's in the work environment that we must teach Millennials how to appreciate the joy in work—joy in accomplishment, joy in personal development, and joy in forming potentially lifelong human connections with coworkers. Sinek advises:

> "Corporate environments care more about the numbers
> than they do about the kids, more about the short-term
> gains than the long-term life of this young human being.

We...aren't helping them learn the skills of cooperation (to) overcome the challenges of the digital world and find more balance...teaching them the joys of impact and the fulfillment you get from working hard on something over a long time. It's the total lack of good leadership in our world today. It's the company's responsibility to teach them social skills. It sucks to be us, but this is the company's responsibility."

I totally agree with Sinek's assessment. I've established numerous meaningful relationships with Millennials both at ICE and outside the office; I derive a deep sense of satisfaction in mentoring them. They want to be part of a team that produces consequential work, in a culture that promotes their growth, values their input, and respects them as people. And they thrive when their energy is properly engaged.

I have always approached our staff from the perspective of a parent with the responsibility that I'm raising the future leaders of tomorrow—*because I am.* Our young workforce is our future and we have a responsibility to treat them with respect, continuing to develop them as the emerging leaders they are. Anything less does not serve them, our community, or our future with the dignity and serious consideration it demands.

Greg Horowitt believes mentorship provides significant opportunity for true global impact; human beings learn many of their key lessons through biomimicry—reflecting others' behaviors. He states:

"Mentorship and apprenticeship allow for that connection and the 'space' to learn through empathy, emulation, and imitation. We are about to experience the largest transfer of private wealth over the next decade in Southeast Asia. It is considered the largest transfer of wealth in all of history, and we not only have an opportunity but an obligation to imbue these emerging leaders to lead with relevance. We need to be teaching life skills, not just enterprise skills. Oculus, a Facebook company, has created a virtual reality exercise to do simulations where we can emulate pro-social behaviors and encounter what it feels like when we experience life through the eyes of others. An example is experiencing life as a Black person if you are White. We've been integrating some of this technology at Stanford to teach empathy, one of the most critical life skills to have as a business leader."[20]

Stath Karras

Stath Karras is one of Greg's closest friends. I've known and admired him for many years. Stath and San Diego are both well-known for leadership that elevates humanity, promoting a higher level of integrity and ethics, as well as intergenerational leadership.

The mentorships Stath Karras received have influenced his mentoring perspective. Stath has a storied history in the real estate industry, serving nineteen years with Burnham Real Estate Services, the last seven as President and CEO. He followed that with seven years as Executive Managing Director when Burnham was acquired by Cushman & Wakefield. Stath is currently the Executive Director of the Burnham-Moores Center for Real Estate at the University of San Diego School of Business, ranked as the number-one real estate college in the United States 2018-2020. Stath received a "Lifetime Achievement Award" from the *San Diego Business Journal* in 2020; it is a strikingly accurate reflection of his success not only in the real estate industry, but in his overall commitment to our community.

President Eisenhower once said, "The supreme quality of leadership is unquestionably integrity. Without it, no real success is possible...." Stath is a lion for integrity and we share a remarkably similar perspective on leadership being based on parental principles.

Stath and I both had the fortunate gift of loving parental involvement as we grew up. We have offered that not just to our children, but to our coworkers. Stath strives to create a family work environment that is as galvanizing as the one he fashioned when raising his own children.

I reached out to Stath on a day when our country was engulfed in the rioting sparked by George Floyd's tragic death. In that context, our conversation had an elevated degree of compassion.

Stath had enjoyed the mentorship of several prominent men in his career. They helped mold his leadership and mirror the support he brings to younger generations.

Stath noted that there are three forms of mentorship:

1. Formal mentor: A conscious interest and effort exists on both sides.
2. Informal mentor: Only in retrospect do individuals realize they were mentored or had a mentee.
3. Mentorship by example: Experienced in a day-to-day work environment, working closely with a manager. It's a natural progression where one day the evolving mentee suddenly realizes the manager's qualities and traits are ones the mentee desires to emulate.

Early in his real estate career, Stath developed a close friendship with his employer, Andy Shearer of Wallace Associates. Andy was a seasoned professional, and Stath worked closely with him for ten years. Andy took an active interest in helping Stath understand the business, suggesting and supporting his pursuing a graduate degree, supporting his community involvement, and treating him as family (including taking Stath and his wife on family vacations). It is not unusual for mentor/mentee relationships to develop into lifelong friendships. They are also mutually beneficial, the mentee benefiting from the guidance and support of a mentor and the mentor benefiting from the sense of joy received in the relationship.

This joy is the lesser known, quiet gift of mentorship that Stath and I—and countless others—have experienced. In service, we discover our true joy. Here, I believe, we all can find and realize our higher purpose. If you remember only one thing from this book, I hope it is this concept of serving others as the road to self-fulfillment and making the world a better place. And not just a better place today—serving others creates a ripple effect to future generations. *Inspiring Generational Leadership* is written as much for today's leaders as leaders one hundred years from now.

While Stath was being mentored by Andy, he also developed an informal mentoring relationship with one of his most active clients, Nick Vidalakis. The two spent quite a bit of time together. Nick taught him many lessons through metaphors such as "Once you've swallowed the jackass, don't choke on the tail." Translation: "Once you've made a decision, no matter the consequences, there's no going back; you have to learn to deal with the outcome."

Nick was very smart and very street savvy, providing a different set of lessons for Stath. This diversity in his mentors' approaches and dispositions made for a broader spectrum of knowledge, understanding, and behavior for Stath; i.e., more tools in the toolbox. Both of these gentlemen laid the groundwork for Stath's most significant mentor, Malin Burnham.

Malin's accomplishments are not only synonymous with the spirit of San Diego's moral belief system, but Malin helped lay the foundation and craft its ethos. A hometown San Diego boy, Malin has experienced astonishing business and financial success. He's chaired nine non-profits and co-founded fourteen organizations, but what defines Malin is the thirty-four years of philanthropic efforts he's advanced *after retirement*. His motto "community before self" is a reflection of his devotion to San Diego to inspire and elevate others. Our City Council honored Malin on his ninetieth birthday, naming it "Malin Burnham Day"! We all recognize the gift Malin has been in increasing and promoting San Diego's philosophical belief system of philanthropy. Malin reflects many of humanity's most admirable values and ethics, and Stath consciously decided he wanted to emulate those commendable qualities.

Stath recalls Malin's involvement in the sale of his family's company, Burnham Real Estate Services. At the time, the Burnham Company was 117-years-old and had established a great legacy in San Diego. Stath was worried about what might happen to a strong local company in the next economic downturn when its client and investment base was far removed from San Diego. Stath realized an alignment, merger, or sale to a national company would be the most prudent course of action for a sustainable San Diego commercial real estate organization. Burnham Real Estate Services was an employee-owned company at this time, so Stath presented the rationale and challenge the organization could be facing to the employees if they didn't shift from being a local entity to part of a national organization that could better weather an abrupt local downturn. After discussing with employees why a sale was in their best interest, Stath engaged with the board to find an advantageous partner. Malin had sold his interest to his senior management team in 1986. He no longer had ownership in the company, but he continued to be fully engaged, serving as Chairman of the Board. Malin represented the legacy of three generations of the Burnham family, and along with guidance from the board of directors and Malin, Stath moved forward with the sale, eventually selling to Cushman Wakefield.

The Burnham name and the Burnham Company was the "gold standard" in San Diego, so you can imagine that the decision to sell your family's 117-year-old company was difficult. Malin understood that the sale of the company was likely the best option for the employees, solidifying what integrity looks like when faced with a watershed moment. To allow the Burnham name and its 117-year legacy to no longer be associated with San Diego's premier real estate company exemplifies the depth of Malin's character. Malin carries a card that states "Community Before Self," and this is an example of how he lives this statement. Malin supported the decision because it was the "right" decision, and it is just one of many examples of how Malin's ethical belief system strongly influenced Stath. Character is only fully realized during moments of crisis, when it's tested.

Trust

Trust lies at the heart of every relationship; it takes years to develop, but can evaporate instantly. Trust allows organizations and communities to flourish, increasing engagement, dedication, energy, and honest interaction. It's defined as "feeling safe when vulnerable"—when trust is present, magic can and does happen!

In his "Millennials in the Workplace" interview, Sinek notes how trust develops in the most casual of exchanges among coworkers and managers before or after in-person meetings. To encourage more conversation between employees, as people gather, management should establish protocols eliminating cell phone usage among employees working within the same building. Leadership can also consciously design offices that encourage conversations and incorporate other mechanisms that nurture hundreds of small interactions that build relationships, honest human connection, and the development of trust.

An old analogy bears repeating: Trust is like an emotional savings account—you make deposits to build your savings, rarely making withdrawals. Over time, you build your savings. Trust grows in the same way with consistent and honest deposits that reinforce your trustworthiness. Over time you may need to make withdrawals but never withdrawals that compromise your integrity. In *The 7 Habits of Highly Effective People*, Stephen Covey puts it this way:

> "If I make deposits into an Emotional Bank Account with you through courtesy, kindness, honesty, and keeping my commitments to you, I build up a reserve. Your trust towards me becomes higher, and I can call upon that trust many times if I need to. I can even make mistakes and that trust level, that emotional reserve, will compensate for it. My communication may not be clear, but you'll get my meaning anyway. You won't make me 'an offender for a word.' When the trust account is high, communication is easy, instant, and effective."[21]

Over the years, Alysse and I made countless withdrawals that tested our relationship, but never once did we make a withdrawal that reduced trust. On the contrary, the trials just continued to build our level of trust. No doubt our relationship is unusually resilient because we both nurture and value the development of ethical virtues. It is why mentors and mentees with high ethical character develop a stable relational foundation—which is most certainly required to build a flourishing mentorship connection. Trust is the foundation of life-changing mentorship and the glue that holds it together during adversarial situations.

The Ripple Effect

One of my intentions in writing *Inspiring Generational Leadership* is to create community and family ripple effects. Influential mentorship has the power to transcend generations and cause a multi-generational ripple effect that can constructively affect an entire community. As we positively influence our work teammates, we are laying the groundwork to positively affect the emotional well-being of our employees' children and even descendants, ultimately imprinting thousands of people. The potential ramifications of this ripple effect when viewed through a more eternal lens are expansive!

The thought of legacy now motivates how I behave every day, most likely due to my advancing age and the grandchildren in my life. Life-altering mentorship is a surefire way to establish generational legacy.

Successful Mentoring Requires Mutual Respect

Let me also reinforce the gift of respectful disagreement. It not only exists at ICE; it's encouraged! Dissenting views contained within respectful conversation and open minds without emotional ties attached to our opinions or beliefs are the keys to successful mentoring. Actually, they are the keys to a successful life!

One of the more gratifying opportunities in writing this book was the opportunity to interview San Diego leaders. It was an incredible chance to better understand my leadership beliefs and gain a deeper perspective of how leaders I admire are leading. I wanted to see if: a) other leaders incorporated my style and approach, and b) if so, could they introduce or expand on concepts I had not considered using? San Diego possesses an interconnected business culture of collaboration; it is inherent in how we view ourselves. Business is a highly competitive sport in every community but California is one of America's most competitive arenas. Yet San Diego continues to maintain the reputation of "America's largest small city."

My interview with Tiffany English, principal of the architectural interior design firm Ware Malcomb, offered many insightful nuggets.

Tiffany has worked for Ware Malcomb since 2001. Ware Malcomb promotes an entrepreneurial mindset and encourages mentorship. The firm's team is so committed to the benefits of mentorship that the firm has a formal program that includes measurable systems and extensive training.

Tiffany was working at the Sacramento Ware Malcomb location when the San Diego location's leader reached out to her to join him in managing his location. Tiffany advised me, "I knew this was an opportunity I could not pass up. I was fortunate that the principal of the San Diego office became my sponsor, mentor, and champion—I will always be thankful to him for his unwavering support. I've been fortunate in my professional journey to have worked with leadership that recognizes my potential, fosters it, and invests in my professional development. They value my abilities and support my ideas—even when they are out-of-the-box."[22]

Tiffany and Ware Malcomb share my perspective that "out-of-the-box" thinking team members are the talent needed to find the most advantageous solutions. Numerous recent studies confirm that diversity of thought created by life experiences, culture, age, gender, and race differences leads to diversity of team members, leading to more creative team initiatives. In the 2018 *Forbes* article "A Study Finds That Diverse Companies Produce 19% More Revenue," author Anna Powers, the first woman to be awarded the Global STEM Leadership Prize, notes that:

> "Diversity boils down to curiosity—diversity also serves a certain function in nature—biodiversity is an important key to the functioning of our planet. Each species and component of biodiversity, no matter how small, plays an important role in the survival of our planet and the ecosystem."[23]

The Boston Consulting Group workplace diversity study Powers cites in her article collected survey results from 1,700 diverse industry companies located in eight different countries and concluded:

> "Companies that have more diverse management teams have 19% higher revenue due to innovation. This finding is huge for tech companies, start-ups, and industries where innovation is the key to growth. It shows that diversity is not just a metric to be strived for, it is an integral part of a successful revenue generating business. Of course, this makes sense because diversity means diversity of minds, ideas, and approaches—which allows teams to find solutions that consider multiple angles of a problem, thus making the solution stronger, well rounded and optimized. Therefore, diversity is key for a company's bottom line."

Tiffany gets energized when she holds a belief or opinion and hears a thought that "flips her judgment." She refers to such moments as "the most exciting times of my life! When I can authentically connect, push aside judgment and ego, and find a new truth, a new alignment."

Tiffany found that her managing principal shared her value of encouraging staff to seek guidance, but not by simply providing solutions. Instead, he modeled the valuable talent of discernment. He encouraged Tiffany's practice of not giving answers, but instead *asking questions*. As a leader, Tiffany makes it clear she's not there to provide quick answers but to promote the development of problem-solving skills by providing thought-provoking questions that lead to the best solutions. This process of asking questions not only teaches problem-solving skills; it leads to an increase in accountability, ownership of outcome, and a heightened sense of pride.

Tiffany, also an enormous fan of Simon Sinek, sees the similarities in leading and parenting. She redefines leadership as "not having all the answers all the time, but by asking strategic questions, then actively listening to answers that expand my mind, we can *collectively* find the most innovative solution." Anna Powers' article adds clarity to this:

> "The study found that instead of focusing on a specific area of diversity, focusing on creating teams that have multiple areas of diversity has more value. So how can companies structure diverse teams? Although there is no 'one fit all' answer, the researchers indicate that the initiatives that come from the CEO's vision coupled with policies such as equal pay, a culture of openness and inclusion help companies create a diverse and well-rounded environment."

Diversity of Thought and Analogous Ethical Belief Systems

While Tiffany and her managing principal were different in many ways, their principles were in complete harmony, especially in areas of personal ethical behavior and social justice. *When seeking a mentee or mentor, this alignment ideally needs to be more than similar; it really needs to be equal!*

Tiffany has consistently affiliated herself with thought leaders *in alignment with her moral values.* She thrived under her managing principal's mentorship because he embraced servant-leadership values, putting aside his ego, and most significantly, judgment. He encouraged her diversity of thought and perspective, reinforcing Tiffany's belief that "To grow deeply as a leader and as a person, you have to expose yourself to many schools of thought. This is how real innovation and creativity is cultivated. When you resign your ego, you will find truth in the middle and create something new in this 'third place,' which isn't necessarily my truth or your truth but an evolved truth based on the merging of both. It all starts with listening intently."

The website LeadershipExpert was formed in the UK in 2000 to provide expert leadership guidance. An article on its website by Anna Martin, titled "The Importance of Ethics in Leadership," advises:

> "An ethical leader works to create open conversation that encourages the sharing of ideas, knowledge and vision to facilitate the group benefit of mutual learning and united purpose aspiration. The leader must also compel others to follow the lead that he/she sets by the standards that are reflected in the way they live, influence and inspire.
>
> An ethical leader is someone who embodies the purpose and values of the company and is driven to perform to the best of their ability, compelling others to do the same."[24]

An ethical leader must set up open communication where the basics of value are routinely discussed and explored to better understand others' views. It is all about setting your ego aside, having an open mindset, and focusing on others. The importance of ethics noted in LeadershipExpert are in alignment with the style Tiffany and I both share—providing the foundation for a fruitful and enjoyable mentorship relationship.

Female Mentorship

Unsurprisingly, most men but only a few women I interviewed had business mentors—exactly what I had personally experienced. According to a 2019 survey conducted by Olivet Nazarene University with more than 3,000 respondents, 82 percent of men have had a male mentor while only 69 percent of women have had a female mentor. Fifty-six percent of all respondents had never had a mentor, yet 76 percent believed mentorship was an important part of their professional and career development.[25]

Dianna Chane is a Forbes Council Member, author, and real-estate expert and consultant. She noted in her 2020 article for Forbes, "The Power of Female Mentors: Why We Need More Women Leading Today's Workforce" the critical and beneficial nature of women mentoring men.

She emphasized the importance of female mentorship in male-dominated industries such as commercial real estate. She argues that women mentoring men can lead to reduced workplace gender discrepancies and has the potential to create equality awareness. She advises:

> "If we want our workplace to reflect a more gender-neutral environment we must create the space by leading the conversation through mentoring men and women equally. I believe it's equally—if not more—important for women to support male colleagues, especially by ascending into more mentorship roles. When women are underrepresented in a business, the entire business suffers. The experience and wisdom we have to offer works to everyone's empowerment."[26]

Equally intriguing is the mentorship research done by Drs. Dave Smith and Brad Johnson of the US Naval Academy. Dr. Smith's research is focused on workplace gender equity while Dr. Johnson is a clinical psychologist and scholar with decades of mentoring research under his belt. They co-authored the book *Athena Rising: How and Why Men Should Mentor Women*. They see women as rising Athenas. Dr. Johnson states, "Athena was the goddess of war, the goddess of literature, and she was a diplomat—she had it all going on. Part of our message to corporate America is that perceptions matter and, if you're a guy in a male-centric environment leading the way, how you choose to see women matters."

Dr. Johnson goes on to advise:

> "Mixed gender teams perform better. They're more creative. Sometimes you have to make the personal case and appeal to women they care about—their daughters, spouses, colleagues, and sisters. For other men, you tie it into leadership and their brand as an inclusive leader. In terms of the issue of pay disparity, I can't think of many

things that are going to move the dial more quickly than having men involved in mentorship."[27]

They believe men need to sponsor and mentor women in the workplace to alleviate gender inequality and note these specific reasons:

1. Women involved in the research consistently advised that men struggle to simply listen; they want to fix the problem.
2. Workplace equality cannot happen until men are equal partners at home and share those responsibilities equally.
3. Data shows that people who are mentored earn more, are promoted more, perform better, and experience increased career mobility.
4. People who are mentored are less likely to leave their jobs.

Supporting the theory of Drs. Johnson and Smith, the Olivet Nazarene University survey confirms that 61 percent of mentorship occurs with both participants working at the same organization.[28]

Saundra Pelletier

Saundra Pelletier is one of San Diego's most courageous, forthright, and accomplished chief executive officers. I met Saundra through the CEO of Athena, Holly Smithson. Athena is a premier women's advocacy organization that fast tracks women in STEM careers through leadership development programs. Many of the women you'll meet in *Inspiring Generational Leadership* are leaders I've met through this extraordinary organization.

As CEO of Evofem, a publicly traded biopharmaceutical company, she is committed to developing revolutionary non-hormonal products that have multiple applications, including contraception and the prevention of sexually transmitted diseases, such as chlamydia and gonorrhea. Saundra noted:

> Evofem Biosciences is a company with a conscience; we call it Science with a Soul. Evofem exists to advance the lives of women, and we believe this work centers around putting each woman in control of her sexual and reproductive health. By providing innovative solutions, such as woman-controlled contraception and protection from sexually transmitted infections, we can move swiftly toward our goal of upholding the purpose each woman chooses for her life. The team members I've attracted are highly disciplined and intensely passionate pharma experts who believe in this mission 100 percent; it is the reason they are at Evofem. The days of just being satisfied with a paycheck are over. Everyone wants to work doing something they believe in and something that gives back.[29]

New York Times journalist Valeriya Safronova certainly captured Saundra's uncompromising spirit in her June 2021 NYT article "The Pill Helped Start the Sexual Revolution: What Will Phexxi Do?" Some of Ms. Safronova's article is noted below:

> The conference rooms in Evofem's offices are all named after women who left a mark on the world: Ruth Bader Ginsburg, Rosa Parks, Marie Curie. A stylized Joan of Arc, in hot pink, looms on a screen in the "war room." In the cafeteria, "feminism" is written on a plaque, along with a definition of the word. A shower curtain…proclaims in bold, uppercase letters, "Here's to strong women/May we know them/May we be them/May we raise them."

Ms. Turner, the brand manager who has worked with Ms. Pelletier for six years, praised the office environment. "My sister works in finance and she was sent home for not wearing the right shoes," she said. "I'm like, 'Are you kidding me? My C.E.O. is running around in this crazy 'My Favorite F-word Is Feminism' shirt. This is an amazing culture to work in."

Though she has always been forthright, Ms. Pelletier said that after battling cancer, she decided she was done with "superficial nicety."

She started implementing 15-minute "reality checks" every other week with her executive team. "I say, 'This is not going well, here's why, and here's what I suggest you do to correct it. Either you take my idea or you come up with a better one,'" she said. "People are shocked. I believe very few people have been given honest, transparent feedback from their leadership."[30]

I greatly admire Saundra as much for her professional accomplishments as her ability to overcome personal challenges with incredible style and unflinching grit. In 2019, she was awarded *San Diego Business Journal*'s Business Woman of the Year. In 2020, Saundra continued to win some of business' most coveted awards. PharmaVoice 100, a premiere life science leadership organization, acknowledged Saundra in its list for the 100 Most Inspiring People in bioscience. She was included in *Inc. Magazine*'s Female Founder 100 List as one of the most influential and efficacious female leaders in America. And in 2021, the organization she leads, Evofem Biosciences, Inc., was named a winner of Business Intelligence Group's 2021 Big Innovation Awards for its product, Phexxi. This annual business awards program recognizes organizations, products, and people that are bringing new ideas to life in innovative ways. Phexxi is breaking entirely new ground as a revolutionary non-hormonal, FDA-approved birth control cream.

Since 1992, Saundra has been a global warrior for women's health rights and well-being. She is especially determined to bring reproductive independence to some of the world's poorest and most underserved villages and countries.

Like most senior female executives, Saundra has never had a mentor. She remarks:

> If I had a mentor who truly cared about my success and trajectory, my ascension as a leader certainly would have been condensed. No doubt there were blocks and bumps I could have avoided. Everyone needs to have some failures, but there were obstacles I could have better tackled had someone selflessly cared about helping women build their careers. Because of this, I'm extremely passionate about being a mentor and role model because if we do not take the time to invest in the next generation of amazing leaders, entrepreneurs, and glass-ceiling breakers, who will? There is a wonderful quote from Amelia Earhart that I always think about with mentoring: "Some of us have great runways already built for us. If you have one, take off. But if you don't have one, realize it is your responsibility to grab a shovel and build one for yourself and for those who will follow after you."[31]

Saundra has always worked within the male-dominated life sciences industry. She learned early in her career that she often had to far, far outperform her male colleagues to receive acknowledgment. She developed a fanatical, seven-day-per-week work ethic while working at G. D. Searle, a company that launched the first US birth control pill. She accepted any promotion the organization offered, no matter the geographic location, and eventually, she ran its global franchise, specializing in women's healthcare products. In a Forbes article, she described this time in her life:

I was making a fantastic income but I felt soulless. I felt like it didn't matter. I questioned, "Am I making a difference, am I bettering someone else's life, am I bettering my own?" It was about looking at my mortality and asking, what do I want to say at the other end? I was only 34 but I felt like 74. I decided I wanted to write a book to encourage women to create the life they wanted for themselves and not wait for a man to do it for them. The skills that women innately have make them good leaders.

Part of my crisis was I always felt like I was on an island. Never did I feel like I was in an environment of team players. And women absolutely did not support other women. On my own journey, it was women who went out of their way to create obstacles for me. I wanted to send the message to women that this should change.[32]

New York Times journalist Valeriya Safronova certainly captures Saundra's sentiments beautifully in the aforementioned article:

"The hardest days are now," Ms. Pelletier said. "It's like being completely naked and walking down the street. Everybody sees what you do and everybody is an armchair quarterback."

But if her directness about sexism and misogyny bothers people, Ms. Pelletier does not care. "I am not going to be a C.E.O. of this company and pretend that I think equality exists," she said. "Because it doesn't."[33]

Interviewing Saundra was one of the highlights of writing this book, not just because of her brilliance and successful career but because we share similar journeys, values, and belief systems. We both made the difficult decision to be single mothers while juggling challenging careers.

Shattering industry ceilings as a woman is hard; doing it as a devoted single mother is life-altering.

Certainly, the obstacles both women and men created for us motivated our passion to mentor young women and not only build, but better design, runways for future generations.

Mentorship—An Organizational Core Value

Similar to Saundra, I was highly motivated to be a force for good because of the challenges and discrimination I detailed earlier. Successfully teaching myself to thrive in sales made me realize it was a teachable skill. I have a burning desire to lift others. It is one of my core values, and it has been influential in shaping my organization's success and the development of our mentorship culture.

Countless books support the science, art, and psychology of mentoring. Their intent and styles vary from highly academic to more enjoyable overviews such as John Maxwell's *Mentoring 101* or the easy-reading parable format of Ken Blanchard's *One Minute Mentoring*. Readers can also pursue deeper learning through podcasts such as *Tribe of Mentors*, hosted by Tim Ferriss, where he interviews the very best mentors.

Mentorship isn't complicated. It can be as simple as having someone you trust listen to your challenges, ask pertinent questions, and help you figure out the best path for you.

English physicist Isaac Newton is attributed with saying, "If I have seen further than others, it is by standing upon the shoulders of giants." The further you can see into your future, the more confident you will become about its possibilities. Mentees, seek out the giants in your circle. Mentors, I encourage you to consider mentorship as an opportunity to honor all those who have helped you along the way, and if no one did that for you, it's time to break that cycle. Mentoring our next generation of leaders is an enormous opportunity to cultivate sustainable change.

Nerissa Zhang

I met Nerissa the end of 2020 through a mutual friend, Laura Lerum. I have been friends with Laura for years through our church 'small group'. Laura joined a new church and met Nerissa through this church and immediately thought to introduce her to me. I've gained a reputation of being a woman that lifts up and mentors' other women. No matter how busy I am, I always squeeze in time to support female professionals that reach out to me. Is it a challenge? Of course, but the 'karma' benefits consistently have reigned supreme.

Nerissa is the CEO and Cofounder of The Bright App, a fitness app that is bringing exercise, health and wellness seamlessly to users by connecting them with fitness professionals. There are so many benefits to this revolutionary fitness model! It benefits both the trainers and the customers. It's an ideal option for the remote workforce, those constantly travelling or for people that are not in close proximity to or do not like going to a gym. The customer only pays for the actual personal training session, not a gym membership.

As a former gym owner and trainer, Nerissa was well-aware of the challenge's trainers experience, especially the nominal financial percentage they retain when working within the limitations of a gym. Not only do they keep more of the money they earn, trainers have access to an expanded, national and international client base, they have higher client retention, and what means the most to many trainers, they have an increased opportunity to support more people meet their health and wellness goals.

When I met Nerissa, The Bright App was in the early start-up phase and struggling to find funding. She and cofounder and husband James had invested all of their personal cash including their retirement and their children's college funding into this company and they were worried. James had left his financially and emotionally secure position as tech lead at Google to create The Bright App. They both believed in the integrity of the product and the ability for The Bright App to improve both the lives of the consumers and the trainers. They were feeling that it might be time to reconsider their options and reassess the personal emotional strain that was being created by chasing their dream. This is when Laura introduced us.

I soon learned that Nerissa is an extraordinarily tenacious woman. Growing up with a lack of permeance and stability as a foster child, she learned to depend on herself. She also has astonishing faith despite her past. She believes that life is good and that we all have the ability to create better life outcomes. She has an upbeat positivity that is not based on circumstances but her faith. She has three beautiful sons that I've also gotten to know. I quickly became committed to helping her grow her start-up despite her lack of venture capital funding. She is a woman with enormous talent, intelligence and determination and because I felt The Bright App was a profoundly useful product, I became determined to support her in whatever way possible.

I'll be honest, not having a tech background or contacts in tech, I felt my benefits would be limited especially because her number one priority was to find investment funding but we forged ahead anyway. My first idea was to connect her with a revenue-based investor which did not generate investment dollars but did lead her to discovering The Alchemist Accelerator, the longest standing tech accelerator for enterprise in the world. Then I tapped Greg Horowitt, the tech investor mentioned earlier in this chapter, but that too was not an ideal fit however Greg did provide exceedingly beneficial connections.

Introductions are often the most valuable mechanism you can provide to an entrepreneur; without influential connections, entrepreneurs often cannot grow. Growing up within the foster child system, Nerissa was an expert in fostering relationships because she learned that was the only thing she could affect and shape, that she had control over. She worked very hard to nurture every connection made on her behalf. Greg's connections yielded substantial benefits but still no funding!

Mentors make introductions that often don't yield tangible benefits but both the mentor and mentee have the opportunity to grow and learn from these failures. Failures often lead to better ideas, allowing you to weed out what doesn't work. I suggest you focus less on what isn't working choosing to learn from it and work as a team to understand what is beneficial. It's helpful for the mentee to provide feedback on what is working and what they need more of.

I learned so much from this experience because I really didn't know how to help, I just knew I *wanted* to help. We realized it was a mutual learning experience and it was a wonderful experience for both of us. Though my efforts felt futile, Nerissa was growing from each effort—learning valuable skills that increased her knowledge on how to ask for assistance and ultimately helped her understand and define what her needs were. She hit a lot of walls but each wall made her realize what her firm needed and who she needed to become as a CEO to grow her organization.

My efforts finally began to yield fruit when I connected her with other women in tech through the Athena organization. From the women she met in Athena, Nerissa made some valuable contacts but even more significantly, they provided her with suggestions on who to reach out to and why, making introductions to significant and influential gate keepers that benefited The Bright App. Previously, Nerissa often could not get past the gate keepers and now with these introductions, she could. This made a significant difference because she now could access the resources she needed to help grow revenue, expanding awareness of her brand at a relatively low cost which ultimately will expand her customer base by working with corporations that promote wellness.

2020 was a physical and emotionally devastating year for so many. Between forced isolation, the closing of gyms, increased drug and alcohol use, skyrocketing health challenges caused by depression, diabetes, weight gain—all these factors were creating an abysmal perfect storm on the general well-being of people. Employee wellness was becoming front and center for many conscious corporations that genuinely cared about their employee's health. One of the central missions for The Bright App is to bring affordable fitness and wellness training to anyone, anywhere, at any time and finally corporations were realizing the benefits of teaming with The Bright App to achieve their goals!

For several months, Nerissa and her team worked around the clock to develop relationships with large organizations that would allow her to generate the new client leads she needed to create a fiscally stable business.

In June 2021, The Bright App grew 112 percent! This was an enormous success. She also started receiving investments from fellow church members that would allow her to hire more employees to manage their hyper growth generated 'overnight'!

If you've concluded her success has much to do with my input, you'd be wrong, but I do know that making valuable connections, such as introductions made to members of the Athena organization, do make a positive impact. Introductions, even some that might seem superfluous, can become extraordinarily valuable. This is the value and power of becoming a "keystone" which I cover in great detail in Chapter 12.

The Ideal Mentoring Partnership

As you enter into this potentially lifelong relationship, take your time. Here are some suggestions for developing this partnership. You can also download this exercise on my website, and more details are noted under Additional Resources at the end of the book.

1. Enter into the relationship with a conscious approach. Clarify and write out your mutual goals. The mentee needs to authentically desire this relationship, realizing they need to live up to the mentor's expectations.

2. This is not a one-way relationship; both need to take the time to make the relationship meaningful and worthwhile. Be thoughtful, considerate, and especially, grateful for the guidance. I detail the benefits of gratitude more in the next chapter.

3. Conversation must be as honest as possible, clarifying the potential of the partnership and of each person in achieving the stated goals. Take some time with this; rewrite the stated outcome and all the goals, and never be afraid to rewrite it again and again as your needs evolve and as you change. Alysse wanted to be in sales, although I didn't think that best suited her skillset, but we

proceeded with that goal in mind. I was wrong—she is the best account executive I've ever experienced—bringing the technology skills needed for today's business demands and expanding and evolving my consultative approach.

4. Each participant must have a desire to hear the truth and be able to discuss the best way to deliver the truth to avoid shutting down. This is an ongoing dialogue. If the mentee truly wants to be mentored, they need to hear, appreciate, and absorb constructive feedback. Change is not easy—altering bad habits and realizing you might have poor analysis capabilities can be difficult to hear.

5. Both parties need to realize a limited and self-limiting perspective serves no one.

6. Be able to take Boomer or Gen X wisdom and distill it in ways Millennials can digest and embrace. Again, this is not a one-way conversation; take the time to figure this out.

7. Keeping in mind the long-term negative consequences of poor decision making is a terrific motivator, so take the time to analyze past decisions that did not yield desired outcomes. Take the time to get to know yourself.

8. Aligned values are critical for any relationship's success. If you both understand the principles of conscious capitalism, that is a great start. Both need to be motivated by a shared definition of success that is mutually agreed upon. For instance, if one cares more about money than stakeholder value, this relationship isn't a fit.

9. Offer a "trust but verify" philosophy—no one is perfect, so if something just doesn't resonate with the mentee, do the research, ask the questions, and seek guidance from others. You should not be afraid to debate findings because doing so can benefit both parties.

10. Seeking knowledge from multiple sources does two things: makes the mentee more confident of the guidance and brings more knowledge to the mentor. By conveying this information respect-

fully, both will grow and trust will develop to support the success of the mentorship.

11. Be forever curious, always interested in learning more.

12. If the mentee is being prepared to lead the organization, they should be able to expand and improve on current business strategies and be encouraged to stretch, even if it leads to short-term failure. To grow, tomorrow's leaders need the freedom to create something new that remains in alignment with the organization's internal compass and belief system. If the relationship is solid, you should be able to openly debate strategies that will lead to company growth.

13. Seek out a mentee who has visionary potential, can analyze data, and has the ability to identify trends that are critical in big picture decision making. The mentee needs to be taught and encouraged to grow as a visionary for long-term corporate stability and health.

14. Be strategic, empathetic, and kind. Develop exceptional listening skills, perhaps participating in the same Toastmasters group. Being unable to clearly articulate ideas, future vision, and how best to manage and direct the team can put stress on the relationship. Anticipate and develop tools in advance to navigate through tough conversations.

15. If you are grooming your mentee as your successor, you must have the ability to delegate and relinquish control. If ego gets in the way, a coach can be helpful. It's not easy for a founder to let go of their baby, and both parties must have the maturity to understand this, working through challenges to maintain a robust relationship.

16. Both must be able to understand the vision of the company in its current state to visualize where it needs to grow to accommodate market drivers. A shared business perspective and background is helpful and can be attained by reading the same books, sharing a business coach, and participating in similar organizations so each is growing their business wisdom.

17. Both must be passionate about the organization's purpose and mission.
18. Both must be dependable, consistent, and not let ego direct their behavior.
19. Both must value, contribute, and nurture the company's culture and contribute to its success.
20. Both must have high respect and value for all employees and understand the immense value in stakeholder relationships.
21. Both need to be able to make hard decisions that are right for the organization.
22. The mentee needs a "pay it forward' mentality, understanding they are now required to mentor others.
23. The mentor must have the ability to inspire and motivate team members.

Finding the ideal person to share your wisdom with, especially with the intention of business succession, is not an easy endeavor, but because I've been able to succeed in this effort, I know it's possible. As I look at ICE more in a rearview mirror, the positive mentoring partnership I experienced with Alysse is what I'm most pleased with, and I look forward to continuing to enjoy her development as a gifted leader.

CHAPTER 3

A Culture of Gratitude Bonds Our Humanity

At ICE, every person in our organization adds to our culture and belief system that we are an exceedingly connected organization of individuals unified with a singular but multidimensional goal to succeed. We strive to succeed as a group and as a community. We have grown to honestly care about each other as people. Do we enjoy each other's company equally? Highly doubtful. Do we get annoyed with each other? Well, of course; any tightly knit unit would. But we genuinely care about each other's well-being and respect each other's contributions to the company. We have developed a corporate culture that promotes gratitude, so we have learned to be grateful for each other's talents and personalities—as parents, siblings, partners, and individuals. We know each other and view each other as *people* more than as *coworkers*.

Bonding in Our Humanity

As you get to know what motivates other people—their history, their dreams, what books they read, what food they eat, the vacations they take, their childbirth concerns—you connect in profoundly different ways. This intimate knowledge creates our interconnectivity. As we slowly became more bonded in our humanness, we began to identify more as individuals than as coworkers. That is the trick to a really powerful and influential corporate culture. It's far more meaningful than superfluous perks such as bean bags or kombucha on tap—options many organizations believe is what is needed to create powerful culture!

We did not consciously set out to create our culture. We slowly built a bond based on this concept of common humanity. Like every relationship, it is ever-changing and grows more connected over time. Like a beautiful stained-glass window, we present to the world a variety of lights and colors, skills and opinions; wholly separate and yet collectively, we've created a singular and cohesive mosaic.

Through the years, we've experienced each other's lives in tangible ways. We celebrate life together and make a real effort to be aware of each child's first step, graduation, or cyber-bullying incident. We mourn the loss of a coworker's sibling or the suffering and survival of cancer interwoven with the promise of a new little life. We affectionately know each other's stories, and we love the physical emotion and act of celebrating each other's journeys. We share them sorrowfully, joyfully, and authentically.

I'm not saying we like each other 100 percent of the time; that's unrealistic. But we like each other a lot of the time, no doubt because we have become so intimate with each other's stories. Our twice-a-month staff meeting and our weekly small team meetings provide the most powerful opportunities to consistently bond and share our individual journeys.

Developing a Collective Mindset of "Team Work Makes the Dream Work"

Several years ago, Project Coordinator Sarah Garcia started using the phrase "Team work makes the dream work." It perfectly reflects how we approach working together. We seek to get along and find shared middle ground. We seek harmony; we don't always succeed, but our leaders tend to be very grounded and laser-focused on consensus building. We like and welcome diversity of thought and ideas. A culture of mutual respect is necessary for the encouragement of ideas, and that culture has evolved because of our desire for excellence.

We work in small teams, with each person providing their specific talent. Our micro-teams consist of an account executive, one or two designers, a project coordinator, and a project manager. Unless the team is failing, they manage themselves. It is uncanny how the team tends to challenge each person to show up as their best self. If someone is failing, they first communicate with their peers, and if that doesn't work, they go to management. They demand excellence from each other because that is the level they are playing at. They advocate on every level for each person to elevate their game. We provide lots of opportunities to resolve issues, offer training, and have open and honest communication. If none of this works, the micro-team communicates with management on how someone can best improve their skills or attitude.

ICE is well-known for demanding and providing a high degree of excellence. Clearly, we are not a fit for everyone, but many are attracted to our culture and stay precisely because they want to work at this level. They want to be considered the best in the industry and they want to work for an organization that strives to be the best. Of course, we still fail at times. I'll cover our organization's worst failure in detail in Chapter 8 because it's important to see how we navigate failure. Failure is the other side of the coin and some of our most meaningful lessons were learned from our biggest failures.

I think how we nurture the art of appreciation is unique; it's one of our foundational beliefs. We seek to be respectful of the value each of us brings to the organization. Our paradigm naturally weeds out those who don't share this collective mindset of appreciation, team work, or commitment to excellence. That leaves us with teammates who share a singular mindset, establishing a model for success.

We seek to set realistic expectations—not for perfection, which is quite harmful to expect—but of always doing your best and being honest with yourself when you need help or you have failed. In many ways we almost embrace failure, which may seem to contradict what I just said, but by the end of this chapter, I suspect it will make sense.

Our leadership team takes the time to listen to everyone, to really listen to ensure all team members are contributing equally and being treated fairly. We strive to spend as little time as possible on drama. Early on we tolerated it, but now we have zero tolerance for manipulative games and personal vendettas. One benefit of our culture is no one tolerates it and we set that expectation early with new employees. At ICE, I believe peers have become even more effective in influencing the behavior of their peer coworkers than have the managers!

One reason I'm so passionate about not tolerating drama is it was often allowed at past companies I worked for, and I found it very disruptive. As a single mother with minimal administrative help, mentorship support, or even support in the way of sales leads, it made my time very precious. Since I was more or less on my own, I had to accomplish a lot during a workday. I have endeavored to create a corporate culture that fully empowers our staff members to become the best versions of themselves. As we expanded our workforce at ICE, we hired outside consultants to ideate and execute a program that would take my belief system to the next level. I could not have created this program alone, so I highly encourage business owners to seek outside consultants who specialize in this process and then to empower staff to implement it. Employee engagement is far more operational when it's internally activated.

Shame Avoidance

We work to avoid mistakes, but they happen. We work consciously and transparently to share our mistakes so others can avoid making the same ones. Since we're all trying to do our best, mistakes are just part of taking on responsibilities, making judgment calls, and growing new skills. Sharing our mistakes openly takes the shame out of the whole process and rebrands it as information. Any mistake is acceptable but it's never acceptable to conceal it; that could very well be grounds for termination. In an effort to promote self-forgiveness, in all circumstances we encourage each other to forgive their teammates. Sometimes our biggest challenge is forgiving ourselves for letting our team down. Sometimes tears are shed, but they're a sign of how much the employee cares.

When you're building a culture of gratitude, you must do whatever you can to avoid letting feelings of shame seep into your workplace. I am eternally grateful to a former employee who introduced me to author and professor Brené Brown's books. This is Brown's take on shame:

> "I define shame as the intensely painful feeling or experience of believing that we are flawed and therefore unworthy of love and belonging—something we've experienced, done, or failed to do makes us unworthy of connection.
>
> I don't believe shame is helpful or productive. In fact, I think shame is much more likely to be the source of destructive, hurtful behavior than the solution or cure. I think the fear of disconnection can make us dangerous."[34]

Shame is such a destructive emotion that we do everything we can to chop it off at the knees!

We are all works in progress. As long as you're giving it your best and learning from your mistakes, there is a place for you at ICE. One more perfect quote from Brown:

> "True belonging only happens when we present our authentic, imperfect selves to the world, our sense of belonging can never be greater than our level of self-acceptance."[35]

Acceptance is a decision and a great gift. I highly encourage you to read anything Brené Brown has written or listen to her TEDx talks on shame, vulnerability, and the lie of perfectionism. Her work is a gift that allows all of us to grow into the fullness and actualization of ourselves.

> Acceptance is a gift we give ourselves; accept yourself,
> accept each other = Increased JOY
> **—DeLinda Forsythe**

In Theory?

When I describe ICE's culture of deep and intimate caring to outsiders, I often receive smirks and quizzical looks—they do not believe what we have achieved.

Trust me, I often ask the staff if I'm imagining it as well. Is my desire to create this culture so strong that I've created an illusion? Do we truly care this much for each other's well-being? When we've asked this question verbally or via an employee survey, the response is generally as high as 100 percent that our workplace is a safe place, woven together in a tapestry of shared experiences—its fibers so intertwined they cannot easily be separated.

> *The energy and spirit of a vibrant family permeates our culture.*

A familial mindset can be defined in many ways, but here are a few analogies:

- You don't choose your family; you inherit them.
- Family is a potential lifetime commitment, whether you like it or not.
- Since you're all in it for the long haul, it's wise to embrace it and make the most of it. "Acceptance is a gift you give yourself."
- We work as a team to improve areas that need development but also focus on each other's positive attributes.
- Not only is focusing on the negative a waste of time, but nothing of value can come from negativity—no one enjoys whining!

Of course, not all families are functional and even functional families aren't functional all the time.

I will note the *striving vs. achieving* theme many times throughout this book because I believe in the journey as much as the destination. Actually, the journey may be the most critical part because if you first don't strive, you certainly won't arrive. As a society, we undervalue striving, focusing only on what was achieved. That is a false narrative.

With this *striving* approach, magic can happen. I've lived that magic at ICE for many years, in many ways, both big and small, intimate and public. Failure and success? Again, two sides of the same coin; you can't have one without the other unless you're not pushing boundaries, reaching for excellence.

What Is Gratitude?

Workhuman, formerly Globoforce, is a social recognition and performance management platform that teaches organizations how to "motivate and empower their people to do the best work of their lives." It has pioneered the growing movement to make work more human. Workhuman substantiates that gratitude is a key element in building a resilient corporate culture.[36] Benefits of cultivating this virtue include the promotion of appreciation, gratitude's sister. Gratitude has emerged as a key factor in living a robust and joyful life. When you apply gratitude as a cornerstone in designing and building your corporate culture, you infuse it with an almost physical energy. I know because client guests who visit us continually say, "I felt your company's energy the minute I walked into your offices—it's why we hired you."

Gratitude creates a physical response that is just starting to be tested and evaluated. What does a brain fired up on gratitude look like? Wharton Healthcare contributor Linda Roszak Burton, in *The Neuroscience of Gratitude*, provides a wonderful overview of the "neurochemical cocktail" created by our brains when we trigger the release of serotonin and dopamine.[37]

When we share and experience the simple act of gratitude for each other, our brains produce this neurochemical cocktail.

Serotonin, often called the "happy molecule," functions as a mood and motivation enhancer. Dopamine triggers optimism, which fosters camaraderie and drives pro-social behavior; both are intrinsically linked and enhance our natural desire for goal setting, which leads to our ability to accomplish personal and professional goals.

When we feel gratitude, our brains trigger this life-affirming, happy brain cocktail. We create new neural brain connections. Yes, we can actually change the physiology of our brains by being positive. This creates a *virtuous circle*—a consistent cycle that feeds itself, generating even more feelings of optimism and a greater desire to experience gratitude.

Think of Pavlov's dog always wanting to push the happy button! In the famous experiments that Ivan Pavlov conducted in 1897 to understand digestion, he found that objects or events could trigger a conditioned response. Pavlov observed that his dogs salivated when they were being served meat.

Pavlov's experiments led to the study of classical conditioning and behavior, the foundation of behaviorism in learning new skills. Bottom line: Gratitude has been clinically proven as one of the key neural creators that contributes to higher organizational performance. Gratitude is one of the most powerful team-building emotions!

> *Gratitude is one of the most powerful forces we can create within our corporate cultures and every aspect of our lives!*

When I discovered Madhuleena Roy Chowdhury's article "The Neuroscience of Gratitude and How It Affects Anxiety & Grief,"[38] I sent it to many of my friends and my staff. Ms. Chowdhury confirms all my intuitive beliefs about the impact of gratitude. Here are a few excerpts:

> "Positive psychology and mental health researchers in the past few decades have established an overwhelming connection between gratitude and good health. Keeping a gratitude journal causes less stress, improves the quality

of sleep, and builds emotional awareness (Seligman, Steen, Park and Peterson, 2005).

Gratitude is positively correlated to more vitality, energy, and enthusiasm to work harder. Grateful workers are more efficient, more productive and more responsible. Expressing gratitude in the workplace is a proactive action toward building interpersonal bonds that trigger feelings of closeness and bonding (Algoe, 2012).

Employees who practice expressing gratitude at work are more likely to volunteer for more assignments, willing to take an extra step to accomplish their tasks, and happily work as a part of the team. Also, managers and supervisors who feel grateful and remember to convey the same, have a stronger group cohesiveness and better productivity. They recognize good work, giving everyone their due importance in the group and actively communicate this to team members.

Gratitude makes a leader compassionate, considerate, empathetic, and loved among others."

And the best part of Chowdhury's article is:

"By consciously practicing gratitude every day, we can help these neural pathways to strengthen themselves and ultimately create a permanent grateful and positive nature within ourselves."

Gratitude is indeed the mother of all emotions, ultimately the emotion that leads to true happiness.

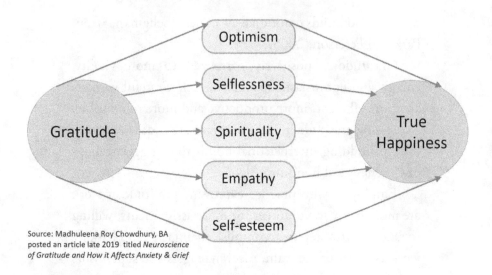

Source: Madhuleena Roy Chowdhury, BA
posted an article late 2019 titled *Neuroscience
of Gratitude and How it Affects Anxiety & Grief*

Reinforcing a Mindset of Gratitude

> *We are what we repeatedly do. Excellence, then, is not an act, but a habit.*

Excellence must be reinforced daily in multiple ways to make it a habit. We can actively reinforce our habit of gratitude, which I'll cover more fully in Chapter 5.

We can permanently change our attitudes by practicing gratitude every day via journaling, meditation, or a gratitude accountability buddy. As Chowdhury notes:

> "Gratitude allows us to celebrate the present. It magnifies positive emotions. Research on emotion shows that positive emotions wear off quickly. We spend so much time watching things—movies, computer screens, sports—but with gratitude *we become greater participants in our lives as opposed to spectators.*"

Thousands of years ago, the ancient Roman philosophers Cicero and Seneca heralded gratitude as one of the most critical of all virtues, believing it was required for the foundational success of a society. Cicero notably stated:

> *Gratitude is not only the greatest of virtues, but the parent of all the others.*

Despite many factors working against us, I believe ICE has experienced higher industry financial success because we share a mindset grounded in appreciation and gratitude. Imagine if organizations consciously implemented programs to create this mindset? What if employers could measure their influence and incentivize people to cultivate an attitude of abundance, gratitude, and appreciation? Can you imagine the positive consequences for our families, communities, and future generations if organizations systematically worked to create this?

Working from Home Since 2014

When Alysse and Elyse first floated the idea to work from home to Tom and me, we opposed the idea. Boomers didn't get that break, so why should their generation? That was our knee-jerk response. We did not see how it could work in our industry.

With a little nudging, we decided to give it a shot. We implemented a work-from-home (WFH) strategy in 2014 when one of our designers moved to Arizona. We had tremendous success with that experience so when another designer moved to Texas, we continued the experiment with more success. Due to COVID-19 restrictions, WFH was mandated in 2020. Having a rigid perspective will not yield flexible results— considering ideas outside our comfort zone has successfully influenced our policies and how we lead.

We realize our business and personal lives have become seamlessly entwined because of how we use technology and our access to it. We now have the ability to be always working, so this policy shift instantly improved employee job satisfaction and engagement. That does not mean the workday needs to extend beyond eight hours; it's just how we carve up and find those eight hours. We allow our staff to make this decision, always keeping in mind they have lives outside of work. The two can and should be mutually beneficial. We have unconsciously modeled for the families of our employees not just the benefits of employment but personal ownership of our own well-being. We encourage positive self-care and behavior, which can potentially stimulate the development of multi-generational gratitude and boundary setting.

It really is important for leaders and managers to understand what motivates the Millennial and incoming Gen Z generations. Living a balanced life is not an indulgence as some from older generations might think; it's a necessity to them. If companies want to attract and retain these generations, they must offer flexible schedules that navigate demanding personal home schedules. Moms and dads can do their "workwork" beside their kids doing their "homework"! It sets a great work ethic example for children. Currently, due to COVID-19, schools are not all open and many parents have added home-schooling responsibilities, adding an additional layer of stress for our staff. When life gets complicated, employers must appreciate what their staff is going through, while employees need to be mindful of the business' challenges. Mutual understanding and gratitude are required.

Finding Happiness at Work

Leading an organization with a gratitude mindset, based on methodology that produces these emotions, is a joyful experience. It is a far more holistic approach and offers the greatest potential for positive and expansive outcomes. This is generational leadership in action, in the real world, with the potential for long-term generational impact.

Forget having free beer, ping-pong tables, and free food—that doesn't reach people deeply and with authenticity. We need to strive to connect with people emotionally, at the most visceral level. The graph on the next page illustrates how gratitude can foster connection.

Connecting at the most visceral level – Love.
Love is by far the most powerful and motivating emotion of all.

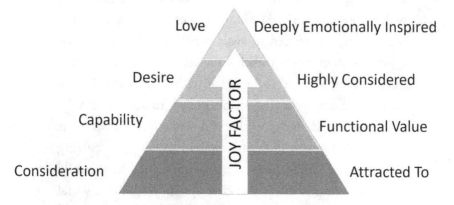

True Generational Impact

When you work for a company that applies this holistic approach, you have a greater opportunity to reach your potential in every facet of your life. The foundation of any society is the strength of the family nucleus, and countless articles have noted the rapid decline and fragility of our family structure. Simple things like flex hours allow single and dual parent families to better raise, educate, and nurture their children.

American workers toil long hours, and how they are treated during those working hours is of immense significance. If our workplace culture and management respects us as unique individuals, valued for exactly who we are, despite our flaws, it greatly affects how we treat others, especially our children. Our children will become the workforce of the future, and if they are socialized to value workplace community and the value of work itself, the concept of human and social capital, our workplaces today will prepare the next generation. How we set that stage is critical but sorely understudied.

Dr. Ian Winters shares my views of how "evolved capitalism" will positively affect both today's workers and future generations. In his 2000 article, "Towards a Theorized Understanding of Family Life and Social Capital," he notes:

"There is now mounting international evidence that social relations of a particular quality and nature are central to creating sustainable communities. Social relationships, which are characterized by high degrees of mutual trust and reciprocity, are argued to sustain better outcomes in the economy, democracy and civil society. These sorts of social relationships are said to be laden with social capital—the norms and networks that enable people to act collectively.

Few would disagree that an ebbing civic spirit is somehow tied up with the fundamental changes occurring in family life. Yet few have actually examined how family life is changing to affect this civic spirit. Within the social capital literature, it is generally assumed that the mere practice of family life will generate norms of trust and reciprocity but the actual circumstances under which this takes place are under researched. Community life, rather than family life, has typically been the focus of social capital researchers. This work has pointed to the 'decline of community.'

Social capital is therefore a means, through social connections, to resources which are keenly sought in capitalist societies. Bourdieu's particular application of the concept of social capital…relates to understanding how individuals draw upon social capital to improve their economic standing in capitalist societies. In such societies, Bourdieu argues, economic capital is the fundamental resource and his concern is with how social capital, and cultural capital, may be instrumental in increasing an individual's economic capital."[39]

There is much to unwrap here. First "What is social capital?" It is a shared sense of identity, a shared understanding through highly functional relationships within social groups such as a workplace. The diagram below helps us visualize the benefits derived from social capital.

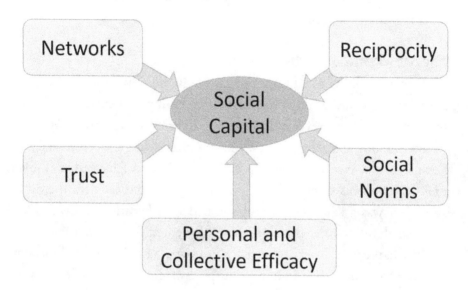

Source: Dr. Ian Winter, *Towards a Theorized Understanding of Family Life and Social Capital*
https://icmhst.wordpress.com/teory-of-social-capital/

Dr. Winters suggests that social capital fostered within a family is critical to a child's educational, cognitive, and social development. His study indicates that social capital helps youths "negotiate their way out of disadvantage," including graduating from high school, attending college, and improving their socio-economic status.

I suspect a direct correlation exists between working every day in a highly functional, respectful workplace and the development of healthy social capital within a family unit. I believe parents who work at an organization that values social capital will teach their children and future generations these principles simply through their behavior. Once valuing social capital is established as normative, future generations will seek organizations that strive toward this ideal. Spending a few hours on social media or reading content published by Millennials reinforces that healthy social capital is important to this generation.

The simple benefit of flexible working hours offers the potential to increase social capital bonds within the family unit. What if how we work, how we mirror the mutuality of family with a balanced work ethic, actually initiates significant change?

The Workplace of the Future

Part of building a culture of gratitude is the mutual appreciation of the value and definition that is work—from both perspectives of employee and employer. We are ever diligent about the stress in our coworkers' lives, always listening and sensitive to working alongside them to create balance. Because we have so many young parents, Tom and I have always joked about the benefits of creating a day care facility connected to the office. Though it was a joke, we certainly wished we'd had the bandwidth and financial ability to offer this immeasurable benefit for our staff.

In Chapter 12, I detail the story of how a San Diego developer saw the need to change the intent and purpose of the physical office and the business park housing the office. They were one of the first developers to implement physical amenities that engage and connect ideas, voices, people, and the community. They intrinsically understood the countless benefits of urban revitalization in attracting young professionals and led an urban evolution of the office workspace in San Diego.

Since then, many San Diego real estate developers have expanded on this concept, introducing placemaking as an approach to create sustainable communities that activate the urban, multi-use business park with housing, restaurants, retail, and creative tech office spaces that spill out into energized open public spaces, beer gardens, parks, and farmers markets.

Kilroy Realty's One Paseo complex in Del Mar takes this concept even further by offering "a deeper notion of mixed use. A spirit of community that, even if you don't live or work here, invites you to meet up, hang out, and join in."[40] Just as the developer in Chapter 12 activated the biotech industry in San Diego, One Paseo has an unprecedented ability to attract organizations, employees, and even tourists. Art and the performing arts have also been woven into many of these business parks and spaces. As Kilroy Realty noted, "Culturally, art is embedded in our very soul."

You might ask: Why this overview of commercial real estate development in San Diego? Great question. This is the work ICE engages in. We collaborate closely with developers in providing furniture, fixtures, and equipment for many of these spaces so we're very familiar with this aspect of fostering community. It is an important element in how we've crafted our personal corporate culture and how we partner with our clients to design their cultures of innovation. The built environment is an integral component of an engaged community, especially if it's a walkable community. Our downtown Little Italy area adds that element to San Diego, feeling very much like an intimate Italian village.

> *Not just the office, but the business park and the neighborhood the office is located in, are all elements of designing an engaged corporate culture.*

An even bigger dream and vision I have is that someday real estate developers will create mixed use business parks that include not only work, live, play, educational, day care, shopping, and restaurant amenities, but also *senior retirement living*. Many seniors move to retirement communities because they can't or don't want to take care of a home, but they still have plenty of life in them! When my father moved to his retirement community, his biggest complaint was that he lost purpose in his life. Many seniors want to give back, but distance, inconvenience, and an inability to drive prevent them from doing so. If they were located in close proximity to families, within the confines of a small village-like community, I suspect many would revel in providing afterschool tutoring or short-term babysitting support to families. Single mothers could benefit the most!

Senior facilities today are very much like resorts with plenty of meeting spaces to facilitate such connections. Seniors love the energy and excitement for life that young people have. Even those who don't have the physical or mental ability to assist in the effort would benefit from just watching children arriving and studying in formal libraries that are unused by the senior residents. Swimming pools are almost never used at these facilities, so offering swim lessons could make great use of pools that are always empty. I remember how hard it was for me to pick up my son after school, take him home, and then head back to the office or to an evening networking event, often with him in tow. I would have been incredibly grateful for this kind of help, and I know how much my son always enjoyed his grandparents.

This could be the natural progression of utilizing the knowledge of our elders, gleaned from decades of life. Instead of wasting our seniors' valuable resource of wisdom, I'd love to see senior-living communities integrated into corporate America, connecting with young professionals and families who would be grateful to have help. Talk about intergenerational leadership!

As work and personal lives continue to merge and become indistinguishable, leaders of the future will seek to find exceptional and unique physical workplaces for their staff that meet the demands of a working family. I, for one, would love to spend my final years still giving back in a meaningful way that positively influences future generations.

A Final Word on Gratitude

Having a gratitude mindset is a choice only you can make. It can only be achieved by adopting an attitude of abundance. The opposite of an attitude of abundance and gratitude is choosing a mindset that the world is unjust. Only you can choose to find good in every situation.

Should you work at an organization that perpetuates your choice to see the world in a negative light? I believe that is unhealthy and will only reinforce your chosen reality.

Creating an organizational outlook grounded in abundance takes effort. At ICE, we actively cultivate a culture where gratitude proliferates. We also work mindfully to consistently refocus negativity through open communication. These conversations can be uncomfortable. At times, even when we are all rowing in the same direction, we still fall short. Working together, we thoughtfully strive to achieve this common mission.

CHAPTER 4

Embrace Workplace Family

A t ICE, we subscribe to five core values. We developed these values together as a team over three months and with many meetings. I've learned that for complete buy-in to occur, it's best to make it a collective effort. We prominently display our core values on a wall in our beautiful showroom. Utilizing a custom heavy textured wallpaper, our core values are emblazoned over a motif of brick and concrete, the foundation of a building and the foundational values of our company. This design feature anchors our office's interior design.

> *DELIVER EXCELLENCE EVERY DAY*
> *LIVE THE ENTREPRENEURIAL SPIRIT*
> *PUSH CREATIVE BOUNDARIES*
> *EMBRACE WORKPLACE FAMILY*
> *CREATE RAVING FANS*

Our core values are not just empty words on a wall. We consistently discuss and actively engage them. How? Every year, we reinforce one by selecting it as an annual theme. *Embrace Workplace Family* is consistently our preferred value because it resonates so well with our team members.

If you don't actively discuss and live your shared values, they become invisible words on a wall.

Defining Workplace Family

Even before COVID-19, we began to navigate disconnection because of our work from home capability; not physically working together makes it all the more critical to connect with each other through these shared values. It's easy to lose track of our shared identity—the wholistic workplace family association we've worked so hard to create. Of all of our core values "Embrace Workplace Family" (again) remains our most treasured. It's the key ingredient in our secret sauce and perhaps the core reason we've experienced such phenomenal success. How we created this authentic culture may be one of the more valuable lessons in this book.

A family is defined as a group of people related by ancestry. However, for many people a family has nothing to do with genetics and everything to do with love, compassion, and support. Family can be your biological family, but it can also be the family you choose. That is how I view my workplace family.

At ICE, we refer to each other as our "workplace family," and as with biological families, we don't necessarily share each other's world opinions or political and religious beliefs; we might not even completely accept each other as we are. But we do try. As in biological families, though we might not completely like each other, we attempt to find our shared commonalities—we endeavor to earn and give respect to each other. We actively make the decision to strive for similar familial acceptance, and as I've mentioned, the striving is as critical as the achieving. All of us, and especially leadership, are dynamically engaged in an effort to develop this level of connectivity.

As in biological families, dysfunction can exist. It's our responsibility to identify specific dynamics that positively and negatively contribute to the functionality of our workplace family dynamic. Each of us is accountable and responsible in this endeavor to interact in a healthy manner and provide emotional and physical connection and support to each other. Biological and workplace families face the same challenges of dysfunction. Dysfunction can become so ingrained that it is perceived as functional. We actively work to identify and reduce those encounters and, as needed, detach individuals who would undermine our efforts. The benefits far outweigh the challenges of creating this kind of working environment.

Getting to Know Each Other

I will cover our staff meetings in detail in Chapter 5, but I'll mention them here because it's important to know what we have done to develop this sense of family. One tradition we developed was "Get to Know an ICE Employee." It has become such a fun part of our staff meetings, and I suspect an underlying sense of competition has emerged because they just keep getting better! We do this activity as frequently as the agenda allows. Let me share the presentation of Carly King, Account Executive, as an example.

Carly started her presentation with her baby pictures, pictures of her home in Connecticut when she was a child, pictures of her three sisters and parents and their relocation to Arizona. But wait, there's more! Her high school experience, pets, cotillion, sorority, meeting her husband, the love she has for her dog, her fairy tale wedding, and Swiss Alps honeymoon. The presentation culminated with a photo of her soon-to-be born baby. Everything was so intimate and sweet. You could see why Carly has developed her positively glowing attitude toward life.

Some presentations have illustrated life starting in a shack in Mexico with dirt floors and the family's heroic transition to life in America. Some stories have given us a glimpse into growing up with a fun, full of life "hippie chick momma," or coming to America as an adult immigrant to seek a better life, or serving our country in the military, or growing up with a mixed racial background, and on and on. We are a diverse organization and our sense of acceptance grows *because we know each other's stories*. We strive to see the fullness of each person, but you can't do that unless you know their *full story*.

Our employees' lives didn't start at ICE, nor will they end at ICE. Maybe we're a lifetime career, but far more likely, we're a moment in their lifetimes. While they are here, we want to do whatever we can to have them fully here, feeling included and appreciated. This simple tradition creates space for this experience.

> *Develop traditions to create emotional space for desired values to thrive!*

Equality

As we seek opportunities at ICE to find our commonalities and the ties that bind us, we start with the mindset that everyone is absolutely equal. Every position at ICE contributes to the organization's greater good. Everyone's work and voice are equal and relevant. We share our common humanity, in all its naked reality, as inherently imperfect. We are all striving to provide ourselves and our families with more security, to put food on the table, save for retirement, perhaps purchase a home or educate a child. Our shared views of equality are infused and create the foundation for our corporate culture.

We are all just people trying to make it in a difficult, often cruel and polarizing world. Our media, especially social media, puts pressure on us to project these images of perfection that are not based on reality. This exercise strips away that false pretense that prevents authentic connection. This authentic connection is foundational to our corporate culture.

Especially challenging are the political and racial divisions the media ceaselessly work to create to divide us. It is our choice to believe there are differences between us. At ICE, we've made the decision not to focus on title or job function but to seek to value each other as *equals*. Each of us offers a specific skill set, and they are all equally critical to the company's success. Our leadership team is here to provide guidance, not condemnation or judgment. Similar to parenting, management exists to help everyone make better decisions, analyze solutions and options, and then share these struggles with the team.

We actively seek the best business solutions together. Getting there can be challenging, but that's all part of the process; it's a practice that requires a great deal of trust and mutual respect. More often than not, we take this feedback and create new processes based on these diverse perspectives.

When viewed through this shared lens, the potential for a disparaging and judgmental approach is mitigated. A judgmental culture creates a highly destructive energy and nothing positive can evolve from that dynamic. Collectively, it's healthier and far more productive to adopt a *solution-oriented approach*, every day, in every situation, especially the most mundane.

While it is easy to write about, it may be difficult to duplicate our methodology unless there is a high degree of authenticity. *The key to this value's success is it must be authentic or it is not sustainable.* You either genuinely value and respect your coworkers and leaders or you don't. You can't just talk it into existence; it is a powerful emotion and unifying feeling that must be carefully nurtured and equally cherished by all.

> *Authenticity is the key—you either genuinely value each other or you don't.*

Authenticity

I have often been complimented by other business leaders on how authentic my leadership style is, as if authenticity were an anomaly. In years past when someone would say to me, "You really are authentic," I found it confusing. I came to realize most people lack authenticity and I was left to wonder, "*Who are they if they aren't themselves? How is that even possible?*"

Simply recalling the truth can be challenging for all of us at times, but it's even more challenging to recall lies or even simple accomplishments that aren't completely accurate. That sounds pretty stressful. Reacting, remembering, and behaving exactly as myself is my only option. Trying to remember who I *should* be and what I *should* say—why would anyone want to live like that? Most people see right through superficial people and the negative ramifications are huge.

Why is it so hard to be authentic? It should be as natural as breathing. Perhaps being perceived as weak, not having all the answers, or simply being different is frightening to people. Maybe benevolence is considered weak by some. Perhaps caring deeply for anyone except our friends and family isn't a natural feeling. Does our upbringing and socialization prevent us from developing compassion and empathy? Whatever the reason, at the core of our company's success is *how we strive to authentically respect each other as human beings*, imperfect as we all are.

A peaceful countenance and a quieter mind results when you are just being you; that leads to more simplicity in every facet of your life. Striving to be a better version of yourself is wholly different than projecting being someone else. I applaud all efforts to "become a better you," as Joel Osteen describes in his book *Become a Better You*. I often think the traits we consider weaknesses are the reasons we develop into our genuine selves. I have no choice but to accept who I am and I've learned to consider this a blessing, turning a potentially debilitating weakness (poor memory) into a strength.

Billionaire and entrepreneur Sir Richard Branson suffered from the challenging learning disability of dyslexia. He believes his infirmity led to his ability to see opportunities that didn't yet exist. Branson shared some of those challenges in a 2019 CNBC post:

> "It helped me think big but keep our messages simple.
> The business world often gets caught up in facts and

figures—and while the details and data are important, the ability to dream, conceptualise and innovate is what sets the successful and the unsuccessful apart. Problem solving, creativity and imagination will be in high demand with the rise of AI (artificial intelligence) and automation,' Branson said.

'We should stop trying to get all children to think the same way,' he added. 'We should support and celebrate all types of neurodiversity and encourage children's imagination, creativity and problem solving—the skills of the future.'"[41]

The skills of the future are here now with empathy often cited as one of the most effective leadership skills today.

Empathy's Influence in ICE's Corporate Culture

One reason ICE's culture has flourished is the high levels of empathy expressed within every department.

Four attributes are commonly associated with effective empathy:
- The ability to see the world as others see it
- The decision to be non-judgmental
- The ability to clearly understand another person's feelings, even if you don't agree
- The skill to communicate your understanding of that person's feelings

Only recently has empathy, the ability to literally feel another person's emotion or situation, become a coveted leadership skill. Many leadership coaches believe Emotional Intelligence (EI) is the most critical job skill, even surpassing technical ability. A Career Builder survey confirmed that businesses actively seek employees with a high EI; 71 percent valued EI over IQ, 75 percent were more likely to promote an employee who displayed a high EI, and 59 percent confirmed they would not hire someone with a high IQ if they possessed a low EI. EI has become a valuable skillset.[42]

Why has high EI become so valuable? According to emotional intelligence expert Harvey Deutschendorf, empathy has become the most important leadership skill for five reasons:[43]

1. Your staff will be more loyal.
2. Your staff will be more engaged.
3. Your employees will work better with each other.
4. Your staff will be happier.
5. Creativity will increase.

Today, empathy is such a discussed and analyzed emotion that it has more than 8 million Google results. Empathy is an integral component at ICE, and ultimately, it led us to the adoption of the workplace family concept. We've taken this leadership skill for granted because it is so intrinsically woven into our culture, but in analyzing why it's one of our stronger skills, I realized it started because of my high degree of caring about others' well-being.

I've always led with empathy, at times to the organization's detriment. One benefit of my mentorship is that Alysse has witnessed the successes and failures of my leadership. Early on, I struggled to have hard conversations that might make an employee feel inadequate. I would even retain an employee despite financial loss to the organization, hoping that person could change. I would also try shifting their responsibilities in an effort to retain them. I tried a variety of options to avoid hurting someone's feelings. Alysse has learned to be more direct, more honest, yet she never lets go of her desire to genuinely assist helping a staff member build their strengths and identify their weaknesses. At twenty, Alysse did not possess a high degree of empathy, but after fourteen years and the natural progression of maturity and seeing the benefits of empathy in action, empathy has become engrained in her personality. It is a teachable skill. More to follow on how to teach it.

I suspect the high degree of empathy at ICE started with me since leadership begins at the top, but I certainly attribute our empathetic culture to the high percentage of women we employ— presently 85 percent.

Seeking more data on the relationship between gender and empathy, I discovered a study conducted by Dr. Marco Iacoboni, director of the Neuromodulation Lab UCLA, and his associate Leonardo Christov-Moore. They used functional magnetic resonance imaging (fMRI) to study the brain activity of people as they reacted to images of pain experienced by others.[44]

They monitored the insula, the portion of the brain that produces the chemical reaction that stimulates empathy. Their data suggests females are better at feeling others' pain because of a higher activation in their insula, the sensory area of the brain associated with pain.

Hundreds of research articles confirm women tend to possess higher levels of natural empathy; perhaps this explains why empathy is second nature within our culture at ICE. It is quite encouraging to learn that empathy is a teachable skill that can be amplified and cultivated and need not be inherent or gender specific. Higher levels of empathy develop higher levels of social bonding. At great peril, our society has moved away from empathetic social bonding. At ICE we actively nurture and foster a culture of empathy.

Our empathy is one more example of how gratitude and the gift of imperfection come into play. We are grateful for and appreciative of our differences, accepting our imperfections and respecting our collective humanity. We are not worker bees. We do not expect people to come to work and do their perfunctory jobs, return home, and repeat it all the next day. We've developed practices that have enabled us to see each other as individuals, and through these practices, we've become more intimately aware of each other's lives outside of work.

Tough Conversations

Our empathy became even more evident during the 2020 COVID crisis. Every decision was based on knowing the situation not just of the business but of each individual's home life. We had been evaluating and considering terminations for a few people prior to the pandemic, so we swiftly acted on those terminations. We knew that not following through with planned terminations based on performance had been affecting our company's functionality and reputation.

We realized our empathy was keeping us from making hard decisions; being kind was becoming more important than being honest. Because we ask leadership to analyze themselves consistently, we were able to quickly make this assessment. By being overly empathetic, we had unconsciously decided to accept poor performance, despite mounting client complaints and financial losses—we were compromising our core value of "Deliver Excellence Every Day" because we cared more for our people than our brand.

I share this example because I want to be clear that we don't always make perfect decisions—we are human and we fail, the same as every other company.

Brené Brown has studied the healing power of empathy. She also realizes when it can contribute to problems. In her blog post, "Clear is Kind. Unclear is Unkind," she talks about what happens when you avoid having tough conversations or making necessary difficult decisions.

> "Of the ten behaviors and cultural issues that leaders identified as barriers to courage, there was one issue that leaders ranked as the greatest concern: *Avoiding tough conversations, including giving honest, productive feedback.*
>
> Some leaders attributed this to a lack of courage, others to a lack of skills, and, shockingly, more than half talked about a cultural norm of 'nice and polite' that's leveraged as an excuse to avoid tough conversations.

…the consequences of avoiding tough conversations…include:

1. Diminishing trust and engagement;
2. Increases in problematic behavior, including passive-aggressive behavior, talking behind people's backs, pervasive backchannel

communication (or 'the meeting after the meeting'), gossip, and the 'dirty yes' (when I say yes to your face and then go behind your back); and

3. Decreasing performance due to a lack of clarity and shared purpose."[45]

If we had chosen not to follow through with our terminations, we would have been sending mixed signals about our striving for excellence. It was difficult to follow through, especially during this crisis, but we realized we needed to be more courageous than we'd ever been before. Courage is the essence of authenticity—being fearless in making controversial decisions!

Striving for and achieving a culture of familial attachment is unique, difficult to achieve, and something many want but have no idea how to achieve. Let me offer a few examples of how we've developed this value.

Staff Meetings

It's time to go a bit deeper into our staff meetings. We devote two hours per month to gather and emotionally as well as physically connect. Connection is critical for keeping the sense of inclusivity we've worked so hard to create. It's a time to understand wins and losses, review corporate finances, and unveil new procedures, but also an opportunity to communicate individual messages, personal challenges, mistakes made, and lessons learned.

Staff meetings at companies where I had been previously employed were not something you looked forward to and certainly not anything you'd try to arrive early for! But at ICE, gathering around our communal tables allows for quality time with each other, much like the traditional family dinner table. Our meetings feel like an opportunity to fully reveal ourselves as individuals and express gratitude for the company and, more specifically, for each other.

Because we've created a very safe environment to fail, at these meetings we also share personal failures with humility and grace. I'll discuss vulnerability in Chapter 9, but know that being vulnerable absolutely influences the accepting energy and mindset of employees, especially during our staff meetings. No one enjoys sharing their failures, but we *respect the opportunity our failures provide to help others avoid making the same mistakes.* We have worked hard to take the shame out of failure and focus on its incredible value! We work consistently to cultivate a sense of being "other focused." In this way, our failure is about helping others, and not "all about me."

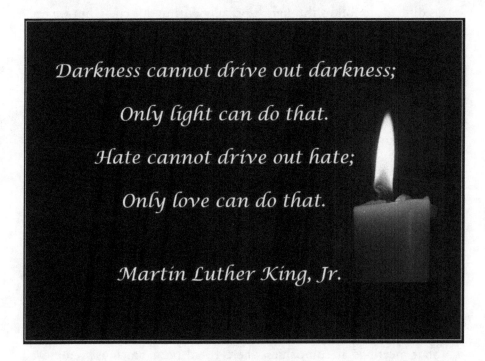

Darkness cannot drive out darkness;

Only light can do that.

Hate cannot drive out hate;

Only love can do that.

Martin Luther King, Jr.

Martin Luther King, Jr. captures the essence of our feelings about failure. We strive to be more accepting of each other, helping one another rather than having anyone hide in the darkness where shame breeds.

We Publicly Share Our Challenges to Educate Others

In our meetings, I sense no judgment from one another. Just the opposite happens: hugs, tears, and words of encouragement and compassion emerge. Negativity doesn't stand a chance to infiltrate the connections we have made with each other.

Sharing failures has become so comfortable that I sincerely doubt anyone would refer to it as "sharing failure." Again, "it's all just information."

We do cover the traditional business topics. I will cover in detail our meeting mechanics, but let me take a moment to stress the powerful influence ignited when we bond during these meetings.

The parking pass handoff has always been extra-special and fun. As a company we are provided only three reserved parking passes for the parking lot just outside our front door. The two additional parking lots are a bit of a hike to our office, so these three passes are uber-exclusive! Mommas-to-be are automatically given one of the parking passes.

The pass is given from one employee to another; it's our ritual for honoring coworkers. I was especially encouraged when one employee honored another because she found her mistakes. "Thank you for finding my mistakes. I so appreciate that!" Genuine gratitude for finding mistakes and publicly telling everyone—that was a first, even for our company! I felt a tremendous sense of accomplishment to see how safe our work environment felt when we not only shared our mistakes, but *publicly thanked someone for finding them!* That is gratitude, trust, family, and vulnerability all wrapped into one story.

By creating this ceremonial coworker to coworker ritual of acknowledgment, we reinforced one of our most sacred, unwritten corporate social contracts: Our shared attitude of "We need each other" and acknowledging each other's work is *foundational.* Without this shared mindset, we would struggle to have a healthy corporate culture. This simple practice reinforces the high regard we collectively share of collaborating together to achieve more. To summarize:

> *We actively draw attention to positive behavior.*
> *We seek activities to reinforce affirming behavior.*
> *We have developed a culture of gratitude for one another.*

On a daily basis, we consciously reinforce our life-affirming belief system so it is who we are and how we collectively define ourselves as a company. This is conscious capitalism in action!

Based on consistent feedback, I've learned most of our employees are grateful to have found ICE and to work among employees they trust emphatically and completely. I say most because it's impossible to have everyone agree on anything. That ideal isn't possible. You will have people who find fault with everything you do; that's human nature. Even if we fail or our intentions are not understood or appreciated, we will never take our eyes off of *trying*. Trying is as priceless as *achieving*.

Creating (Physical) Space to Transcend the Ordinary

The way an office is designed and furnished should create community, serendipity, and creativity. Interior design and layout are integral in building a corporate culture that transcends the ordinary. Interviewing Maria Martinico, principal of world-renowned SmithGroup, many of the considerations I had were addressed.[46] Maria noted:

> "The office environment has always provided a social, communal scene but post-COVID this sense of belonging and community is becoming even more prevalent. Working remotely is becoming a new paradigm for how we will work in the future. WFH has been a positive shift toward flexibility. It has been a positive impact in both personal and professional lives.
>
> Yet creativity and successful innovation involves collaboration—the sharing of ideas and teamwork. I was very appreciative of the tight connection I had with my team during the pandemic. Prior to the pandemic, we worked together in person to build these connections of collaboration and trust. During the pandemic, we were fortunate to hire new employees, but it was more challenging to build these brand-new relationships

remotely. During the initial phases of the pandemic, we relied on past long-lasting relationships built on trust to keep the momentum of business moving forward. New relationships were a challenge to establish and grow without our previous in-person encounters. We communicate through tone, body language, impromptu exchanges and without a physical presence, it became harder to build a culture of trust that was limited to a Zoom call.

This shed an even brighter light on the importance of trusting relationships. Trusting relationships are the key to innovation and a successful business. There are creative ways to build relationships virtually without in-person engagement. I am seeing a shift in how workplaces are designed post-COVID to an increase in more communal and informal spaces that facilitate socializing and collaboration. Our clients are moving away from enclosed and confining conference rooms and more toward larger open spaces with varying shared work settings that incorporate outdoor access to natural ventilation for meetings, collaboration, and social connections. There is an increasing purpose of the workplace to be a place to foster collaboration and to socialize, while incorporating a concern for safety.

Social distancing remains a concern. We are designing workstations that give people more privacy and proximity. Small touch phone rooms were previously designed to allow for quick personal calls but now they are also being used for focus/heads down work and to provide additional physical separation from others. We are seeing furniture solutions with a softer residential look and feel. Our client TuSimple provides nap rooms allowing employees to have a place for privacy and to recharge. Lab spaces also have been redesigned to allow for more collaboration and for informal personal areas adjacent to the labs. Even the previous notion of a main headquarters is evolving to the development of smaller, more numerous hubs and to buildings having fewer stories.

The hospitality sector is also changing, and developers are building more bungalow style hotels that offer more privacy and separation and fewer elevators. Hospitality spaces now must offer larger common areas both indoors and outdoors for conferences, socializing and interaction with others. Developers are integrating more access to the outdoors through operable windows and private patios. Rick Caruso, a developer and previous client, created the Miramar Beach Resort in Montecito, California that decidedly reflects this casita style design.

I don't know if people will ever have the same feeling about sharing space as they did in the past. People may always have a sense of fear of being too close to others. 9/11 changed how we travel; it changed everything and so has this pandemic. There might always be an element of social distancing in the office. We just fought a war with an invisible enemy and many people are suffering from a trauma because of it.

I believe we will see the emergence of HR professionals that simply address the psychological impacts caused by COVID-19. I think we will see the emergence of peer groups that facilitate conversation about people's COVID fears and of future outbreaks. There will be a need for an outlet that allows people to share their "war stories." The reluctance to return to "normal" may take years to overcome. Some elements of working from home are here to stay. Employees not only were productive and saved money and time, but they also saw how it positively impacted the environment and that is becoming ever more important to people.

Companies have been incorporating wellness strategies into the built environment for many years and it continues to emerge as a more critical element. Tenants and developers are finding LEED WELL accredited buildings are more desirable than ever. WELL-certification offers a holistic approach to wellness in buildings through design strategies that address ten concepts in how we measure and address issues that impact the health and comfort of occupants. This includes air, water, lighting, cognitive health obtained through healthy eating and physical activity. These are strategies that focus on impact and driving positive change for people through interventions in building design, operations, and organizational policies. As a principal with SmithGroup, I have seen how we continue to emerge as a leader within this movement."

As San Diego's most creative office and hospitality furniture dealership, ICE has partnered with some of the most forward-thinking real estate developers, designers, and architects to co-create some of San Diego's most iconic commercial environments. Collaborating with these highly creative organizations has continued to push our ever-increasing imagination, which takes into consideration many of the concerns Maria noted. Our spaces are never cookie cutter; each environment is suited to the property and the client's character.

We take great care to research and explore unique options, but this approach can be a gamble. By consistently discovering and trying out new and unproven vendors, we take a risk on their performance, putting our reputation in jeopardy. Often, we have to pre-pay manufacturers for products that do not ship for three to five months, taxing our economic resources and cash flow. It takes our designers longer to create project proposals because they research multiple options with little known product lines, consistently pushing them out of their comfort zone to be ever-more creative. At times this leads to incurring additional upfront design specification costs we frequently are not compensated for. When these new vendors fail, we often cannot recoup costs.

You can see why our competitors might want to shun this approach—it's not necessarily fiscally responsible. However, it is absolutely the only way to create physical spaces that transcend the ordinary. We have earned our reputation as San Diego's most creative dealership because we have bravely taken financial and reputational risks. But did we really have a choice?

When we entered into a partnership in 2017 with Teknion, a well-known international manufacturer, we were already well-established. Partnering with a highly-respected, environmentally sustainable brand added a formidable dimension to our business' artistic capabilities, making growth far more scalable. Through our partnership, we can continue to furnish some of the world's most creative spaces but now on a larger scale that includes some of the most beautiful and functional furniture available in our industry.

Prior to this partnership, to stand out in the market, we had to take risks and implement ideas that weren't mainstream. Being non-aligned forced us to take a chance and develop our creativity, despite the risk. If you look for it, most adversity generally has a silver lining.

Creating (Emotional) Space to Transcend the Ordinary

As I noted when discussing our staff meetings, our culture encourages staff to share even uncomfortable information with others so we can learn from each other and avoid repeating those issues. Everything is a learning opportunity, which is how we approach our daily work challenges.

Providing office furniture is what we do to make a living. What we do to make a life and to make our work lives meaningful has become equally as important to our company. While we create physical spaces, we also have created a distinctive emotional space that allows people to thrive, not just survive. We actually enjoy how we collectively develop new strategies and procedures to do our jobs better. We strive to evolve as individuals, to reach our potential, and to help others do the same. We seek and enjoy collaboration and we take great pride in our growth and the growth we see in others. We are inspired by others' achievements. If you have dreams, we'll help you achieve them, even if it means your leaving our company.

Even when mistakes are encountered that bring financial loss to the company, our safe emotional space applies. Often, the only person struggling with discomfort from a mistake is the one who experienced it because they feel they let others down. To a degree, failure is baked into our culture and business model because we push our staff to develop projects that stretch our knowledge or experience. We could not do what we do effectively without safe emotional space.

The Destructive Nature of Fear

The alternative to creating safe emotional space is an office culture based on fear. This is an old leadership model that absolutely will not work with younger generations. Fear is a debilitating emotion and a destructive force; nothing good can come from creating a fear culture.

Arizona State University Professor Blake E. Ashforth studied the pathology created by a culture of fear and reported his findings in a paper titled "Petty Tyranny in Organizations." In the abstract for his paper, he states:

> "A petty tyrant is defined as one who lords his or her power over others. Preliminary empirical work suggests that tyrannical behaviors include arbitrariness and self-aggrandizement, belittling others, lack of consideration, a forcing style of conflict resolution, discouraging initiative, and noncontingent punishment. A model of the antecedents of tyrannical management and the effects of tyranny on subordinates is presented. Petty tyranny is argued to be the product of interactions between individual predispositions (beliefs about the organization, subordinates, and self, and preferences for action) and situational facilitators

(institutionalized values and norms, power, and stressors). Tyrannical management is argued to cause low self-esteem, performance, work unit cohesiveness, and leader endorsement, and high frustration, stress, reactance, helplessness, and work alienation among subordinates. It is further argued that these effects may trigger a vicious circle which sustains the tyrannical behavior."[47]

Fear stifles creativity. It kills productivity, period. At ICE, we have no place for fear.

When You Care About Your Coworkers

While fear is toxic and debilitating, love is the exact opposite. Love encompasses a broad range of strong and positive mental, physical, and emotional states. Many consider it the most significant human emotion. Remember the saying, "You might not remember what someone said, but you always remember how they made you feel"? That is love in action; it's compelling.

Our species' very continuation is dependent upon love. What could possibly be more effectual in any environment, including an office environment, to bring people harmoniously together?

> *When you harness the power of selfless love, you can unleash another's highest potential.*

What if you could create a work environment where love was felt more profoundly and more completely? In an office, non-leadership individuals interact far more frequently with other non-leadership individuals, from preparing lunch in the kitchen to attending project team meetings. The time coworkers spend with each other can be far more influential than time spent with managers, and the relationships they build with one another can be more significant. At ICE, we capitalize on that reality.

Our workplace family value evolved by embracing all the good juju derived from a foundation of mutual respect and love in its purest form. A company can encourage this familial bond by hosting work get-togethers that include children, dogs, and partners; and celebrating life milestones that include not just employee birthdays, but children's birthdays, personal business accomplishments, seasonal changes, and holidays. Our celebrations encourage attendance by everyone and promote close interrelationships. Every interaction allows people to get to know each other as individuals; these meaningful and heartfelt connections make going to work a source of joy.

We closed our offices during the COVID isolation period and mandated a full-time work-from-home policy. The overwhelming feeling during this crisis was that our teams began to value their relationships with each other even more. They realized how much they missed and appreciated the honest, intimate friendships they had forged, but they also missed our collaborative problem-solving culture.

An authentic caring culture creates employee engagement and increases trust and employee performance. In 2020, it solidified our workplace family ethos with a shared mindset that we are all in this together with a common goal of surviving a crisis.

How to Create a Sense of Family

Here are some ways we have created a sense of family at ICE that you can try in your own organization.

1. Decide that a sense of family is the foundation for your corporate culture. You'll need whole organizational buy-in. Don't just make the decision unilaterally; have open and honest conversations with the team and collectively decide if you all want to participate in this effort.

2. Define what a workplace family feels and looks like for your organization and be very specific—if you can't verbalize and visualize what it means, you cannot create it. The use of storyboards and small group breakouts can help define it for your organization.

It should be an optimistic and exciting change for the company, but don't be disappointed if you don't attain 100 percent buy-in because that might be an unrealistic goal.

3. Start by sharing your personal stories as a group. Make it a slow, comfortable process; don't force it. People will share what they're comfortable with sharing. Whether the sharing is in-depth or superficial, both are fine. We all need to break down the barriers we've constructed around our hearts. Sharing can be really painful for people if there is discomfort or shame around their personal stories. This exercise has an added bonus of potentially opening a door to individual healing. We're all as strong as our weakest link, so do what you can to support growth, but also be aware that the efforts may not be worth the results you're achieving. You can only help those who want to help themselves. Recognize that just one discontented employee can negatively affect the entire organization.

4. Be patient. It will take time to develop a healthy workplace family, but the effort is worth it and the results are incredibly gratifying!

5. Remember it's all about authenticity. If leadership doesn't see the value in this process, don't bother because it is highly likely your efforts will result in frustration and failure.

6. Hold movie nights, staff and micro meetings, and fun company get-togethers. Celebrate life milestones. Gatherings can be as simple as a Thanksgiving potluck, a pancake breakfast, or a group activity, such as bowling or going to the beach or a park—physical activities you'd do as a biological family that create a sense of community, inclusion, and personal connection.

Conclusion

Work is important, but so are all our values and our family-centric culture. We've tried consciously to integrate our workplace family and our actual families. Our teammates actively embrace this unification, which has changed how they view the workplace. I think this unification has a lot to do with how Millennials have redefined the concept of success.

CHAPTER 5

Staff Meetings Build a Collective Mindset

In 2020, we modified our weekly one-hour staff meetings to twice a month; we found weekly meetings were actually less impactful. This change gave our staff two extra hours per month to accomplish their daily tasks, providing the potential to shift from an "obligatory" attitude to an "anticipatory" mentality. We wanted to elevate and transform our staff meetings into a more mindful and meaningful practice.

> *Everyone benefited from creating more time in the month!*

I encourage leaders to consciously look for opportunities to improve and change practices that might even be considered unassailable. Engage an empathetic approach. Ask questions of yourself and your leadership team. Here are a few ideas to generate open-ended dialogue:

- Are there opportunities at our organization to implement small or large modifications that can provide significant benefits?
- How can we better seek input from all departments, all levels of the organization with an equally open mind?

- As a leader or manager, do I maximize each exchange with my coworkers for the benefit of the organization more than my benefit, status, or ego?
- Do I listen to what my intuition is telling me?
- Am I okay with being wrong?
- Do I nurture a culture where those I manage feel comfortable pointing out flaws in my thinking, processes, and solutions?

Opportunities do not have to be huge. Sometimes a small change can yield substantial benefits! Alysse and Elyse consciously chose to craft a staff meeting "experience." Just as we want to engage our external customers, it's important to engage our internal customers, our coworkers. Our meetings have become anticipatory and unique because we are eager to learn what will be *experienced* because each meeting is so well-planned and executed. The team consistently puts in extraordinary effort to improve and foster personal connections. The icing on the cake is that an element of fun is always mixed in!

> *Our leadership team plans staff meetings as if they were meeting with the highest revenue-generating client.*

Another small but significant shift was changing the start time from 8 to 9 a.m. to allow for childcare considerations and long commute times. This extra hour also increased the opportunity for more personal connections to happen. We now have created casual time to gather early in the kitchen reception area to share both business and personal life updates. To help foster these personal connections, we worked with our design team to create an engaging and open space. We don't have a traditional reception area; you literally walk right into our communal living space, which is very welcoming and firmly establishes our corporate Workplace Family value. We chose this suite and office campus specifically because the park-like exterior unifies seamlessly into our interior spaces. The office environment and how you design and set up your space is an integral part in the development of a conscious culture.

Our office feels very much like a home; new customers always comment about the positive energy our space exudes, and it is often one reason they hire us! In 2020, because our employees were unable to come into the office, they grew even more appreciative of the investment we had made in our physical office environment. Of course, creating office space is what we do for a living, so yes, we did it really well.

More showroom images can be found at www.icesd.com

How We Designed Meaningful Staff Meetings

Even prior to the COVID pandemic, we offered work from home flexibility, which always made our staff meetings and connecting as a group significant. Staff meetings provide the opportunity to share everything going on with the company and our projects in a consistent messaging format. It has become not only our most dependable method to convey information but also a way to nurture individual, departmental, and micro-team growth. Our staff meetings continue to evolve.

In our staff meetings, we:

- Promote a gratitude mindset
- Share in-depth financial updates
- Discuss project highlights
- Distribute the much-coveted parking pass hand-off
- Discuss key dates for upcoming events and marketing initiatives
- Validate each other
- Get to know each other
- Share good news of the week
- Teach and promote our core value connection

Below is a staff meeting agenda to help you visualize the content.

Team Meeting 11/12/19 Agenda

Housekeeping/Announcements
- Parking Pass Handoff
- 11/19: Cavignac safety presentation @ 8:45
- 11/21 @ 12 p.m.: Thanksgiving Potluck
- 11/21 @ 4:30 p.m.: ARE Welcome Party at The Park

Staff Meeting Mix-Up - 1 activity per meeting
- CEO Message
- Expressing gratitude, share your win, or angel card—everyone shares, 2 min or less
- Accounting Financial update—controllable and uncontrollable losses
- Sales quotas and objectives/projections
- Manufacturer quotas
- Get to know an ICE employee
- Core Value connection—how you personally connect with our core values—everyone shares, 2 min or less

Discussion Items
- Secret Santa draw – 11/12
- Teknion new products training overview

Upcoming Vendor Presentations
- 11/12 LUUM L&L 12-1 (sales, design)
- 12/3 HEM Design Studio 9:30-10 a.m. (sales, design)
- 12/10 OFS Appreciation lunch 11:30-1 (all)

Quote of the Moment

> *"Integrity is choosing courage over comfort; it's choosing what's right over what's fun, fast, or easy; and it's practicing your values, not just professing them."*
> **—Brené Brown**

The Staff Meeting Mix-Up

Prior to ICE I had never experienced what we call the staff meeting mix-up. We try to incorporate one of the activities noted in the agenda every meeting. The CEO Message might happen every two to three months, the Get to Know an ICE Employee once a month, the financial update was once a month but during COVID we incorporated a financial review in every meeting—we truly mix it up!

Our meetings allow us to share lofty visionary ideals that provide a bigger picture of our corporation's purpose, communicate personal thoughts and our personal history, express gratitude for each other, and share personal perspectives. We attempt to live and engage the company's core values. All of these activities are designed to bind us together.

We strive to offer activities to engage staff, especially our more introverted team members who can otherwise be overlooked. It's been especially gratifying for me to see personal growth happen with our more introverted female employees as they find their voices—we all see this and help them celebrate this accomplishment. Introverts don't want to toot their own horn, but often, they are the ones receiving the most accolades. That is really empowering!

The Power of Shared Stories

As previously mentioned, sharing our personal life journeys during staff meetings has effectively broken-down barriers that prevent true connection. Enduring bonds have developed and been elevated in part because of this practice. Some stories have absolutely revealed our softest underbellies. This has led to the development of empathy and understanding needed for improved communication. As we express our individual journeys, we are *laying the necessary groundwork for constructing a new, mutually crafted narrative.*

The power of shared stories during our staff meetings produces the glue that purposefully bonds us. Sharing how we personally experience our corporate values keeps our values top of mind. Each employee is asked to select how they experienced one of the core values and "Embrace

Workplace Family" is overwhelmingly selected by staff as their most-valued ICE practice. As each employee recalls what and how they experience working within our communal workplace, beautiful stories are always tearfully and emotionally shared.

Storytelling is a powerful driver of our collective mindset and corporate culture and organically fostered the development of our strong familial bond. Our connection with one another is inseparable from the actual work we do; it's infused in every aspect of our work environment. If you compared a human body to a workplace, with each cell living off another cell and in harmony with each other, that would be how our work family environment feels. We're reliant on each other!

Tight friendships continue to evolve from working at ICE. One reason might be because so many have shared the pregnancy and parenting trek. The bonds that develop from celebrating life milestones such as baby showers, baby parties, and baby's first word or first steps, and all the challenges that come with becoming a parent are significant. Several teammates have even vacationed together. Several are linked through biological relationships. Current employees often recruit their friends to interview and join our team—a true sign that what we offer is authentic! You wouldn't recruit friends and family members if you didn't completely believe in the work we're doing and the culture we're striving to create. I've been advised that both current and past ICE employees appreciate the tight friendships forged at ICE more than any other experience at our company.

Collective Mindset Creation

You might think this emotional space we've created, where everyone thrives both professionally and personally, is just *theoretical*. It might sound impossible, unrealistic, or more aspirational than actual, but I assure you, it's quite real and *you can create it too*. It requires awareness, desire, emotional intelligence, maturity, and patience. It requires everyone infusing mindful intentionality in every decision made from the smallest to the most impactful.

> *Creating a collective mindset starts with building awareness that evolves to sincere desire that transforms into personal commitment.*

Let me provide a tangible example. During one of our Thanksgiving staff meetings, everyone shared their gratitude and joys through tears—almost every single employee was crying joyful tears. It was so incredulous that I thought to myself:

> *How is this even possible? I know I imagined a safe office space motivated and inspired by abundant gratitude, but never in my wildest dreams did I imagine this!*

When my husband joined ICE in 2014, after a thirty-six-year career at MetLife, our staff meetings shocked him. He could not believe I struggled with controlling my emotions in a business setting and it made him incredibly uncomfortable, but within a few months, even this tough Irish New Yorker was choking up, fighting back tears from the overwhelming gratitude he felt in working at such an empowered and joyful workplace.

In February 2021, Alysse asked everyone to identify a situation, relationship, or experience they had at ICE and to share their feelings of gratitude via email with the team. The full list of messages can be found on my website www.DeLindaForsythe.com. This activity is so easy to do and reaps such tremendous organizational benefits that I encourage business owners to adopt it.

During Times of Crisis

Let me share with you a journey that is no doubt still fresh in everyone's collective memory. March 12, 2020 was the most disconcerting day of my career; that's when I realized we were in a very dire situation with the COVID-19 virus pandemic. We needed to issue decisive statements both internally with our staff and externally with our customers. I've managed ICE through many challenges, but I did not possess the expertise to navigate anything so complex or anything that affected every single person in America so profoundly.

We worked feverishly to craft the most appropriate message. As always, let me stress the word *we* here; our executive leadership team worked together seamlessly and intelligently. The generational influence was tangible, integrating my thirty-five years of business wisdom with Millennial perspective and technology acumen.

The information was coming at us so quickly that we had to rethink the message we would convey in our next staff meeting multiple times to keep it relevant. As the CEO, I remained very calm and felt it was my responsibility to reinforce our core value of being a workplace family. I felt obligated to convey as much information about the COVID-19 virus as I could in an effort to reassure and console our staff.

By March 31, our next virtually held staff meeting, we had much to discuss! We started out as we always do with our tradition of expressing gratitude and sharing "Our COVID moment, good or bad." Here are a few of those moments:

- "As part of the ICE book club, I chose *Stillness Is the Key*, in which I learned that great companies are transformed by crisis; they rise to higher levels of excellence because of them. I learned so much from this book on leadership during crisis, and I look forward to leading during this time to discover opportunities for all of us to be transformed for the greater good."

- "I'm impressed every day by everyone's willingness to go above and beyond their normal duties; we can't get through this unscathed without your selfless daily sacrifices. I am grateful for our amazing team."

- "I appreciate the potential of reading to change my ability to make sense of the world and life. Knowledge is transformational."

- "I'm finding pockets of joy…. I love spending more time with my kids and family, really being present with them. I have time to cook and love on my spouse."

- "I love that I'm accomplishing things I never dreamed I could accomplish. I'm grateful for the new skills I'm learning."

COVID taught us that we were more capable than we thought we were; what a thing to be proud of!

One employee was raising a caterpillar she had discovered coming out from under her bed; she was looking forward to its transformation into a butterfly. After a nice long pause, as we soaked this story in, we wanted to know if she'd named it, which she had. No matter what is going on in the world or in our company, we always find time for levity!

One team member had immigrated from a Third World country and was incredibly grateful to be in a First World country during such a global crisis.

Even in this nightmare situation, we were connecting in *gratitude*! Then we moved to a more serious posture as we discussed the challenges we could anticipate and ones we could not.

- We were able to share how our clients were reacting, which was overwhelmingly positive.
- We shared our updated "worst case" budget planning, which supported why we thought financially we were in a solid position, even though we anticipated a steep decline in sales.
- We detailed our 25 percent cost-cutting plan that included very creative ways to reduce overhead without losing staff. We emphasized one of our five core values, Live the Entrepreneurial Spirit, by reinforcing with our staff why losses from preventable mistakes had to be avoided.
- We iterated that recent terminations were not layoffs and that layoffs would be the last option.
- We redefined success as zero layoffs.
- We had completed the installation of developer Kilroy Realty's One Paseo project and took time to enjoy this highly successful and extremely complicated two-year project that had brought our dealership to a new level.

We focused on the positive every chance we could, but we never avoided or sugarcoated the hard truth. We provided each person with the opportunity to share their personal challenges through this crisis. This activity united us in a profound way. The following statements capture some of their viewpoints.

- As in every generation, perspectives varied based on "family of origin" and life experiences from optimistic and unrealistically rosy to fear centered and severely depressed. We realized with precise clarity the importance and the benefit of having safe "emotional space."
- Some lost faith in our system, our government, and the world; there was a reflective loss of naiveté and perhaps a shared mourning by many.
- Some thoughtfully responded, bringing extraordinary wisdom beyond their years in providing insight but also positive solutions and options for our organization to move forward, and many asked "How can we grow from this experience? Where is the organizational value in this crisis?"
- Many were surprised by how proactive our leadership was, comparing us to organizations with thousands of employees who were not putting out statements or action steps.
- They realized their behavior and commitment to excellence had a direct correlation to the emotional and especially, the financial welfare of their coworkers.
- We all linked our day-to-day tasks back to our personal responsibility for each other. This responsibility is what business owners feel every day; it drives how we make decisions, based on the collective whole. We are indeed our "brother's keeper."

In times of crisis, the need for leadership becomes evident. It is the most telling time. Tough times bring out the best or the worst in us, teaching us who we are, including our core values and personal character.

As previously mentioned, we had planned terminations and we continued through with this decision, knowing timing and optics were terrible but because of our transparent culture, they were not unforeseen by our staff. We provided more generous than usual severance packages.

This was an extraordinary opportunity to cultivate leadership skills, fully integrating multi-generational perspectives during a most horrific experience. Could there be a more challenging incident? Our Millennial leaders were undaunted through this crisis and Alysse as ICE President, became even more focused and tenacious.

I leave you with the words of one of our country's most courageous civic rights leader, Martin Luther King, Jr.

> *The ultimate measure of a man is not where he stands*
> *in moments of comfort and convenience but where he stands*
> *at times of challenge and controversy.*
> **—Martin Luther King**

Living the Entrepreneurial Spirit

In our meetings at ICE, we are transparent in detailing our corporate financial snapshot. We are transparent to the point of wondering if we're too transparent! Early in 2020, we experienced the most challenging financial month in our history. Alysse weighed the advantages and disadvantages of being too transparent, then decided to let the staff see the impact of controllable losses to help them foster a business owner mindset. One of our core values, "Live the Entrepreneurial Spirit," is not always easy to understand.

We chose this as one of our values because we wanted to cultivate a company culture that encouraged every employee, in every area of their lives, to develop effective leadership skills. These skills transcend day-to-day work activities. As noted previously, because of our whole human perspective, we care equally about what happens to our team during non-work hours as we do during workday hours.

Our desire and ability to ignite an entrepreneurial spirit—a *spirit of independent thinkers*—also appeals to Millennials. Entrepreneurship isn't possible for every person, but *intrapreneurship* certainly is. Intrapreneurship is a system that allows an employee to act like an entrepreneur. Intrapreneurs are self-motivated, action-oriented individuals. We've worked very consciously to develop this dynamic, and it flows seamlessly from ICE leadership to our coworkers, hopefully diffusing throughout their personal lives.

What does it mean to have an "entrepreneurial spirit" and to live an emboldened life energized with this animated energy?

Fred Engelfried's 2020 book *Defining the Entrepreneurial Spirit* provides a comprehensive overview of what this entails. Engelfried covers crisis, participative management, and corporate leadership, noting more than twenty characteristics he's observed in entrepreneurs he's known or worked with. Below are a few of the most telling attributes he found of those who had an entrepreneurial disposition.[48]

- Committed to the success of all and inspires others to embrace the same and mentor those willing to learn.
- Sponsors "ownership." Doesn't do others' jobs or solve their problems without their participation.
- Loyal to a fault. Shows an unwavering commitment to those who have tirelessly "shared the ride," a trait that can be severely tested when performance issues arise.
- First to disrupt. An architect of paradigm shifts designed to meet crisis and opportunity—head on.
- Is candid about what he/she doesn't know. Seeks professional input as needed from subject matter experts but, in the end, makes the final call.
- Makes it a priority to know as many associates as possible by name but more importantly, *to know "who they are."*
- More interested in listening than being heard.
- Passionate about his/her responsibilities, sometimes to a fault.

These qualities struck me as particularly similar to how we strive to capture our hutzpah; all reflect our supportive inter-generational, *participative* leadership style.

Transparency in Action

When you have a transparent corporate culture, you foster trust and foundational understanding of why decisions are made. Others might not understand or even agree with those decisions, and you can run the risk of being too transparent, but I think erring on that side is far better.

At ICE, we share project overviews that include definitive details such as lead source, design firm, scope, and profitability of a project, which includes very nuanced details of mistakes made and lessons learned. We also present specific products and manufacturers used. Each presenter takes the time to compile a customer-worthy PowerPoint with images of the furniture installed. Most of our staff never experiences the final project completion so sharing these stories and images breathes life into everyone's work and fosters a rewarding sense of accomplishment. It increases our sense of pride and has been a phenomenal benefit to our staff meetings.

We share our upcoming business development snapshot, which includes planned internal (employee) as well as external (client) interactive events, presentations, marketing efforts, and short- and long-term goals. The snapshot fosters a great deal of excitement and provides knowledge of how much effort business development requires. At dealerships where I previously worked, a disconnect always existed between sales and other departments. Resentment resulted because of this misunderstanding and lack of appreciation. Our sales executives are hardworking, deadline-driven, and very competitive; they push the other departments to help them win projects. We have learned to rely and appreciate each other.

Having members of the sales team share their challenges in finding and securing sales opportunities has increased commitment and buy-in between departments. This exchange has reduced conflict. Do team members still complain about the deadline-driven demands our sales executives put on them? Yes, but it does reduce some of that tension, providing reminders that we're all playing for the same team.

We share equally the humiliation and the benefits of failure; failure that leads to personal and corporate growth. Here are a few tips based on what we have shared in our staff meetings:

- Focus on new procedures, asking for input on what works and what doesn't.
- Discuss reemploying old processes that were eliminated, analyzing if they offer more benefits than previously realized.
- Analyze the value of taking more time to do a job upfront, to avoid mistakes at the end of the project. This increases the potential to lose opportunities because proposals can't be turned around as quickly.
- Analyze and co-create upfront checklist procedures that reduce mistakes in the back end of a project—sales can get resentful of this because it can delay the creation of proposals which might lead to lost opportunities.
- Discuss in detail what went wrong, educating others so they can avoid making the same mistakes.
- Share why a new opportunity was lost and, in rare instances, a client loss—this can be really painful—and embarrassing.

It's all about increasing understanding and communication between departments. This approach of slowing down and thoughtfully going through these details accomplishes so much. It lets everyone know we do not have all the answers, we are all works in progress, and we genuinely value each person and their input. We don't simply offer performative words. Even the most experienced people make mistakes, so we strive to remove the shame and turn mistakes into opportunities for growth.

We stress that every single team member brings enormous value, no matter their position. And everyone is given the opportunity to share their stories and advice, thereby growing in their ability to speak publicly and communicate their feelings and thoughts. The confidence that blossoms within the most introverted individual is quantifiable. This entire exercise continues to spring forth significant individual and corporate benefits.

Knowledge Empowers—Start a Book Club!

I am a huge proponent of reading and spent much of my youth absorbed in books. In fourth grade, I worked as a librarian at a local library on the military base where my parents were stationed in Salina, Kansas. I spent my entire summer reading Nancy Drew books, visualizing myself as a detective, learning strategic and analytical thinking skills.

I've always encouraged others to read business books. Alysse became a voracious reader and took reading to a far more expansive practice than even I have as a career professional. I was pleasantly surprised when she introduced in a staff meeting the ICE Book Club with a pre-selected reading list. Each person selects the book that appeals to them and is encouraged to read it in their personal time. We even added a financial incentive to encourage personal growth—part of their annual bonus is based on their engagement in the book club. The ICE Book Club became an immediate hit! Below is our 2020 reading list:

TITLE	AUTHOR(S)
Stillness Is the Key	Ryan Holiday
Helping People Win at Work	Ken Blanchard and Garry Ridge
Pick Three	Randi Zuckerberg
Onward	Howard Schultz
People Over Profit	Dale Partridge
Conscious Capitalism	John Mackey and Raj Sisodia
Essentialism	Greg McKeown
Insight	Tasha Eurich

I was struck by the diversity in the list. There were business books but also life skills books such as *Essentialism: The Disciplined Pursuit of Less*. Here is an overview of what you'll learn from *Essentialism*:

"Being an essentialist is about a disciplined way of thinking. It means challenging the core assumption of 'We can have it all' and 'I have to do everything' and replacing it with the pursuit of 'the right thing, in the right way, at the right time.'

By applying a more selective criteria for what is essential, the pursuit of less allows us to regain control of our own choices so we can channel our time, energy, and effort into making the highest possible contribution toward the goals and activities that matter."

This is what you'll discover from *Stillness Is the Key:*

"In this book, Holiday outlines a path for achieving this ancient art of stillness... Drawing on a wide range of history's greatest thinkers, from Confucius to Seneca, Marcus Aurelius to Thich Nhat Hanh, John Stuart Mill to Nietzsche, he argues that stillness is not mere inactivity, but the doorway to self-mastery, discipline, and focus.

More than ever, people are overwhelmed. They face obstacles and egos and competition. *Stillness Is the Key* offers a simple but inspiring antidote to the stress of 24/7 news and social media. The stillness we all seek is the path to meaning, contentment, and excellence in a world that needs more of it than ever before."

So many demands are placed on our time, especially when you're juggling parenthood. Persistent, destructive myths that promote a "do it all, have it all" mindset perpetuate this false narrative. By adding books that encourage balance and the adoption of healthier habits, you are encouraging lifelong skills that benefit not just the person gaining this knowledge but future generations.

Many of the readers selected *Stillness Is the Key*. The shared experience of reading the same book encouraged engagement of a mutually experienced story. This increased the opportunity to further share ideas learned, the applicability to our everyday lives, individual growth, etc. This provided yet one more opportunity to design connection into our corporate culture.

New knowledge led the way for increased wisdom in better understanding ourselves, our leadership, corporate principles, social justice issues, societal challenges, etc. The list was intentionally diverse, and all the books offered insight into how others see the world with the prospect of transforming narrow perspectives.

> *We actively strive to influence an informed, positive mindset.*

Our book club creates opportunities to achieve multiple aspirations. Like good parents, we want to foster the ability for each person to grow as an individual within a variety of positive proficiencies. We want the journey of personal development to include time management, the redefinition of success (which is again, less about stuff and more about personal relationships), conflict resolution, and options for gaining leadership and business wisdom.

The book club also offers the opportunity to increase appreciation of each other's perspectives. It was one more tool to increase unity among our teammates.

Each person was then required to write a book report that they provided to their manager. They were able to increase their bonus based on how much they embraced this practice, how much they wanted to grow. Each book equaled 5 percent of their annual bonus with up to three books for a total of 15 percent of their bonus. *A guaranteed 15 percent could be earned simply by reading!* I thought it was ingenious to build financial incentives into the book club; that just reinforced how seriously management valued the book club.

Should you consider adding a book club at your organization, I would recommend offering more opportunities to increase the bonus by asking each staff member to verbally present their book review to their micro-team. If they feel comfortable, also offer the opportunity to present to the entire organization during the team meeting. This would increase the potential for everyone to gain new perspective, but it would especially benefit the reader/speaker. Reading, writing, and *then teaching* is closing the full learning circle. That's when the lessons are fully absorbed. We have not tried this yet. Most of our team members are quite uncomfortable with public speaking, which is why I promote Toastmasters as a personal growth tool.

Alysse experienced increased business acumen and the ability to understand others' realities and perceptions simply by reading, so she wanted others also to be incentivized to grow through the gift of reading. Our book club is still in its infancy, but it is already becoming a positive, influential driver at ICE. It illustrates not just the benefit of having a mentor leading by example and experience but the long-term positive outcome derived through mentorship as Alysse took my love of reading to an entirely new level.

Group Exercises

A few times a year, we have interactive group exercises. Sometimes our consulting team joins us, and sometimes we host these on our own. We mandate all employees read *StrengthsFinder 2.0* by Tom Rath and take the assessment test when they join ICE so we can determine their strengths for their benefit and ours. According to Rath, people who have the opportunity to focus on their strengths are six times more likely to be engaged in their jobs and three times more likely to report having an excellent quality of life. It always brings extraordinary engagement when we incorporate our strengths in our day-to-day interactions.

We use this information in team assignment evaluations to balance micro-teams with appropriate individual strengths. We endeavor to keep assessment results relevant by consistent discussion of each other's strengths. In the three years we've done this, it has maintained its effectiveness and continues to increase in popularity.

Through continuity and reinforcement, these exercises have become relevant learning opportunities. This is how you build a team culture: constant incremental reinforcement. Each year, we pick a corporate value and ask them to personalize it. Each year, we request everyone select a personal strength to build on. These group exercises encourage individual growth as well as discernment. This leads to the entire company improving and growing.

Bringing Individual Strengths to Life

Alysse and Elyse developed the following interactive and fun experience to increase awareness of each individual's strengths. They decided not to give any advance notice of this exercise to engage the employees' ability to think outside the box quickly, but also to learn to be fully engaged and anticipatory at meetings. They were encouraging spontaneity and honest feedback, believing with too much advance preparation that the most authentic responses might not ensue.

Not everyone considers and values their strengths. These exercises build appreciation—gratitude for who each person is as an individual and gratitude for ourselves. When you lead a high-achieving team, sometimes you need to help them step back to give them a chance to reinforce their appreciation of themselves! Our team is so committed that we actually have a problem with people obsessing over things going wrong and having unrealistic expectations. This particular exercise was designed to reduce that pressure and build connectivity.

Here is a summary of our strengths fellowship-building exercise:
- Ultimate goal of exercise is to reinforce strengths and focus on the positive by learning to honor and respect each other as individuals.
- It requires 60-90 minutes to conduct.
- Break out in departments or micro-teams and engage in this activity twice a year with each category.
- Start by identifying each individual's strength; provide summary of strength description.

- *StrengthsFinder 2.0* identifies five core strengths per person. This exercise requires the selection of one strength chosen by the employee.
- This exercise increases awareness and efficacy of the strength in day-to-day scenario applications.
- The team member then identifies and details how they applied their strength effectively or ineffectively in an actual scenario with a focus on increasing mindfulness on how to maximize the benefit of their strengths for the company, but more significantly, for their personal growth.

Following is a summary of how this day's exercise went. The group was split into departmental teams, shared their five strengths, and selected one to expound on. I joined the project management team. Here is their narrative:

> **"Restorative, Adaptability, Context, Intellection, Learner**: This project manager selected Intellection as her most valued strength because she enjoys taking a deep dive into problem solving, analyzing problems in minute detail to ascertain the best solution. She has the capacity for intense introspection. She starts by gathering as much information as possible early on, asking that extra question no one is asking to do this deep analysis for the benefit of the company and to understand how all the puzzle pieces work together—even pieces that aren't our organization's responsibility. She detailed how she coordinated one of the most complicated deliveries in the history of ICE with more than eighty different manufacturers' shipping over an eighteen-month time frame and how she was able to coordinate this project seamlessly with almost no punch. She also noted that when she leaves a meeting or has new ideas, she dictates them, capturing ideas in the moment

when they're fresh and when time allows; then she returns to her recorded comments and writes them down. She keeps a record of ideas to improve processes with an eye on how to better use current resources such as software programs. She concluded the exercise by suggesting ways for her teammates to use their strengths more, and she also asked for input on how they thought she could use her strengths more efficiently.

Consistency, Intellection, Content, Input, Learner: As a new addition to ICE, this project manager picked Input because he wants to collect as much data as possible since he isn't intimate with our organizational processes. As he's learning, he's been archiving information to create his own organizational system that's adapted around ICE procedures. He's created spreadsheets to capture every step of the process we're currently using to stay organized but also to ensure he performs each step in sequence. He hadn't thought to share them with the team, but then he realized they would be highly beneficial for current and future hires. The director of the project managers also suggested ways to improve this process by asking him to share ideas to improve current processes as they bubble up, while capturing the detail of each process. Again, this was not something he had thought of doing, but in the group setting, they collectively agreed how helpful this sharing would be for the entire organization.

Achiever, Empathy, Adaptability, Competition, Includer: This project management leader selected Achiever because he is achieving the implementation of new processes and new forms and seeking front-end opportunities to improve project execution and improve training programs. His ultimate goal is to create new processes to increase efficiency and decrease losses. He discussed the new program, Plan Grid, he had introduced to ICE and discussed how much it has improved our communication pathways since we invested in it. He noted Go Formz is a future mobile program to consider when funds allow, and the group hashed out its efficacy. He reinforced the need to have access to all our forms in the field, enabling our project managers to perform their tasks in real time. They agreed it all comes down to costs, bandwidth, etc. as we consider changes, so these may be longer-term changes to implement. He asked his team for input, which as noted, is one of our project managers' strengths. By already capturing every step of the process and, at the same time, including opportunities to improve those processes from field experiences, internal meetings, etc., we already were creating vehicles to facilitate improvements. Since this was a new employee, we were encouraging this consideration of having a new set of eyes to see how we can make those improvements not just for one individual, but to benefit the entire company. Specifically, we were questioning if we have repetitive ICE processes or holes that can be filled."

Results from This Exercise

By simply sharing in detail with specific field examples on how they had or were implementing their specific strength, the group members naturally moved into acknowledging how they had experienced each other's strengths, noting the overlap and affect each one brought to each project, their project management department and the organization as a whole.

Although not planned, what this exercise ultimately revealed was an opportunity to build awareness of what they were doing individually and how they might consolidate their efforts as a department. The exercise revealed how they each use their skills and the personal tricks they had developed for themselves and collectively for the project management department. It was a wonderful observation and aha moment.

Final Outcome

They discussed how many processes or ideas could not be implemented because of costs or lack of personnel, but they also noted how open the company was to implementing new ideas. They took it to the next step by planning for additional costs to be included in future budgets. Since we are always so transparent with costs and encourage an entrepreneurial mindset, they approach business challenges *from an owner's perspective as much as an employee*! We work consciously to help each other see our company through an owner's eyes, with real world challenges and limitations. Since intrapreneurship is the act of behaving as an entrepreneur within an organization, this exercise encouraged our "Live the Entrepreneurial Spirit" core value because it encouraged staff members to become intrapreneurs.

They understood that as profitability increased, we would be open to incurring costs for software and tools to make their lives easier—*they realized future potential.* This understanding is key because people want to be heard; they want their input to be valued and, in every way, we strive to create this sense of appreciation for each other and the organization.

They also gained an increased awareness on how their department was functioning currently and how it could better function with a long-term blueprint for success. This was a huge positive outcome because it presented an exciting opportunity *that they collectively could create.* It's often said when positive change is developed from within the team, the success ratio increases dramatically!

A sense of personal contribution and acknowledged respect for each individual is highly empowering; imagine if your individual efforts were acknowledged in such an affirming manner how that would motivate you to do more, think outside the box, and experience a sense of value and inclusiveness.

Inclusiveness is a hot business topic right now, but it's not rocket science. These interactive, simple exercises consistently reinforce our inclusive belief system.

Finally, this sharing provided a very specific opportunity to discuss efficiencies and tools and to analyze current and future software options. As a department, they decided they'd each explore the introduction of new software applications. Since it's difficult to stay up-to-date with what is available, they realized if each person did a little bit of homework and shared with the group, they could stay current with options.

Sharing Findings as a Group

As these individual breakout sessions ended, we reconvened as a group to share with the entire company what each department had learned. Two people from each group came up. One wrote the group's findings on huge sticky sheets attached to our windows, and the other discussed in detail the results and their conclusions. Questions and comments were encouraged!

Our project management group shared:

- New potential processes and information gathering and compared it with current procedures to figure out how to streamline to reduce redundancies.
- How best to collect field information to decrease the time it takes to download this information to our project coordinators; their goal was to request feedback from the project coordinators to streamline this process.

Unexpected benefits of this exercise included:

- When you have an opportunity to call out and name not only your strengths but your weaknesses, you actually find humor in your weaknesses and shine a light on them; you bring your fears out of the basement, which provides an opportunity to collectively work on improving your weaknesses without shame. As noted, shame is a highly destructive emotion we actively, not passively, avoid.

• Realization that we are all works in progress, and when leadership makes it clear they're in the same situation, it really relaxes the emotional environment and creates space for people to "emotionally transcend the ordinary"!

We found it invigorating to discover actionable steps as a team that led to goals and a clear path we could collectively achieve. You can imagine our excitement and how positive everyone felt. We went from focusing on inefficiencies—which is human nature—to possibilities for how we could constructively design a better company together.

We absolutely did not minimize the importance of the individual or their strengths and ability to improve and grow. We found opportunities and actionable steps to hold each other accountable by understanding what everyone is working on. We discovered ways to improve, honor, and acknowledge the extra work they're individually doing. These extra efforts not only will help everyone achieve their goals but improve the organization from the foundation up!

Watching and Observing—Parental Pride

I observed all of this as an outsider. I wasn't prepared or briefed on what the meeting would entail. I did not contribute any content to the exercise. If you've experienced parenthood—watching your child take their first step, stand up for injustice, etc.—you know what I was feeling. I had such pride in this group, in our leadership, but really in every single person as they excitedly contributed. Experiencing an empowered staff is an astonishing, almost fictional, occurrence. Watching those you've lovingly pushed (though they might not see it that way) reach their potential creates a sense of accomplishment words really cannot capture.

Conclusion

As we finished this exercise, a major theme emerged from management on how passionately they wanted to develop others. As their knowledge increases from ICE-encouraged reading, they are establishing goals for themselves they never imagined—goals that will help them grow as young professionals and young parents. They expressed their passion to encourage the same emotional evolution for their teammates.

Our company continues to learn this lesson of being other-focused, becoming and displaying clarity of purpose, continuity in thinking, and behavior and goal setting. It's a process, but one definitely moving in a positive direction!

CHAPTER 6

Deliver Excellence: We Are What We Repeatedly Do!

This chapter reinforces how we consistently live our values and fortify our culture.

Modeling Experiential Excellence

Our goal is to build a robust, highly interconnected culture, so we actively work to maintain the "begin with the end in mind" principle. Everything we do, both significant and insignificant, is designed to develop and maintain culture. It's a lot of work, but once you make it a habit, it becomes integral to how you approach daily challenges and internal corporate messaging.

In 2020, in our effort to ingrain our core value of "Deliver Excellence Every Day," we designed an employee experience to visually share and teach our staff how they can improve the bottom line and deliver excellence in their day-to-day work.

As discussed in the previous chapter, we added the Project Highlights portion to our meetings to bring our projects to life for every staff member since most employees do not see the final completed installation. We realized we were missing the opportunity to make projects more personal and real because very few team members had the opportunity to experience more than their piece of the project. The final installed project was frequently only seen by the Project Manager or perhaps the Account Executive. When we added the Project Highlights PowerPoint, we brought "field reality" to our paperwork.

This addition led to an increased sense of accomplishment and a reduction in errors. Our team members have such a strong desire to perform at a high level. They took what they learned from the Project Highlights presentations to further analyze their projects with an eye toward identifying opportunities for improvement. This soon led to enhanced procedural checks and balances. As a group, we discuss how mistakes add costs to every project, specifically in the design and project coordination phases. Often, it's not until the final installation phase that mistakes are identified.

This simple practice validated the company's financial requirements to remain a profitable entity and how each person could best support this end result. We implemented this new practice in late February 2020 because in January we had sustained the largest monthly loss in our fourteen-year history—a whopping *255.54 percent loss*. We had never sustained such a hit, and in February, the bleeding continued. Then COVID-19 hit in March—can you imagine how concerned we were? We realized we had to do something and do it quickly.

By simply increasing awareness of controllable versus uncontrollable losses and measuring accountability, we encouraged everyone to become better financial stewards at ICE. As COVID dragged on, we reinforced the belief that each person was their *brother's keeper*, and we made the goal to reduce controllable losses very personal, *very other-focused*. Though our 2020 sales revenues plunged 59 percent, we avoided layoffs partly because we increased project profitability by simply showing everyone the magnitude of controllable losses.

Even though we were focusing on individual mistakes, we made it a positive, shared practice that was non-threatening and completely eye-opening. At all costs, we endeavored to avoid shame and fear and instill the sense that we are all in this together.

This chart illustrates the financial success we experienced once we implemented this practice of analyzing controllable losses and personalizing everyone's responsibility in this effort.

ICE ERROR LOSS AS % OF TOTAL PROFIT

- JANUARY: –255.54%
- FEBRUARY: –93.48%
- MARCH: +0.86%
- APRIL: –15.75%
- MAY: +3.68%
- JUNE: +2.76%
- JULY: +3.26%
- AUGUST: +0.37%
- SEPTEMBER: +0.52%
- OCTOBER: +0.36%
- NOVEMBER: +3.14%
- DECEMBER: +4.01%

Let me note once more that we avoided layoffs, even though revenue *plummeted* during the COVID crisis. I give all the credit to our incredible ICE family. They stayed positive, motivated, and dedicated, despite significant childcare and emotional challenges. And in the middle of all this stress, we all took a 10 percent pay cut to further reduce costs. How can that not be demotivating? By focusing on avoiding layoffs more than the pay cut and focusing on keeping us all together, we hoped to take the sting out of the loss of income. By December, we were back up to full pay.

We achieved this as a cohesive family team with each person performing their role as error-free as possible. We did it for ourselves, for each other, and for our company, and we kept our attention on our new definition of success: zero layoffs. Millennials have redefined success. COVID-19 redefined how ICE measures success. Our new definition drives home how effective an organization can be when conscious leaders are at the helm.

I have never experienced a more successful way to inspire and motivate another individual than by simply valuing the work they do—appreciating that they want to work for our company and treating them as equals and individuals—critical to the success of the whole.

Breaking Down Project Highlights

While you most likely are not in our industry, I hope detailing our business practices clarifies how you can also improve your corporate culture and staff connection and teach financial literacy and best practices.

Our Project Highlights include:

- **Project Stats**: Team members' names, lead source, profitability or loss on project, station and office typicals, overall floorplan, and manufacturers used.

- **Lessons Learned**: Punch list issues created by manufacturer, freight carrier, or our design team, such as specification oversights. Installation notes to include onsite staging, stair carry, and elevator details, especially with oversized items that would not fit in the elevator. What the installation team and project manager might have learned on the project such as: general contractor issues to include overlooked column locations; columns the contractor furred out that were not included in the construction documents; jobsite measurements that were not done correctly; walls added that were not on construction documents; floor cores not in the correct spot; and very small details such as which walls to hang markerboards on and how high to hang them, wire management minutiae, and how to position area rugs and throw pillows. One of the best stories is how our installers had to place a large reception desk outside and on top of the elevator, and ride it down manually! We get very creative in finding solutions, and by sharing issues, we learn what to avoid on projects.

- **Project Images**: This is the most anticipated portion of our Project Highlights section because everyone is eager to see the beautiful, completed installation for obvious reasons, but also to collectively analyze, "What could we have done better? What finishes, products, and solutions actually function well, and what can we learn from what doesn't work as well?" We all examine and comment on opportunities for improvement that might include a better table base design to increase knee space or conference tables that need only one base and appear to float in space. We focus on aligning directional wood-graining patterns on tops and drawer fronts to create a more pleasing design aesthetic. Contrasting top stitching on chairs and feather content in pillows that create a better crease when karate-chopped down are details we discuss.

We get into the *weeds* where with most organizations, there could be hurt feelings or defensiveness. However, it's just the opposite because *we all share this mindset of striving for excellence*! We all feel terrible when we've missed these small details because we truly want to be the most detailed and most respected dealership in town.

Project Highlights reinforce and expose our staff to so many expansive concepts, such as popular design trends, what products we offer that are low-cost but high-design, what factories perform consistently well, and how to better improve communication and procedural processes between departments. We have seamlessly infused team member knowledge exchange, which for most companies is a humiliating experience, into a robust interchange of opportunities to increase excellence for everyone and learn from each other's mistakes.

Becoming San Diego's Most Creative Furniture Dealership

We have been designing and manufacturing elaborate custom furniture for years. The process can get very complicated. In the beginning we often lost money as we taught ourselves this new skillset. Most dealerships only specify furniture; they don't design it. *Manufacturer's* design and fabricate furniture; dealerships generally simply order furniture from manufacturers. Our goal in 2013 was to become San Diego's most creative dealership; therefore, we had to become furniture designers.

We improved quickly because we've always embraced the skill of deep analysis. Consequently, we learned to produce even more detailed shop drawings, reducing our errors. As we became more knowledgeable in furniture construction, we became as much a manufacturer as a dealership. This established a deeper knowledge of furniture, making us more appreciative of what our furniture manufacturing partners endure. We also learned which factories to partner with to improve our capabilities, often partnering with factories in Mexico. This partnering was an enormous advantage due to the proximity to our warehouse just north of the border. Our ability to literally build anything envisioned by a client's design team solidified our reputation of being "San Diego's most creative office and hospitality furniture dealership." It certainly helped us weather the 2020 business tsunami because, while office and systems furniture sales dropped significantly, amenity furniture for outdoor spaces, informal gatherings, and reception areas increased.

Sowing Excellence Leads to Satisfaction

Every person in your company can and should be a sales ambassador, and when every employee can visually see *what* your company produces and *how* it affects and improves others' lives, you create excitement, pride, and deep understanding. This leads to a natural sharing of what we do with friends, family, and others—a natural pride of ownership. It's surprising it took us thirteen years to realize how powerful it is for the team to see the final installed project come to life with images of the completed project, but now that we know, we rarely let a team meeting go by without sharing at least one Project Highlight.

Since our industry is fraught with unlimited opportunities for failure, this simple exercise led to increased respect and gratitude for what each department and each person does. Learning from each other's mistakes and seeing how each department can influence and improve the work of others offered enormous opportunity for personal and cross-departmental growth, leading to that sense of connection that we all naturally crave as humans. Again, the mindset that we're all works in progress is quite helpful here!

Undoubtedly, your industry offers the same option to humanize/personalize your work and make it meaningful to everyone. Look for activities to increase connection between individuals and departments; make it meaningful and fun—that is the simple secret to the creation of a healthy corporate culture based on the foundation of gratitude; it's very difficult to disrespect or dislike each other when you experience a day in your coworkers' shoes and see what they go through to deliver excellence.

Nurturing Fiscal Community

After reading several articles and working with our consulting firm, Equal Parts, it became clear that very few people, including business owners, understand "corporate financial literacy"—even managers and directors often do not take into consideration wide-ranging financial matters. I know when I first started ICE, I was not financially literate. No previous employer had taken the time to educate or personalize my individual fiscal responsibility for the company other than to tell me, "Be profitable on every project," which only focused on the markup. If you want fully engaged employees, you need to share your organization's financial snapshot. It is our responsibility to educate our staff about the importance of cash flow, deposits, how our vendors often require 100 percent payment in advance of receipt of goods, how payables work, etc.

It's understandable why small businesses are reluctant to share financial knowledge; however, it all connects back to building a culture of trust through transparency. If you desire to have your team adopt an entrepreneurial spirit, teach them the most basic facts about corporate finances. By teaching financial literacy, we reinforce our core value of "Live the Entrepreneurial Spirit." In establishing an ownership mindset, our intention is not to pass on the burden of ownership but to develop knowledgeable and engaged employees.

Initially, we *unconsciously* developed this habit of striving for excellence based on a uniform mindset of integrity, ethics, and trust. Over time, we've made a *conscious* decision to thoughtfully invest our time in teaching financial literacy.

All our efforts to develop our empowered culture are interconnected, attentively designed to reinforce what we stand for as an organization. Your values and higher purpose cannot simply be words on a wall; to bring them to life and internalize them within your team, you need to create an emotional connection. We reinforce our values every day—we live them in the smallest of ways possible to make them become habits, not just words. All our "business hacks" and habits are designed to support our higher purpose and our five core values!

Mike Norris, from my Toastmasters club, lives a life inspired by this Aristotle quote: "We are what we repeatedly do. Excellence, then, is not an act, but a habit." I've learned a hundred lessons from club members, but this one has stuck with me the most. So how do you make excellence become a habit?

Making Excellence a Daily Habit

We also increase financial awareness through our book club by recommending business books that teach corporate literacy and policies. We've suggested podcasts or blogs that offer insight to corporate objectives. But it is again within our staff meetings that we truly bring this to life by discussing honestly the finances of our organization and every project.

Typically, only the accounting department and the owner care if Client X pays their bills or not, or if Factory Z needs 100 percent of their money upfront six months before shipping their products. That's not glamorous, especially to creative types! So, we were challenged but determined to make this information relevant for everyone. Often, it's the sales department, the engineer, or the product developer who gets the attention, not the accounting department. We bring proper recognition to this less visible area of business. To increase financial literacy, we added a monthly financial update to our meetings. Some of these topics include:

- A corporate snapshot: monthly, quarterly, and annual sales goals are compared to actual booked sales. Our targeted gross profit versus actual gross profit
- Transparency in project losses due to large revenue growth
- The instability of the year made *every profit percentage point matter*
- Importance of individual accountability
- Encouraging sales and design to specify products to meet factory quotas

In 2020, we became fiscally literate as we examined our corporate snapshot, elevating everyone's desire to be more profit-focused and to deliver excellence.

Creating a Risk-Free Environment

The staff created highly visual graphics and charts to simplify these details and make them easy to understand. Additionally, they appeared eager to learn new skills and be engaged in these traditionally management-level-only conversations. Employee engagement is a major concern with Human Resource professionals and business leaders. If you want engaged employees, you need to engage their minds and their talents and challenge them. Small opportunities like this create highly engaged employees. Highly engaged employees become emotionally attached to clients—they learn to care as much about clients as top management does.

Financial losses can teach valuable lessons. By sharing loss trends that occurred due to high revenue generating months, we were able to shift the focus into a positive experience.

No one has arrived; we're all learning. We don't avoid the hard conversations; we simply embrace a more human-focused, wholistic mindset that illustrates how profitability affects us all, and we do not need to create an atmosphere of blame.

Shane Jackson

I met Shane through a virtual program sponsored by Conscious Capitalism Inc. in late 2020 and immediately requested an interview with him. Shane is the President of Jackson Healthcare, one of the three largest US healthcare staffing firms, with more than $1 billion in annual revenues. The *Atlanta Business Chronicle* named Shane as a local "Leader in Corporate Citizenship" because of his commitment to corporate social responsibility. Under Shane's leadership, Jackson Healthcare has earned numerous awards, including one of the Best Places to Work specifically for Millennials and women. They have integrated societal concerns into their core operating strategies for the benefit of their employees, customers, and the metro Atlanta community.

Shane developed a strategy that has fostered a corporate culture very similar to ICE's that exemplifies philanthropy, employee volunteerism, and engagement, and is committed to inspiring and developing Millennial leaders. Shane states:[49]

> "We tend to hire inexperienced people so you know mistakes are going to happen. To develop a culture of continuous learning and a climate of innovation, you have to create a risk-free environment where failure is acceptable, so we purposefully designed a culture that allowed mistakes to occur. You need to make people feel safe in taking those risks. They need to know they aren't going to get punished if they screw up; this is how they're going to learn. If you punish failure, you are never going to get innovation. There is nothing more powerful than a safe culture that

ultimately leads to a culture that fosters innovation. This is at the heart of Jackson Healthcare's business.

We have formal mentorship and training programs, but if you ask our associates why they are successful here and what has been the most important training they've experienced at Jackson Healthcare; they will tell you it's the spontaneous conversations they have with their coworkers. They were the recipient of someone else's generous informal training and time. It's a very caring environment—it's been ingrained into our culture to care for others and to put 'others first.'

Giving back is part of our DNA and our corporate mission: to improve the delivery of patient care and the lives of everyone we touch. That starts with our associates and our customers and extends to communities across the country and around the world."

Shane is an extraordinary leader, and it was gratifying to learn how similarly we practice conscious leadership principles. Jackson Healthcare has fifteen hundred employees; ICE has under twenty-five, but these basic principles work seamlessly no matter organizational size or reach.

Cultivate Empowerment

I cannot say all of this financial education of our staff was completely well received. If you want your employees to understand the dynamics of layoffs, pay cuts, bonuses, and salary increases, take the time to teach them how and why these decisions are made. Build that connection between their work and negative outcomes; make it personal and encourage accountability.

I see a direct correlation between how we decided to approach financial transparency and how Stath Karras early on taught financial responsibility to his children by literally opening up the family's books. It's not an easy thing to do because the information can certainly be used against you, but the benefits of experiencing what personal accountability looks like and the potential to forge strong bonds far outweigh the negatives.

The generational impact we're seeking isn't necessarily limited to our staff. If we are modeling honorable business ethics through our actions, those principles will likely influence our staff to reflect similar behavior for their children. We want our business practices to encourage positive parental behavior. I look at this through the same lens I analyze the global warming question: "Are human activities influencing global warming?" I have no idea, but why not adopt proper actions that can potentially reduce the impact of global warming? Why not err on the side of caution? What if our business actions don't create a ripple effect for future generations? There is no downside to doing the right thing, no downside to striving to be a person who has integrity, but there is certainly a downside in not possessing this characteristic.

Once again, it's not all about the achieving; it's all about the effort. For the most part, I have little to no control over many outcomes, but that doesn't change how I act. Most of the principles in this book are very simple to live out in small ways, which is where the potential lies. It's always in the small, seemingly insignificant opportunities that you have the chance to shift others' perspectives. How you tip and thank your waiter, how you treat your suppliers, if you smile and say good morning to your coworkers and check in on how their kids are doing with homeschooling or with that issue with the bully, how you pay commissions on time and pay for your staff's book club books—very small things that over time leave an indelible impression of honest integrity and caring for each other.

One of the biggest differentiators we made in having this candid financial conversation was not just how we presented it, but who presented it. The overview was offered by a peer versus an owner or executive management; peer-to-peer engagement dissolves invisible societal lines and solidifies our respect for every staff member. We encourage individuals to think and behave like leaders; titles don't make you a leader, behavior does.

> *Titles don't make you a leader, behavior does.*

Toastmasters

I joined Toastmasters because I had a deep-seated fear of public speaking based on a series of false narratives I had internally created. All these fears were based on real experiences, so a measure of truth exists in my internal narrative. I needed to retrain my brain to focus on a new narrative. I knew the company would suffer if I didn't develop a more constructive mindset using daily affirmations.

Eight years ago, we made the very short list for a multi-year contract that would offer ICE a tremendous growth opportunity. We were asked to present our capabilities in front of a panel of fifteen industry professionals. It was the most critical presentation to date for our company. I was responsible for leading our presentation. I did quite poorly, and after, one of the panelists (a client and dear friend) gently advised me I had introduced everyone but myself—I literally forgot my own name! I was so disappointed in myself; I vowed I would never let ICE down like that again.

Determined to overcome this debilitating fear, I joined Toastmasters. They teach the fundamentals of speaking—such as the power of three—tone, body language, and effective facial expression. As we identify and focus on "filler" words like "um, so, you know, ah," we become aware of how such words reduce a message's impact. Speech writing, preparation, delivery, and practice, practice, practice are additional skills you learn as you realize communication is not about you but your audience. Toastmasters' trains speakers to use the power of persuasion. The gift of oratory is a benefit to speakers and can be a major influencer in others' lives. A story told is a life lived, so we need to learn to share our stories!

Speaking is as much about listening as speaking. Toastmasters absolutely improves communication skills because members are taught the fundamentals of listening. If there are fifty annual club meetings, you might actually give a formal speech five to ten times a year, but at every meeting you are asked to participate in various functionary roles such as Ah Counter, Timer, Humorist, Grammarian, Speech Evaluator, Meeting Evaluator, Table Topics Master, and the grand role of leading the meeting as Toastmaster. All of these roles provide opportunities to improve your ability to speak extemporaneously, which is far more reflective of daily communication.

Toastmasters also teaches you about accountability. It's a weekly, ninety-minute session that requires people to sign up and commit in advance to taking on the functionary roles or commit to presenting a speech. The Toastmaster leads the meeting, and when members fail to show up, it falls to the Toastmaster to fill those roles.

Toastmasters taught me what leadership in the community looks like, especially when I was asked and accepted the role of club president right as COVID-19 hit. It was a time when I often felt overwhelmed, underprepared, pessimistic, and fearful. I learned a leader has all the same challenges as everyone else; they just choose to manage through them; they choose to lead themselves out of those dark places so they can lead others out of them.

Toastmasters taught me you can be completely vulnerable and exposed and feel utterly safe. It is a place where you are encouraged to fail and fail miserably. And then feel honored to hear, in great detail, exactly how you failed. Toastmasters encourages you to keep giving the same speech until it's your version of flawless! They embrace my same philosophy of failure being a gift.

Toastmasters showed me what joy and accomplishment feel like when I made a decision to overcome a debilitating fear, one that had limited me my entire life. As my confidence increased, I learned not only what it means to face and overcome a mindset that did not serve me or my greater purpose in life, but how to share this knowledge and experience with others.

Over the eight years I've been a Toastmasters member, I've stopped attending countless times, but a few members would always ping me and say, "Hey, we miss you; come back; you bring a lot of energy to the club," and those nudges made me come back. They never gave up on me. It was like yoga ten years ago; I initially hated it, but I learned to love the health benefits. Similarly, I did not like Toastmasters, but I enjoyed the pride I felt in delivering an effective message.

Early on, one of the members, Ryan Birdseye, asked to become my sponsor. Through the years he became my biggest cheerleader. His one-on-one coaching was perhaps the most significant influence in the development of my speaking skills. He's been in our club for more than twenty years and has become not only a proficient speaker but has won several speaking contests. He participates not because he needs to improve his speaking skills but because he enjoys helping others develop their speaking gifts. My ability and confidence soared because of Ryan's coaching! More information about working with Ryan can be found on my website.

Seeing opportunities for personal growth by participating in a Toastmasters meeting opens a person up to the potential of helping others develop. And when you make yourself this vulnerable and improve such a visible skill as public speaking, you inspire others to grow and improve their capabilities in speaking and other areas.

> *Through this personal experience, I learned in a very intimate and profound way that the only real happiness one can have is in service to others.*

Toastmasters enables you to build socially, culturally, and generationally diverse friendships because each club is a real mixture of our society. The potential to develop lifelong, authentic relationships is incredible. These folks really know who you are because you reveal your soft underbelly as you deliver your speech. The friendships are as far from superficial as possible. We encourage each other to identify their goals and purpose and to acquire the life skills needed to attain them. Toastmasters also demonstrates how to overcome public speaking fears.

No one comes to these meetings as an accomplished speaker; they're here because they are not accomplished, and many share the same intense fear I had. English is the second language for some members, which makes it even more of a challenge, but they are all welcomed, encouraged, and appreciated.

Why this focus on Toastmasters? In Chapter 10, I will cover how we identified opportunities at ICE to increase awareness of social injustice—the best way to increase awareness is through communication. You can't increase communication unless you learn how to communicate. Conversations around racism are fraught with potential friction, so they can be uncomfortable. Delivering a speech with content that is potentially polarizing edifies a very complex skill, and that is exactly what we want to encourage. It's what our society needs if healing and unity are to happen.

You never want to avoid the tough conversations, not at work, not in your non-profit volunteer efforts, and certainly not with your children. Social injustice, racism, gender identity, sexual orientation—the controversial content list is endless, especially during 2020 when everything became a political hot potato. Real leaders emerge and are evident during crises because they don't avoid these conversations.

What does all this have to do with excellence? You develop excellence in others when you aren't afraid to show how flawed you are, and you publicly share how you are striving to develop excellence in yourself. Equally as valuable a lesson here is that you take your flaws as just information and opportunities to improve—they don't define who you are.

Toastmasters' nurtures individual growth by encouraging each person to become the best version of themselves and to grow their skills to become better communicators, problem solvers, and listeners.

StrengthFinders

When you focus on someone's strengths, you build their natural skills. In Chapter 5, I described an exercise we conducted to teach excellence by focusing on each team member's individual strengths; hence, we started providing every employee with a copy of Don Clifton's best-selling book, *StrengthFinders 2.0.*

Cathy DeWeese, in her 2018 Gallup article "Learning about CliftonStrengths from Don Clifton Himself," clarifies this perfectly.[50]

"CliftonStrengths coaching and performance stem from a revolutionary question Don Clifton asked: 'What would happen if we studied what is right with people instead of focusing on what is wrong with them?' ...

What if every manager and leader looked at each employee and asked, 'What do they do well?' and then put that person in a role that best suited their unique contributions? What if they coached and mentored that person to do more of what they do well? What if they created teams full of people with complementary talents? How would that transform organizations? ...

A focus on what is strong isn't just nice and engaging, it's efficient. There is too much untapped potential in our world for us to spend our time fixing problems and filling gaps. The power of talent is too promising for us not to focus our energy on learning more about it, making the most of it and putting it to immediate use."

Our staff heartily embraces Clifton's perspective of focusing on one's strengths, building our teams around each individual's skill sets. We take every opportunity to emphasize their talents, and they enjoy the training around these employee development programs. By focusing on strengths, we've gained greater appreciation for each person as an individual. It also builds tremendous confidence within that person.

I highly recommend using this exercise and training with your personnel.

CHAPTER 7

The Higher Purpose Journey

The two most important days of your life
are the day you were born and the day you find out why.
—Mark Twain

In the past decade, thousands of articles, books, and blogs have been written about the transformational power of having a well-articulated higher purpose in our personal lives. Additionally, billions (yes billions) of references on Google pertain to the benefits of establishing a higher purpose in business. Contributing to something bigger than ourselves that is not simply profit-driven has proven to be one of the most powerful motivators for not only performance, but life satisfaction, physical well-being, self-esteem, and happiness. All of this content confirms that discovering our purpose leads to fulfillment in both our personal and our work lives.

Why Is Understanding Your Purpose So Meaningful?

Discovering your "why"—your purpose—and being able to articulate it and move it to actionable engagement, thus breathing life into your words, is the single most influential developmental task a company and a leadership team can engage in.

> *Organizationally crafting a meaningful higher purpose motivates every aspect of your company, but activating it, galvanizing it— therein lies the challenge!*

Fewer than 20 percent of organizations and executive leaders have a strong sense of their own personal and organizational purpose; why this enormous disconnect, and how do we change it?

According to a study conducted at Gettysburg College, over the course of our lifetime, we spend 90,000 hours working, which equates to one third of our lives.[51] Since we are spending a large majority of our lives in a working environment, how can we make that time more fulfilling? I believe it is business' job to understand and embrace this responsibility.

The 2018 Gartenberg study encompassed 500,000 people across 429 firms.[52] It indicated the positive influence experienced when purpose was clear on both operating financial performance and ROI. The study also evaluated more forward-looking "soft" measures of performance. When purpose is communicated with clarity, the result is far more than a feel-good statement. Organizations experienced real financial implications on their well-being and competitiveness. The study also found that when a clearly articulated sense of purpose existed, the experience of high camaraderie rose significantly between workers. They felt more connection with management, punctuated by more clarity in communication of organizational goals, leading to both higher organizational and stock market performance, and even improved hiring practices. It is evident that when an organization shares a common set of clearly articulated beliefs and those beliefs are embraced by staff, it leads to employee actions and a perception that their work is more meaningful.

Health Benefits

People and organizations need to be well-informed to become committed to change. They have to understand the "what's in this for me?" in order to become passionate about changing patterns, belief systems, and mindsets. So, let's focus on something meaningful.

Health benefits result from living your life with a higher purpose. Doctors have found that people with purpose in their lives are less prone to disease. Purpose has been noted as the key to navigating this ever-changing ambiguous world we live in. Purpose stimulates goals, promotes healthy behaviors, and gives meaning to life.

In the *Newsweek* article "People with a Sense of Purpose Live Longer, Study Suggests," Kashmira Gander notes:[53]

> "The data revealed that the stronger the participants felt they had a purpose in life, the lower their risk of dying. This result remained even when the scientists adjusted their calculations for factors that could affect their score . . . It is as though the mind and body can draw on a pool of immune responses, and a healthy mind allows the body more immune response, in some way that we simply do not understand in 2019. Remarkably, a number of studies seem to show that happy people and people with a sense of purpose live longer."

Former US President Barack Obama wisely advised that "Focusing your life solely on making a buck shows a certain poverty of ambition. It asks too little of yourself, it's only when you hitch your wagon to something larger than yourself that you realize your true potential."

Based on research by the Center for Disease Control, only 21 percent of adults strongly agree their life has a clear sense of purpose. In two other studies, 90 percent of alcoholics and 100 percent of drug addicts thought their life was meaningless. In numerous polls, over several time periods and countries, when asked what was *very important*, "having a purpose or meaning in life" was chosen by 89 percent of the respondents while money was chosen by around 16 percent. All this according to a website that is no longer accessible, but the data is interesting nonetheless. A common belief is Americans are completely motivated by money, but such polling results confirm that is a false narrative!

Jeff Fenster

Jeff Fenster is a serial entrepreneur, having founded ten organizations. At age twenty-four, he started CanopyHR, his first venture and a successful payroll company. The desire to treat others with dignity and respect drove Jeff to found CanopyHR *specifically because the organization where he had been previously employed did not value him.* As CanopyHR grew, he realized the number-one challenge organizations face is attracting talent, so he expanded his services to add recruitment, making CanopyHR more recession-proof.

After Jeff sold CanopyHR, he founded Everbowl, a craft superfood restaurant focused on producing acai bowls with the clever tagline "food that's been around forever." He founded Everbowl in 2016 with no food service experience. Even during the COVID-19 pandemic, Everbowl remained remarkably resilient.

Jeff used the same resiliency-building model he incorporated in building CanopyHR to build Everbowl. He created WeBuild, a construction company, to reduce his restaurant build-out time from two months to two weeks. WeBuild continues to grow, adding other clients. Continuing this trend, Jeff created JFEN Holdings, a disruptive marketing agency with a focus on building the remarkable Everbowl brand; it has also expanded its client base. Superfuel Coffee, coffee injected with the health-promoting benefits of superfood acai, soon followed, as did his acai-importing company, Real Happy. By taking control of the costs of his key ingredient, Jeff was able to sell acai bowls more competitively, but more critical to Jeff, his clients can now better afford the long-term benefits of the acai berry!

Jeff didn't just create a restaurant; he created a system—a system that could easily and profitably be franchised, which is how Everbowl has expanded. Jeff has never solely focused on financial success, and his ability to now offer franchises was fostered because he believes in the benefits of ethical entrepreneurism. Jeff gets choked up when he tells the story of his employee who started with him as a shy nineteen-year-old and is now the proud owner of his own franchise, at twenty-three!

Jeff also strives for excellence in every way, much like we discussed in Chapter 6, and he uses the word *kaizen* to encapsulate his desire to seek daily improvement. Kaizen is a Japanese term meaning "change for the better" or "continuous improvement." Jeff seeks improvement in productivity and personal development as a gradual and methodical process. He explains:

> "People say they're too busy to learn a new language, gain a new skill, learn something new, but that's because they're approaching it as a mountain. What if you found four minutes a day to develop a new skill? By the end of the year, you would have dedicated twenty-four days to learning that skill. It starts with making a decision to evolve, to become "the best you" possible. Break it down into a system; then commit to doing it."
> (as quoted by Jeff during the November 6, 2020
> Awaken Church Conference)

Jeff is prosperous because he's a smart guy, but for Jeff, financial accomplishment without respecting and including your higher purpose will never define his success story.

Higher Purpose Is a Call to Action

> *This is the true joy in life, the being used for a purpose*
> *recognized by yourself as a mighty one.*
> **—George Bernard Shaw**

In addition to stating your purpose, your why, you must live it by incorporating your purpose into your daily activities and envisioning the impact it has on your employees, customers, and all of your stakeholders to fully live your purpose.

To build an inspired, committed workforce, everyone must understand how they personally are a purpose-driven driver, no matter their role or position; everyone can be a *purpose champion*. Your organization's purpose will have more sway if your team understands and can not only articulate but are personally connected to your mission. They need to embrace your corporate vision. For maximum efficacy, your purpose needs to permeate every aspect of your corporate culture, literally shaping individual behavior and reinforcing your organization's collective mindset.

Leaders who still think "old school" will approach purpose with varying degrees of skepticism. I urge them to reevaluate this antiquated thinking. Unless you have a *clearly articulated, authentically lived, higher purpose*, you will struggle to create an extraordinary company with today's younger workforce. I am convinced of this because I've personally experienced the positive results; we are consistently contacted by potential employees because of *what we stand for* and our well-established brand of offering an empowering corporate culture.

In this chapter, I want to focus on *how* we crafted and ingrained our higher purpose at ICE. Because we care about the personal lives of our employees, we encourage them to discover their personal higher purpose. Sometimes, that might result in them leaving our organization to pursue their purpose, but that's also part of the journey.

Conceiving our higher purpose was quite the undertaking. We worked on it as a group. It is a statement created by staff, management, and our consulting firm Equal Parts, over the course of six months and hundreds of hours.

I may sound like a broken record, but *it all started with reading a book....*

Reading *Conscious Capitalism* shifted my understanding of business, specifically my business. I had difficulty understanding why we had experienced such growth and financial success. In discovering the attributes that comprise a conscious business enterprise, I was able to clearly understand what ICE is, how we had achieved our success, and how to articulate that message to the rest of the company to ensure the continuation of our values. Alysse and current employees understand these values, but will they be known fifty years from now? Conscious capitalism is never a short play, but a long one, and thinking in those terms further inspired me to capture our story.

By actively and enthusiastically embracing the four tenets of the conscious capitalism movement—conscious leadership, conscious culture, integration of stakeholders, and higher purpose—we were able to fully understand another ingredient in ICE's secret sauce! We inherently knew we existed for reasons beyond just making a profit, but now we had a language to express our values that defined ICE.

As frequently noted, I believe strongly in the power of capitalism. Over the course of history, no other economic system has lifted more people from poverty than capitalism. Let me quote from the Conscious Capitalism Credo (from www.consciouscapitalism.org):

> "We believe that business is good because it creates value, it is ethical because it is based on voluntary exchange, it is noble because it can elevate our existence, and it is heroic because it lifts people out of poverty and creates prosperity. Free enterprise capitalism is the most powerful system for social cooperation and human progress ever conceived. It is one of the most compelling ideas we humans have ever had. But we can aspire to even more.
>
> Conscious Capitalism is a way of thinking about capitalism and business that better reflects where we are in the human journey, the state of our world today, and the innate potential of business to make a positive impact on the world. Conscious businesses are galvanized by higher purposes that serve, align, and integrate the interests

of all their major stakeholders. Their higher state of consciousness makes visible to them the interdependencies that exist across all stakeholders, allowing them to discover and harvest synergies from situations that otherwise seem replete with trade-offs. They have conscious leaders who are driven by service to the company's purpose, all the people the business touches, and the planet we all share together. Conscious businesses have trusting, authentic, innovative and caring cultures that make working there a source of both personal growth and professional fulfillment. They endeavor to create financial, intellectual, social, cultural, emotional, spiritual, physical and ecological wealth for all their stakeholders.

Conscious businesses will help evolve our world so that billions of people can flourish, leading lives infused with passion, purpose, love and creativity; a world of freedom, harmony, prosperity, and compassion."

Reading *Conscious Capitalism* inspired me to write this book; behold the immense influence of reading!

I realized sharing the ICE journey had the potential to increase awareness of the power of an inspired Millennial workforce, and because we've always employed an unusually high percentage of Millennials, we had a unique opportunity to intimately learn, and share, what does and does not work.

The Process for Developing a Higher Purpose Statement

Here are the steps we took to develop our statement.

1. After reading *Conscious Capitalism*, we realized the only principle we had not articulated was our higher purpose.

2. We worked with Equal Parts to craft a "heroic" higher purpose. We were unclear about the process in drafting this critical statement and immediately realized just how very necessary they were

in helping us figure this out. They consult with organizations to drive institutional change that leads to improved performance and productivity by collaboratively and strategically aligning stated business goals and culture for maximum ROI.

3. Alysse introduced the leadership team to yet another great book, *It's Not What You Sell, It's What You Stand For: Why Every Extraordinary Business Is Driven by Purpose* by Roy M. Spence Jr. This book clarified how to create our higher purpose.

4. We had several leadership-only meetings to discuss strategy in introducing the higher purpose exercise to staff. We wanted to be very clear on what purpose meant to us before we articulated this effort.

5. In our company meeting, we informed our employees of our goal to design a higher purpose that resonated with everyone, captured what we do on a daily basis, and inspired us to the highest level possible—the heroic.

6. We met with our consultant to analyze what we had all learned. We saw the correlation in what we do externally as a company (create physical spaces for our clients) and what we do internally (creating a nurturing emotional space that fosters creativity, a sense of ownership, and freedom). Our higher purpose literally wrote itself.

Some of the meetings were held off site to better focus and inspire creativity. We worked very consciously to make this an enjoyable and memorable experience, and at the end, we realized how much we had enjoyed the entire process. It was a very organic process that resulted in a most accurate and impressive Higher Purpose statement!

Unveiling Party

Following through with this intention, we were excited to create an unveiling celebration that reflected the hard work we'd done, truly celebrating a milestone accomplishment. We moved the meeting from our conference room to the fireplace in our community kitchen area. And as we gathered around our communal table, the atmosphere was anticipatory because this was an unveiling of something valuable we had all participated in creating. This process cannot be a top-down decision or it loses employee enthusiasm.

We set the stage, adding to the excitement and family-centric ambiance we created for this much anticipated "great reveal."

Alysse and Elyse offered their perspectives on why the higher purpose was important to them. Elyse's speech really touched our hearts. Let me share portions of it here.

> "I graduated from the Johnston Center in 2006. When I left, I was devastated that part of my life was over, and I didn't think I would ever find another place that encouraged such development and a communal approach. I found ways to make it happen in other areas of my life to help me get by, but nothing really stuck. Fast forward to 2013 when I was hired by ICE. Seventy percent of ICE employees were brought on by some referral source. I was referred by Alysse's mom, who is still ICE's outside accountant. I was employed by her at the time as an accounting assistant.
>
> Within the first month of that growing exposure to ICE, I realized DeLinda had created an open environment that welcomed other ways of thinking, and she was reading a lot about the value of the Millennial generation in the workforce. She was the first Boomer I had heard refer to my generation as 'capable.' She wasn't hung up on the idea of entitlement or dependency; it was all about learning about them and how to appeal to them. Truth be told, she didn't have all of the answers within herself to apply to ICE, but in some ways, I think she knew that, and that her best bet would be to leave it up to us.

Looking back, I'm sure there are a few points in time that led to my progression. After Tom joined ICE full time, he and I worked side by side for several years. His day-to-day involvement helped pave the way for the growth the company had always wanted but didn't know how to support. Before I knew it, Tom had me participating in meetings and conversations. He copied me on emails and people were asking me what I thought about different ideas and what I said mattered. I was starting to bring my own opinions and thoughts to the table, and I realized I had found a place where I could contribute to the company's future in all the ways important to me—the things that had been important to me all the way back in college.

I loved being part of a community and fostering a certain kind of environment, one where I could watch the people around me develop, and we could all find ways to support one another as we're collectively striving to excel. ICE was, and is, anything but an ordinary company. And it's really only when I sit back and reflect that I realize ICE inadvertently had created that open, encouraging space to transcend the ordinary.

And as I have been reflecting on the creation of the Higher Purpose, my role at ICE, and my direction in 2020, I realize that ICE has allowed me to become the best version of an employee, and of myself, that I could ever wish to be."

Elyse's speech defined and acknowledged everything Tom and I had worked so hard to create; hearing it was one of the more gratifying moments of my career.

In typical ICE tradition, let me note our missed opportunity—what we could've done better here. I highly recommend you have a sign to physically share your purpose with your team because it would have strengthened our message during our unveiling party.

What Is the ICE Higher Purpose?

When we finally revealed our higher purpose statement and what it meant to our company, it was enthusiastically received. We incorporated all the elements of our inclusive corporate mindset that I have detailed in this book of family, team work, transparency, our staff meeting format, our public celebrations, and our deep respect and high regard for younger generational, peer-to-peer input.

What is our stated higher purpose and the meaning behind it?

Creating Space to Transcend the Ordinary
*We not only create beautiful, functional physical spaces,
but emotional space to thrive!*

It includes what we produce, what we do for a "living," which is providing furniture for our clients. We help create *physical spaces that transcend ordinary*, encouraging innovation and creativity to thrive—but equally what we do *internally to provide emotional freedom to thrive*. Both spaces are equally important to us because we know emotionally safe cultures create an environment for people to find happiness in their daily lives.

Creating an emotionally safe environment was a major motivator for me personally. As I detailed in Chapter 2, throughout my career, I never had a safe working environment. My past leaders had never been exposed to the concept of conscious leadership, so how could they create emotionally safe work environments? They were taught just the opposite—that workplaces are competitive and could be hostile environments.

Our higher purpose reflects *who we are* as highly motivated and inspired individuals and *what we do* as a group of dedicated employees sharing a collective mindset to create client spaces that transcend the ordinary. Both are equally important within our workplace family.

Love the ICE Higher Purpose, But What About Me?

I've painted a picture of how we've designed a culture that sparks individual growth that reaches into every area of a person's life. We encourage staff to explore concepts, and belief systems that support their personal growth and their increased awareness of self, the world, and one's place in it. In early September 2020, we introduced another engaging exercise to encourage staff members to identify their personal higher purpose.

Prior to the meeting, I sent a thought-provoking article with the intention of helping them identify: "What does it mean to live a purpose-driven life? Is there value for you to understand your own personal purpose or your purpose in relationship to ICE's purpose? What if you really don't care about purpose?"

We realized some people would not feel comfortable having this conversation or find it useful. We knew others would be intrigued by the concept of identifying and living their own personal higher purpose. We wanted to spark their awareness and engagement in finding their higher purpose for a number of reasons, many already mentioned.

Additionally, we posed these questions, "Why am I here? What are my greatest natural gifts, and how can I tap into them not only to improve my life, but to serve others?" We identified the exercise's purpose was to help them define their personal higher purpose and how management could help them find it. Here is some of the content from the article:

"Let's define purpose: Purpose is that sense that our efforts and our passion will lead us to create something that has significance and benefits the lives of others. Our purpose lies somewhere in the intersection between what we care most about, what our true passion is, and where we can contribute in helping others. *Purpose is very other focused.*

Research confirms that people who are more focused on others' happiness actually experience far more happiness themselves and that "a sense of purpose" is a strong predictor of happiness and a powerful antidote to depression.

Margie Warrell noted in her Forbes article "Pursue Purpose Over Success: The Science Behind Mark Zuckerberg's Advice to Harvard Grads"[54] that Zuckerberg's Harvard commencement speech emphasized this message to 'find your purpose—find your joy.' Warrell quotes him as saying, 'Purpose is that sense that we are part of something bigger than ourselves, that we are needed, that we have something better ahead to work for. Purpose is what creates true happiness.' Not money, not status, not how we look, not how many Facebook 'Likes' we have— *purpose is the main ingredient to living a fulfilled, joyful life.*"

Consider these statistics, noted in Warrell's article, that purpose-driven people are:

- Four times more likely to be engaged at work
- 50 percent are more likely to be leaders
- 64 percent have a higher level of career satisfaction
- 42 percent have a higher feeling of overall contentment
- Purpose-driven people live seven years longer

ICE management is here to serve you. We want to help you discover the value in having a higher purpose. Having a sense of purpose not only benefits ICE; it's also beneficial for your family, your personal development, and your community. For those of you who are parents, we also are motivated to help you find and live your purpose for the benefit of your children. This can help teach them the value of their purpose so they, too, can live life authentically and with great passion.

These questions will help you determine your purpose. We ask you to work on them prior to our team meeting. During the meeting, we will cover this concept in more detail and answer questions to help you complete this exercise.

Write and date your response under each question and keep this document to update over the years as you get to know who you are because your purpose will evolve. This process is a great way to document your personal growth.

Identify Your Gifts
1. What are you good at both personally and professionally? For example, what part of your job or role at ICE comes naturally to you? What outside activities that you engage in or would like to engage in encompass your natural gifts?
2. What advice would you give your younger self to determine your purpose?
3. After high school or college?
4. In your first month at ICE as a new hire?
5. What hard-earned wisdom or advice would you share with others at ICE today?
6. When was the last time you felt your passion ignited?

7. Where and how do you provide service to others by using your talents? Please offer a suggestion for how your gift improves the lives of your coworkers as well as others in your personal life and steps or things you can do to kindle your purpose.

Why both personal and professional? Because a seamless overlap exists in our personal and professional lives, we should not separate them. Our family upbringing and how our culture and society values us all play a big part in how we value ourselves. Our daily work, the income we earn, and how we support ourselves and our families is a tremendous source of pride; it increases our confidence in our personal worth. You might not realize how valuable your work is to our organization and to each of us as individuals. If you are feeling more disconnected due to COVID isolation, it's because working with others gives your life meaning. It's why when people retire, they often flounder—because their self-worth was defined by their careers.

The definition of success has changed. We are beginning to realize career success does not define our value as people. It's also time to rethink how we see money. Money and success are not evil; they offer us an opportunity to inspire others and help our children attain their goals to reach their potential. Money in the hands of a person with a kind and generous heart is an enormous multiplier that helps both strangers and friends alike.

In her article, Warrell states, "only when we shift our focus from 'looking good' to 'doing good' can we truly thrive in life. So, think about the problems you are naturally great at solving, the needs you are uniquely positioned to fill and the people you are uniquely positioned to help."

Businesses are not responsible for their employees' personal dreams and aspirations, but I do think business can encourage self-awareness. Starting conversations that encourage self-reflection benefits everyone. We encourage personal accountability and repetition as a habit for achieving goals. Our goal was to plant a seed and introduce the concept of a lifetime journey of self-discovery.

Inspiring Entrepreneurism

In August 2020, as Elyse and I prepared to lead the personal higher purpose exercise, she let us know she was leaving ICE to follow her passion and start her own firm as a workplace consultant. Of course, we were disappointed to lose such a valuable long-term teammate. She had been instrumental in developing our corporate culture, crafting our higher purpose, and developing our leadership team strategies.

Elyse came to us with limited workplace experience. We encouraged her to learn new skills, and as a result, she taught us new skills. She introduced us to new perspectives and new ways to lead organizations. She gained knowledge, inspiration, and confidence while with us and always gave us her very best. She taught us who we were and how to become the best version of ICE, and we'll always be grateful.

Our dedication to developing people to reach their potential might necessitate them leaving our company, and that's encouraging. Elyse was not the first employee to leave us, and she certainly won't be the last. We encourage entrepreneurism. We consciously strive to make ICE the best furniture dealership in San Diego, a place that continues to draw incredible talent that we can mentor and positively shape. If that means our workers are inspired to leave us to create their own great American success story, that's actually a wonderful accomplishment for everyone! People come from all over the world to live the American Dream, raise families, and pass on generational legacies; ICE is proud to create and be part of this life-affirming American legacy.

Redemption Plus—One Company's Path to Higher Purpose

In conclusion, let me share the journey that the firm Redemption Plus traveled in seeking their higher purpose. In 2020, I joined a Conscious Capitalism Inc. (CCI) Mastermind group led by Ron Hill. Ron is the former Chief Enrichment Officer and Founder of Redemption Plus. He started his firm from the ground up, launching out of his parents' basement in 1996. Ron recently sold his $20 million company and now has more time to follow the passion and commitment that he developed as an ethical entrepreneur over those twenty-five years of owning a small business.

Like me, Ron was practicing the principles of conscious capitalism years before he was introduced to the movement. After a chance meeting with John Mackey, Founder of Whole Foods and Co-Founder of the Conscious Capitalism movement, Ron discovered his untapped passion in being an instrument for changing how business gives back. Also similar to my experience, Ron not only learned a language to better share his internal passion with his coworkers, but he found his tribe through CCI! He discovered other entrepreneurs who were equally determined to help business reach its untapped potential as the most powerful force for good! He realized while enjoying retirement that he could devote even more of his time to this effort.

Although I had known Ron for several months, I didn't know the details of his story until I heard it on *Good Business Talking* with Ravi Rai. That is also when I learned of the higher purpose experience his organization went through; I was eager to interview this like-minded peer!

Ron's journey as a conscious capitalist is quite inspiring, and the journey Redemption Plus traveled in crafting and engaging their higher purpose was quite different from ICE's. They went through this process in 2016, before higher purpose had come to define organizations. Ron learned about the concept of higher purpose at a retreat where they defined it as purpose above profits, tied with lived values, reduction of waste and rework, and understanding the customer's unspoken needs. It was not defined in relation to the principles of conscious capitalism, which he did not learn of until 2017. One reason he was so motivated to draft an organizational purpose statement was he intuitively knew business' purpose was about people. He noted "It's about all of the people in our care—that is the greatest way we can give back, by caring for their well-being. Business is about advocating for our employees, removing roadblocks in their way, and inspiring them to become better people."

At Redemption Plus, they used a top-down approach with leadership defining their purpose and then modifying their behavior to reflect their purpose. They hoped their staff would be inspired by how leadership had changed and would want to follow their example and become a part of this change. Within three years, he lost 50 percent of his employees, including 50 percent of leadership! Redemption Plus had a high percentage of Boomers, which might have been a factor in the lack of success in engaging their mission to elevate humanity through their business. Ron described it this way:[55]

> "It was not so much that it was tough to convince our people to align around the purpose of 'enriching lives through insights that empower,' it was our previous history with not being aligned. We knew that everyone on the team had to be focused on fulfilling our purpose and living our core values. When people thought it did not apply to them, they were reminded a couple of times, then coached out to find their purpose elsewhere. We had others who had grown as much as they cared to and with our new value of adopting a 'growth mindset,' they realized they could never align with this value of continuous growth. At this point, Redemption Plus was sixteen years old, and the only way to keep growing the business was if everyone was willing to grow. It was a natural sluffing off process that helped us to build a stronger team of coworkers that already shared our values and behaviors and were eager to be aligned with our purpose.

Lastly, I would not be honest if I did not say I was in a way protecting some people who had been around a long time. As I continued to hire employees who were in alignment with our stated values and purpose, it caused people to leave, revealing the disconnect between their words and their behaviors. In the end, it worked out beautifully because there was less friction and we created an amazingly aligned team. Going through this process was absolutely worth it, even if it was painful."

You can download and personalize the complete Higher Purpose Employee Exercise at: www.DelindaForsythe.com.

CHAPTER 8

Create Raving Fans

K en Blanchard's popular 1993 book *Raving Fans* is about the radical importance of delivering the highest level of customer service. When you provide this level of service, people will not be able to stop talking about their unforgettable experience with your company. It's an "unexpected gift" to receive a high level of service. If your company develops a reputation for delivering extraordinary service, you will potentially experience tremendous growth.

A company can grow in a multitude of ways, including acquiring other businesses. ICE grew organically, adding one valued client at a time. Our average seven-year growth from 2013-2020 was 32 percent. Our industry average is in the single digits; our revenue growth is an unprecedented industry accomplishment, but it did not come without some severe growing pains.

While this chapter's title, "Create Raving Fans," infers a focus on what we did correctly, I want to first share failure. No one wants to admit or talk about failure, but only failure will teach you about success; they are two sides of the same coin. Social media focuses on success; we want others to admire us, to desire to be more like us. If you're posting about your failures, especially *epic* failures, how do you then attract the adoration so many of us desperately need?

Although we fear and avoid failure at great peril, even the greatest leaders experience it. Here is what some of our most visible leaders have to say about failure.

- "It's fine to celebrate success, but it is more important to heed the lessons of failure." —Bill Gates
- "Do not be embarrassed by your failures, learn from them and start again. Failure is a wonderful way of learning. As an entrepreneur, if you're not taking risks, you're not going to achieve anything. If you give something a go and it doesn't work out, you certainly haven't failed; you just learned." —Sir Richard Branson
- "Develop success from failures. Discouragement and failure are two of the surest steppingstones to success." —Dale Carnegie
- "Success is not final, failure is not fatal. It is the courage to continue that counts." —Sir Winston Churchill

I genuinely believe in the power of failure to inspire in every way. Nothing has greater ability to grab us by our proverbial throats and shake us to the core. Failure has always been a huge motivator for me, especially the *fear* of failure. I also honor the humility it can create in each of us.

Humility is not an easy virtue to attain, and acknowledging failure can encourage humility to grow within. Humility is the center of a moral life and can be a powerful quality in a leader. Humility is not easily forged through success; failure forges humility!

Bill Taylor, cofounder of Fast Company, in his *Harvard Business Review* article, "If Humility Is So Important, Why Are Leaders So Arrogant?" focuses on the virtue of humility.

> "In reality, of course, humility and ambition need not be at odds. Indeed, humility *in the service of ambition* is the most effective and sustainable mindset for leaders who aspire to do big things in a world filled with huge unknowns. Years ago, a group of HR professionals at IBM embraced a term to capture this mindset. The most effective leaders,

they argued, exuded a sense of "humbition," which they defined as "one-part humility and one-part ambition." We "notice that by far the lion's share of world-changing luminaries are humble people," they wrote. "They focus on the work, not themselves. They seek success—they are ambitious—but they are humbled when it arrives…They feel lucky, not all-powerful." We live in a world where ego gets attention but modesty gets results. Where arrogance makes headlines but humility makes a difference."[56]

Bill provides amazing clarity by questioning the benefits of humility and just how elusive it is for ambitious leaders. Humility and ambition are often at odds with each other.

Epic Failure

Maintaining focus on poor performance might seem odd, but most organizations that analyze their failures will gain immense understanding of more effective solutions. There is value in analyzing both failure and success, and I encourage organizations to do both.

In retrospect, our "epic failure" was the first time we dedicated innumerable hours to analyze how our processes failed. We chose to make this failure valuable—because until you fail, you assume everything is going well, and you are as wonderful in reality as you are in your head!

Let's analyze this particular failure, involving a company I'll call Company X. ICE did many things wrong, from ordering the wrong color panel frames and not measuring the space correctly to missing columns that affected station placement and also missing product. This was the greatest financial loss we have experienced at ICE, with an even more significant potential loss of our brand of excellence. The chart shared in Chapter 6 that indicated a negative 255.64 percent loss in January 2020 is highly reflective of Company X's installation. This project revealed opportunities within our systems for failure to occur. This project was the perfect storm.

How did we manage this account once all of this failure came to light? Not well, initially. It occurred when I was turning over management to Alysse, and simultaneously, Alysse was developing our value of "Live the Entrepreneurial Spirit." This entailed letting staff take on more ownership. We believe if you do not let others fail or succeed on their own, you will never have an organization of leaders, strategic problem solvers, and thinkers. Consider this quote:

> *Mistakes are the growing pains of wisdom.*
> —**William George Jordan**, writer/editor

How will any of us gain wisdom if we prevent failure? That's why I value failure so much.

As I've indicated, we are always striving to improve ourselves and our processes. We don't just accept status quo; our culture is one of continuous improvement. We embrace change and new ideas of looking at old problems. But because we have had mostly success with minimal financial or brand loss, we simply didn't realize we needed to dive into a deeper level of understanding; this loss solidified the value and need for meaningful internal scrutiny.

We chose to reevaluate everything we were doing to include our practices, people, organizational structure, and the way we sell and manage client relationships.

Fortunately, we do not frequently fail because if we did, we wouldn't have a business to be writing about!

Company X's "Dis-Satisfaction"

One night, I received an unsettling email from the Senior Executive Assistant to Company X's CEO/Chairman. She is a remarkable individual, having experienced extraordinary responsibility and past success. She was responsible for the furniture acquisition process and was the liaison between our firms. She quickly became an ICE "champion," advocating on behalf of our firm in the selection process. When I received her email,

"My Dis-Satisfaction with ICE," it shook me to the core. It detailed information I was aware of but believed we were handling efficiently and effectively; we were not.

In addition to our mistakes, she was equally disappointed with Alysse and me. Since we were aware of the situation, she expected us to be involved in the resolution. She was disheartened that we were so hands-off in seeking solutions.

The most critical lesson we learned from this experience was to engage upper management at the onset of a significant challenge. Early engagement with the client is paramount, because:

> *Relationships are everything!*

We failed to keep our eye on the personal connection we had developed with her. Some of my dearest friends started out as business clients; it was one of the things I enjoyed most when I was in sales. This experience reinforced the value of personal connection that we develop with our clients. It's critical never to lose sight of the power of connection, regardless of the level of confidence you may have with your Account Executive.

Our ability to create deep relationships was a possible factor in avoiding the kind of failure we experienced with Company X. So why now the hands-off approach? Due to our tremendous growth in the past seven years, our infrastructure was changing rapidly. These new teams were just beginning to solidify, and we wanted to encourage more autonomy for them to fail or succeed. Both Alysse and I dislike being micromanaged; therefore, we discourage it as a leadership tool. We painfully learned that with nascent teams, this isn't the best idea.

With the Millennial generation, it is tricky to know when to be more hands-on. It can potentially offend your team and make them feel "less than," but it can also undermine their ability to develop as leaders. There is a balance here and knowing how to strike it is dependent upon each situation and individual. As often referenced, I equate managing to parenting, so I've worked toward making myself unneeded. As a leader, your job is to give those you lead the latitude to become independent thinkers; that is how I have best learned to support and mentor this generation.

We learned from this experience to explain the long-term benefits that develop when we all nurture personal relationships and when to let management know when things are not going well. It provides a powerful opportunity for management to build a stronger bond with the client. It is not a reflection of management's lack of confidence in the team or individual. Had we simply conveyed this message to our team and stayed in touch with Company X, perhaps we could have avoided a lot of pain for everyone.

Everyone had a part in this failure. Here are the biggest lessons we learned:

- Never underestimate the scope of the project, especially more complex projects that extend the time frame needed to complete the project.
- Don't take shortcuts in processes just because of time constraints; due diligence is never something that can be compromised.
- Be sure if you streamline your process that it doesn't cause you to miss mistakes because you eliminated old procedures.
- Standardize your field measurement process.
- Never rely on the accuracy of existing plans. Always take the time to field verify accuracy.
- Always feel comfortable in questioning client direction. This leads to a more collaborative approach, especially for less experienced staff.
- Realize everyone's work is open for contemplation. A more collaborative, reflective approach will be used to manage all future projects.

We ultimately lost this client, but we did not lose our commitment to do whatever we could to make them a Raving Fan. Reputations are all about the long game, about always doing the right thing, no matter the cost or effort. The only way to sustain growth is by building a brand and reputation on a foundation of honor.

We will always remain hopeful of a future relationship. When a vendor is contrite and acknowledges the depth of their mistakes, it can often lead to future opportunities.

Repeat Customers

Let me share why we've experienced such industry-defying growth—it's because we're committed to our customer in a way that makes them commit to us. The dedication our staff demonstrates to our customers has evolved because of how much we value our staff. The culture I've written about and all the efforts we take to empower our team has solidified what the feeling of being valued is. We also know what we're not and what we are, and we ask ourselves the hard questions: Why did we fail? How can we do it better? What are we really good at?

In 2008, we had our first project with California State University San Marcos (CSUSM). Since then, we've won every significant project they've had, as well as countless small projects. We estimate we've completed fifty to seventy-five projects with CSUSM in the last twelve years. Large projects are actually easier to be successful at than small, time-consuming projects. Our attention to their less significant needs is one reason they continue to work with us. Our daily work on these small endeavors and maintaining service consistency with the same project team has provided CSUSM the dependable service they've come to rely on. ICE is the "easy button," and we all lean toward simplicity.

Building and Designing Community Within the Office Environment

We actively endeavor to Create Raving Fans not only within our client base but especially within our own organization and, as I've noted many times, we achieve this through a variety of techniques. I mentioned in Chapter 7 how we unrolled our higher purpose festivities in our front lobby, and I included those images in Chapter 5 and noted you can view more ICE showroom images at www.icesd.com. We specifically designed our front area to include a well-equipped and frequently used kitchen, an inviting fireplace surrounded by comfortable lounge chairs, and a sofa that define a welcoming family room—all of this is what delineates a traditional reception area! We mindfully created this communal gathering spot to celebrate life and welcome in the San Diego community. This space spills outside when we open the six sliding glass doors, offering an invitation to step outside and fully integrate the amazing San Diego climate inside the office.

We have many pieces of locally made "live edge furniture," as well as an entire wall constructed of cold rolled steel and wood slats interspersed with faux succulent plants. When we first started designing the space, many questioned why we were leaving a third of our showroom sparsely furnished when we should be using all available footage to show furniture. We explained we had created space to invite the community into our offices, to host gatherings for local causes. Our design direction was influenced by real estate development partners. They inspired us to create space that builds community and super-charges corporate culture.

Doubters quickly embraced the impact our office emanates, exuding a warm residential energy. Days after we completed our build-out, Scott Deugo, former Chief Sales Officer Worldwide Markets for Teknion, our major vendor partner, visited us as our guest speaker for a series of intimate educational industry conversations. He could not stop commenting about the vitality our showroom radiates. His comment was "This has to be the best Teknion showroom I've seen yet; there is something very special about the energy, the feeling of your space." I know he couldn't quite define it, but I believe it's not just the built environment you sense at ICE; it's the positive energy of the people who choose to work at ICE.

I suspect you would probably have to visit ICE to feel the difference that everyone comments on!

Scott Deugo delivering his message on the impact of compelling furniture design within a work environment.

Scott and Teknion are industry leaders in designing and manufacturing office furniture that makes a space feel fully-human, fully-alive, and welcoming! Teknion published *The True Measure of a Space Is How It Makes You Feel* in 2015, and we decided to memorialize those words on a column in our conference room so we would not forget that in our work we have the opportunity to provide furniture in the built environment that, above all else, elevates humanity.

> *The true measure of a space is how it makes us feel.*
> —**Steve Delfino,** Teknion

Community Starts Within, but Radiates Out

We have created a palpable community spirit within and outside of ICE through the use of our space. We offer it free of charge to organizations because we know the tremendous benefit created when you bring people together and increase communication, knowledge, and friendship. When these groups are in our building, they sense our corporate culture and commitment to a higher purpose. By hosting not-for-profit events and board meetings in our corporate headquarters, we provide a tremendous benefit to the San Diego community, and subsequently, we've developed lifelong friendships with these organizations and their committee members.

Among the organizations we've hosted has been transcenDANCE, which benefits underserved youth in some of our most marginalized San Diego neighborhoods. It's an organization I'm deeply committed to. I've also developed some very meaningful relationships with its members, specifically Pat Zigarmi, who served as transcenDANCE's Board Chair for several years. Pat is an accomplished writer, and as my interest in writing has evolved, she's become a valued mentor. She's also been inspired through our relationship, specifically in how our space reflects our corporate brand. This reflects the serendipitous virtuous circle that transpires when you give back to the community.

Alysse has hosted events for the National Association for International Office Providers (NAIOP) and the International Interior Design Association (IIDA)—both national associations that serve local commercial real estate brokers and interior designers. She's worked extensively with the NAIOP Developing Leaders, a program designed to develop and connect commercial real estate professionals under thirty-five in a formal mentoring program as they gain access to leaders in their industry.

Athena, a non-profit organization that powers the leadership journey for women in STEM (Science, Technology, Engineering, and Mathematics) has selected ICE to host numerous events and meetings. I've always been an enormous advocate for women's organizations. Athena, with its ability to promote, bond, and educate STEM leaders not only in San Diego but through its efforts with the United Nations, certainly offers women in every country the ability to grow their network of influence.

COVID sidetracked our Women in Defense (WID) meeting, but we'll host that after the pandemic has passed. We are especially focused on supporting women in the defense industry because we know an office environment such as ours reveals a hugely different perspective of how an office environment should look and *feel*. The defense industry has had challenges attracting younger generations, partly because of the sterile design of most government spaces. I believe that design perspective is also shifting in an attempt to attract young inquisitive minds.

Other events that were cancelled due to COVID included speaking engagements with my publishing coach Christine Gail and Ryan Birdseye, my Toastmasters mentor. Both are advocates for the power of the female voice in leadership and how finding and using our voices holds the greatest opportunity to create unity.

Opening up our office to promote a sense of community both inside and outside of ICE is a significant part of our corporate goal to create raving fans, and one we're all proud of. It is an integral part of how we identify ourselves as civic partners.

Real Estate Developers

We are especially proud of our work with San Diego's most influential real estate development corporations. They have repeatedly partnered with us to design furniture solutions to further solidify their unique brands. Our past award-winning hospitality furniture success has fueled our growth and engagement with them. Their curated amenity spaces often fuse work, play, and live ecosystems. These mixed-use complexes seamlessly merge the office environment with retail, hospitality, and outdoor spaces that can include farmers markets, parks, and recreational facilities.

These are best-in-class, mission-driven developers that are changing our society by providing collaborative laboratories, buildings, and campuses. These clusters of innovation are creating life-changing technology that is reshaping our world! These spaces support scientists as they work to develop cures for diseases to bring healing to the world and they promote health and wellness among the scientists themselves with farm-to-table restaurants and fitness options to reduce stress.

Their buildings are more than buildings; they are environments that shape human creativity and productivity, creating hubs of life-changing innovation. They foster the same kind of community that ICE fervently promotes. We are proud to be a part of this important work.

Developers often stretch themselves, pushing the envelope and creating projects that may have never been tried before. We are a vital partner in designing solutions that set a project apart from the competition. In an extremely competitive industry, real estate developers do not want ordinary or cookie cutter. They want their projects to evoke emotion, create social media chatter, and ultimately design an unforgettable experience. Furniture is just one way a project stands out, but it is becoming ever more significant in creating Raving Fans!

CHAPTER 9

Vulnerability in the Workplace

When you show up every time as your most authentic self, speak your mind unequivocally, and care more about the *message* than your *image*, you increase the potential for others to be more authentic. When others realize they don't have to be guarded and the space is safe, you increase the potential to influence positive transformation within people, in the community, and in your company. In earlier chapters, I made the correlation between how safe space can foster innovation and creativity. Let me also link how showing up as the authentic person you are creates a safe workplace for creativity to thrive. Conversely, showing up in a more authoritative manner can establish boundaries of differences.

In 1992, the *Harvard Business Review* published "The New Boundaries of the Boundaryless Company,"[57] which details how traditional hierarchical boundaries of occupational titles have drastically changed and dissolved former differences of power and authority. This rigid structure is no longer effective due to technological advances, global competition, work-from-home flexible schedules, and a more informed workforce—all have blurred the traditional boundaries that previously defined corporate management policies.

This redesign of former corporate structure has been occurring for at least thirty years, yet most organizations remain reluctant to change. The article calls out for the replacement of "vertical hierarchies with horizontal networks; linking together traditional functions through interfunctional teams; and forming strategic alliances with suppliers, customers, and even competitors." This sounds a lot like "equal stakeholder value," espoused as one of the four tenets of conscious capitalism. The article continues:

> "For many executives, a single metaphor has come to embody this managerial challenge and to capture the kind of organization they want to create: the 'corporation without boundaries.' General Electric CEO Jack Welch has eloquently described this new organizational model. 'Our dream for the 1990s,' Welch wrote in GE's 1990 annual report, 'is a boundaryless company...where we knock down the walls that separate us from each other on the inside and from our key constituencies on the outside.' In Welch's vision, such a company would remove barriers among traditional functions, 'recognize no distinctions' between domestic and foreign operations, and 'ignore or erase group labels such as 'management,' 'salaried,' or 'hourly,' which get in the way of people working together.'"

I have a singular goal to improve the lives of others by sparking synergy, collaboration, and connectedness in everything I do. That is part of my personal higher purpose, and to accomplish it isn't easy. For most people, outside forces—such as financial and family obligations, careers, health and well-being maintenance, and life responsibilities—all pull us away from thinking in terms of serving others. As I moved into retirement and my life situation changed, for the first time in my life, I realized I had a real chance to live my purpose. I'm not going to slow that down by worrying about my image and what others think of me.

I have often been told that how I speak my truth is quite refreshing. It makes others feel that they too can be vulnerable, and even though it might feel uncomfortable, they are encouraged to also speak their truth. This is a great starting point to develop authentic relationships built on trust.

Figure out what works best for you, but always, be as true to your nature as possible.

Leadership Skills Have Evolved

The softer leadership skills I reference appear to be more effective with younger generations. From my experience, they also seem to come more naturally for many female leaders. The rising emergence of female leadership is expected to continue. Kim Elsesser, in her January 2020 Forbes article "Goldman Sachs Won't Take Companies Public If They Have All-Male Corporate Boards," quotes Goldman Sachs CEO David Solomon as saying he won't take any company that he represents public unless the company has at least one "diverse" board member.

"Starting on July 1, 2020 in the U.S. and Europe, we're not going to take a company public unless there's at least one diverse board candidate, with a focus on women,' Solomon told CNBC from the World Economic Forum. He added, 'And we're going to move towards 2021 requesting two.'

Solomon suggested that one rationale for Goldman's new policy was to 'drive premium returns for their shareholders,' and told CNBC that in the last four years, 'the performance of IPOs where there has been a woman on the board in the U.S. is significantly better than the IPOs where there hasn't been a woman on the board.' The actual numbers are striking. Companies with one diverse board member saw a 44% jump in their average share price within a year of going public, while those with no diverse board members saw only a 13% increase in share price.

Goldman is highlighting the importance of diversity and holding those companies without diverse boards accountable. That's how change happens."[58]

Why this push for female leadership? Numerous studies are confirming that women have a natural ability to increase team collaboration. Women in most families, and certainly in US culture, have been socialized throughout their lives to be cooperative, collaborative, and relationship-driven. This transcends into the ability to create work cultures that make others feel valued and heard. They employ traits such as empathy, communication, and vulnerability to open up avenues to improve connection, where people feel valued and heard.

Barack Obama famously stated, "If every nation on earth was run by women for two years, things would be better." I tend to agree!

It's ironic that historically men have often criticized women who lead with these softer skills and have often disparaged women as being less successful leaders, unable to make tough decisions.

The Power of Vulnerability

In Chapter 2, I introduced Saundra Pelletier. What I didn't tell you is that she battled cancer while leading an organization. Here, in her own words, is what resulted from her sticky courage:[59]

"In July 2018, I was diagnosed with Stage III breast cancer. This was a total shock to me—with no family history, a clean mammogram the year before and a meticulous attention to my health and diet—it was the last thing I anticipated hearing. At first, I advised my doctor that "she may have the wrong chart"; she advised denial would likely kill me. My company, Evofem Biosciences, was in the midst of a Phase 3 clinical trial for our first commercial product, Phexxi, the first and only non-hormonal contraceptive gel for women. We were getting ready to finalize the trial, submit it to the FDA for product approval, and embark on a major capital raise to support the product's commercial launch.

After the initial shock of the news from my oncologist, I made a series of calls to my family and staff; then I called Thomas Lynch, Evofem's board chairman. I requested an in-person meeting; I needed to share the news with him personally. I've never felt so exposed, so vulnerable. Not only was my health in jeopardy, but I also felt the job I loved so passionately was in jeopardy too. I was convinced I might be asked to take a leave of absence, or even worse, the board would want to replace me.

I shared with Tom that my prognosis was not terminal. I hoped I had proven how resilient I was and he would recommend I remain in my role as CEO. My prior experiences had always revealed to me that the minute someone was weak, they were kicked when they were down, then discarded. Without missing a beat, Tom assured me, "If there is anybody who can beat cancer, it is you." His absolute and complete support of my continuation as CEO was more than just reassuring; those were the words I needed to facilitate and aid in my healing. I've never more appreciated or understood how words of support can change a person's life.

I embarked on the most aggressive regime possible, undergoing a double mastectomy, a hysterectomy, and an oophorectomy with intensive chemotherapy every twenty-one days. My chief of staff would show up an hour after chemo started, and I would dictate to her nonstop. She helped facilitate conference calls. I would get chemo on a Thursday, be off the grid for two days, then by Monday, I would start calls again. I had investor calls at 6 a.m.—they didn't know I was sick.

I couldn't travel due to risk of infection, so my team attended every conference in my absence with my chief commercial officer conducting my presentations. Delegating my conference responsibilities was by far the most difficult thing for me to relinquish. For the first time in my life, I had to get comfortable with being utterly vulnerable, requiring help and surrendering all control of critical outcomes to others.

This experience changed everything, not just who I am as a leader and a human being, but it altered many of our organizational operational practices, and for the betterment of all. Now I know without a doubt that I can depend on my team; I don't have to participate in everything. I can receive executive team meeting updates with complete confidence. This has procured me more time to visualize long-term strategies and philosophies that no one else can do more effectively than me, which included launching our product Phexxi in September 2020, leading the way to potentially unrestricted commercial success for Evofem.

Would I want to go through this again? Oh, hell no, but I have learned to find gratitude and purpose in life's most challenging times. It is in these moments we learn who we are, what matters, and we are provided an opportunity to rise to the summit we were destined to reach."

I think you'll see why I said previously that learning Saundra's story was one of the blessings of writing this book—it reinforces my work. Brené Brown in her book *The Power of Vulnerability* captures this sentiment well:

> *Vulnerability is the birthplace of connection and the path to the feeling of worthiness. If it doesn't feel vulnerable, the sharing is probably not constructive.*

Matt Valentine of Buddhaimonia provided a simple blog overview that covers the five most inspiring points of Brown's 2010 TEDx talk "The Power of Vulnerability."[60] Here are the key points:

1. Don't bottle up your emotions, become self-aware.
2. Vulnerability takes courage.
3. Show up, face fear, and move forward.
4. Seek excellence, not perfection.
5. Dare to be yourself.

He concludes: "Dare to be yourself in all your glory—your strengths, skills, and beauty as well as your flaws and insecurities. In doing so, you can realize true strength of spirit."

Men and Vulnerability

In Chapter 2, I mentioned how Steve Rosetta supported me in launching ICE. He does not view his leadership style as being necessarily vulnerable, but by reading Brown's *The Power of Vulnerability*, he grew to better understand it. Steve inherently understands Covey's value of "Seek First to Understand, Then to Be Understood" and makes exceptional efforts to expand his perception by first understanding another's perspective. Breaking it down further, Rosetta's version is less about being emotionally vulnerable and more about being transparent in mistakes made or capabilities. He considers this "honest leadership"—leadership that is open in terms of exposing personal flaws and weaknesses and sharing one's human side.

As previously noted, Stath and Steve worked together during the merger of Burnham Real Estate and Cushman Wakefield. When the merger occurred, Steve was Cushman's incumbent manager. His less vulnerable style was well-known and possibly the reason Steve was named as the Market Leader and Vice Chairman, a title that exceeded Stath's. Steve was younger than Stath. This never posed a problem for either, and Steve was grateful for Stath's humble and thoughtful approach to leadership; it taught him so much at a very young age. Stath became a mentor and role model for Steve and, most significantly, he became a trusted advisor.

The merger was especially difficult because it came in 2008, in the early days of The Great Recession when tough decisions had to be made. Steve confirmed, "They say it's lonely at the top; I will attest to that! It was a tremendous gift to have someone to run ideas by and to assist in making and executing these types of decisions." Steve will always be grateful for Stath's wisdom and depth of character. Stath never was competitive with Steve. He never undermined him in any way; he took on this "reverse mentorship" role with incredible maturity, grace, and zero ego. Stath had a clear understanding of what was best for everyone and the organization.

Stath modeled vulnerable leadership that builds corporate community and a fun culture. He always gives everyone their time; he's very personable and kind. This was never Steve's skill; he's highly task and goal oriented, but he saw how valuable Stath's qualities were, and he quickly learned to surround himself with others who could fulfill this need. Socrates wisely noted "To know thyself is the beginning of wisdom." Steve and Stath both consciously integrate this wisdom in how they lead.

What I found so refreshing was that though this was an uncomfortable story to share, both realized the value in sharing their true personalities and potentially perceived weaknesses. They did this not only to highlight that men can and need to be vulnerable—that it's really okay to ask for help—but to show what transparent and transformative leadership looks like. We need more men in all leadership roles to understand the immense value for change that is possible when they are courageous and willing to share that they are not perfect. Much of this book breaks down the deception and destruction of the myth of perfection; this is just one more nail in perfection's coffin!

Benefits That Evolve in a Safe Workspace

For those who just lack the ability to appear accessible, whether due to family upbringing, societal influence, or personal beliefs, let me share the benefits of what you can create when you decide to let everyone know you are not invincible, right, or perfect.

1. When you allow your defenses to fall consistently, it can signal a safe zone for others' defenses to fall. They then have the opportunity to be their authentic selves.
2. When you don't care who receives the credit and you allow ideas to be free-flowing, it can produce a galvanized and synergistic energy.
3. When you give up your need to be authoritative, it allows others to find their voice and can encourage leadership growth.
4. Maintaining an image that is not in harmony with who you are is exhausting and will give you less energy to be creative.
5. Genuine relationships can only be nourished in a safe and trustworthy workplace.

Inspirational poet Maya Angelou perfectly captured this sentiment: "I've learned that people will forget what you said, people will forget what you did, but people will never forget how you made them feel." How do you make someone feel good? By caring more about connecting with them, and finding their worth and greatness at the possible expense of your own.

Do Organizations Need to Evolve into Self-Development Trainers?

I've attended Toastmasters for many years to improve my communication skills; becoming a professional motivational speaker never interested me until that seed was planted by my publishing coach, Christine Gail.

During our higher purpose exercise at ICE, in which we worked with the team to identify their personal talents and purpose, I revealed my desire to reach others through keynote speaking. I had a negative association with this new endeavor. When I revealed this very vulnerable feeling, I could see it made people uncomfortable to see me so uncomfortable. I ignored that feeling and the ensuing pause as they contemplated my position. Then the advice started flowing:

"Most keynote speakers are highly successful and are coming from a place of helping others more easily navigate life's journey by sharing the successful path they forged."

"Why don't you reframe your perspective and consider associating keynote speaking with successful examples?"

"Think of Marianne Williamson; she is changing others' lives. How cool would that be?"

Immediately my mindset shifted—this was the perspective I needed to hear and to adopt.

While I was close to finishing my book, I had yet to make a formal declaration on social media announcing my efforts in writing my first book. Although I hesitated, I understood the power in actualizing goals by making a public declaration. It became even more apparent after attending Nick and Megan Unsworth's *Life on Fire* virtual challenge.

The Unsworths recommend several steps for finding your purpose, passion, and path. The first is to "know thyself" by recalling a time when you felt accomplished, confident, and full of energy—they call this your "moment of fire." Then they ask you to refine this moment by answering what you felt, why and when you felt it, and attach a meaning to why this moment was so significant. They take you through several steps, one being to declare your goals on social media.

The step that resonated with me was creating a vision board to help visualize a twelve-month plan with a specific deadline. The Unsworths also encourage posting your vision board on social media along with a stated deadline to achieve goals. Their message is clear: "Power comes when you make a stand and commit to what you *will* accomplish, declaring it to the world!"

I had never attended anything like this, so it completely changed my perspective of what having a life coach meant. I started to realize just how hard it is to change yourself without having someone teach you the necessary steps and methodology to take you through the process.

At my present age of sixty-three, writing a book felt like a stretch goal for me, but hosting training sessions and giving keynote speeches would require me to learn even more novel skills. It was intimidating that at this stage in my life I would purposely choose to move out of my comfort zone and potentially fail so visibly. I realized as I prepared to lead my organization's higher purpose exercise that if I wanted to authentically and fully live my purpose, I would need to shift my mindset from "What I can't do" and "What if I should fail miserably?" to "Where and how can I do the most good in service of others by using my talents?" and "Should I succeed, I will model to my team the benefits of extreme vulnerability."

Going through this self-development training session planted a seed that perhaps organizations could reach their highest and greatest good by encouraging and teaching their employees to also strive to reach their greatest potentials as individuals—outside of work as much as inside the corporate environment. Perhaps the next level of employee engagement was to provide educational tools and training during working hours to assist in employee personal development? Perhaps leaders need to evolve into motivational counselors and personal development coaches? Could that lead to higher levels of employee engagement and commitment to the organization? I think it would.

The Science of Neuroplasticity

While researching my book, I was introduced to the neuroscience of emotional connectivity and neuroplasticity. It is a fascinating study based on the concept of emotional intelligence, first introduced in 1995 by Daniel Goleman in his book *Emotional Intelligence: Why It Can Matter More Than IQ*. Goleman believes that EQ (Emotional Quotient) is a more accurate predictor of success in life than IQ (Intelligence Quotient). EQ is the ability to understand how your emotions and behavior affect those around you and how you can adapt your behavior to encourage more positive behavior from others.

Your EQ is useful in every area of your life, whether it's encouraging your kids to eat broccoli by renaming it "superhero building trees," or in avoiding confrontational encounters at work by not inadvertently triggering defensive postures in your team mates. Asking yourself "What am I doing to make them defensive?" becomes a natural internal dialogue.

Your brain's amygdala interprets incoming senses such as smell, touch, hearing, taste, and sight. If it codes this input as positive feelings of relaxation, joy, and satisfaction, it triggers the release of oxytocin, dopamine, or serotonin. If it codes this input as negative feelings of stress, fear, and anxiety, it triggers the body to release stress hormones such as cortisol. These emotions and the resulting hormonal release can either optimize the body's ability to be creative, reflective, and curious, or negate the brain's ability to think rationally or creatively, resulting in more impulsive, shallow, and negative responses, such as frustration or bursts of anger.

This research led me to attend John Assaraf's six-hour-plus Brain-A-Thon, which details the new and evolving science of neuroplasticity. John is one of the world's leading behavioral and mindset experts. I met John in 2000 through mutual friends after he moved to San Diego. He shared with us the most powerful vision board story I have ever seen. Approximately fifteen years before moving to San Diego, John created a vision board that included a picture of a house in Rancho Santa Fe, California. The vision board was relocated when the family moved, and after they arrived in San Diego, his son Noah remarked, "Dad the house on this board looks just like our new house!" It was indeed the *exact same house* as he had on the vision board! The immense power of a vision board!

During the Brain-A-Thon, I learned John had become fascinated with the developing science of neurodiversity in 2010, collaborating with countless neuroscientists, psychiatrists, and other brain experts. Similar to my desire to write this book to understand why ICE had exceeded every industry standard for revenue growth, John invested a million dollars into understanding how to harness this knowledge for the benefit of others. He wanted to help others do what he had done naturally—he wanted to learn how he could teach people to physically change and retrain their brains. He knew if he could understand the science behind this, he could help others recognize the mental and emotional obstacles preventing them from reaching their potentials.

Internally, we create a narrative of how we see ourselves. Then we unconsciously choose to accept that is *the only truth* and we cannot change. John offers a full program through NeuroGym called Innercise—brain exercises designed to realign this internal narrative by strengthening mental and emotional abilities to remove mental blocks we've unintentionally created. He describes Innercise as follows:

> "As a constantly working organ, the brain is in charge of various cognitive functions, from processing and perceiving sensory stimuli to motor control and memory storage. Habits and beliefs, that are stored in long-term memory, can be challenged when one engages in a novel, learning experience; this "aha" moment results as a rapid shift in neural activity takes place and allows for a new habit or belief to be formed. This is exactly what NeuroGym's Innercise methods do; they help one adopt new perceptions and behaviors that can solve old problems efficiently. Moreover, the Innercises apply practical mental exercise techniques scientifically shown to improve mental and emotional functioning. The benefits are far-reaching and have resulted in providing upward spirals of positive emotion to counter negativity and unproductive behaviors, relieve fatigue, decrease stress levels, and increase positive behaviors to achieve success. These proven techniques can train the brain to adopt a healthy lifestyle, release undesired thoughts and habits, and tune the brain to triumph in life."[61]

To live the fullest life possible, including having better health, more wealth, more happiness, and a life with an abundance not scarcity mindset, you might want to take the time to invest in the only thing you have control over: *you*. Let me reinforce this point: Investing in personal growth and learning to retrain your brain to become "the best you possible" is worthwhile. I recommend you identify and break the old habits holding you back. Many coaches and products can help with this; Innercise is just one option.

Encouragement Only a Coach Can Offer

Becoming a proficient speaker is like any other skill and can be improved through consistent practice. Serving as our Toastmasters club president in 2020 and speaking weekly in our meetings developed my speaking skills and helped me find my voice. The enhanced perspective I gained by attending the self-development training and the Brain-a-Thon shifted something in me and clarified the decision to become a keynote speaker. I consciously made the decision that the negative internal dialogue I had with myself of "I don't have the skillset to become a keynote speaker or life inspiration coach" no longer served me.

By early 2021, I began to enjoy public speaking and committed to speaking as frequently as possible. My fellow Toastmasters loved the vulnerability naturally infused in my speeches. They are a kind but brutally honest group, and when they insisted my vulnerability was one of my most enduring qualities as a speaker, I decided to embrace their feedback. Acceptance is indeed a gift you give to yourself. They became my speaking coaches!

Hiring my book publishing coach to help me craft this book proved to be an invaluable investment in me because it starting me on a road of personal growth through personal development. It solidified the process of identifying, achieving, and having someone holding you accountable to achieve your goals. I have participated in leadership programs such as The Chairman's Roundtable and Vistage with tremendous benefit, but neither offered the same personal attention and results I achieved when I hired Christine Gail. When you invest in yourself, you make the conscious statement "I am worthy. I deserve to reach my potential." If there is a book inside you, no one can help you more easily realize that dream than Christine!

Christine introduced me to performance coaches Nick and Megan Unsworth's' *Life on Fire Challenge* virtual event, which led me to spend a Saturday attending John Assaraf's life-affirming training sessions. Having made an initial investment with Christine, I started a process of self-development that would reveal my potential in ways I had not anticipated.

Christine Gail, Nick and Megan Unsworth, and John Assaraf are all coaches who want you to succeed, and they find great purpose in helping you do so. Please see the Additional Resources at the end of the book to access more information. At a minimum, you might want to visit their websites to access free content that will shift your perspective. I encourage you to sign up for newsletters and training events to help take your first step toward self-valuation.

Despite my age, I still choose to invest time in personal growth. You are never too old, too busy, or too anything to decide you want to become a better you. One of the best outcomes in sharing your decision to be a "lifetime student of life" is the potential to inspire others to become their best versions of themselves.

CHAPTER 10

Doing Well and Doing Good Need Not and Should Not Be Mutually Exclusive

A primary driver for Millennials is seeking to "be part of something greater than their own work." They crave and seek association with organizations that postulate higher purpose, shared values, and a commitment to responsible corporate citizenship. They want to work for companies that are not simply profit-driven but focus on and enable societal transformation.

Ingrained in my personality is a desire to implement change—to be a force for good. I suspect my mother influenced this philosophy of mine. My mother grew up in Poland. When she was seven, she was taken from a Catholic church by the Nazis along with her five-year old sister to work in a munition's factory in Germany, packing bullets for the German war-machine. Despite never seeing her parents or siblings again, she always maintained an enormous ability to forgive with an understanding for "disregarded" people.

My desire to help the marginalized has influenced much of my lifetime behavior. Beginning in elementary school, I found myself defending those being bullied. Improving the human condition has always been instinctual to me, so I naturally engrained those principles into ICE's foundation. The values of JEDI (Justice Equality Diversity Inclusion) will continue to progress as the only sustainable path forward for business leadership.

The 2019 Deloitte Millennial Global Survey reinforces the positive effects of being a force for good. It surveyed 13,416 Millennials and 3,009 Gen Z across forty-two countries.[62] As discussed in Chapter 2, in capturing this diverse data for many years about Millennials, and now Gen Z's belief systems, the survey has been able to track shifts. It noted an alarming trend of a lost trust and optimism in our young people, plus their disappointment that business often misses the opportunities to be forces for good.

One of the survey's key findings was that *younger generations believe business must be a positive influence on society*—46 percent of Millennials are attracted to organizations that espouse this as one of their key values. They make it very clear they prefer not to work for organizations that do not support or prioritize these issues. Deloitte notes that 59 percent of survey participants were planning to leave their current employers within two years, and 74 *percent planned to depart within five years simply because their employers did not care about their community*!

In 2017, 76 percent of Millennials believed businesses were responding to this call for improved societal progress influence, but in 2018, that fell to 61 percent, and in 2019, it slipped to 55 percent; *our youth are losing faith in their belief that business is or could be a dependable catalyst for social justice initiatives.*

Why do businesses need to care? Why must they change? Quite simply, the survey reinforced that our younger generations will not frequent or support companies that do not align with their values. Thirty-seven percent said they have stopped or minimized a business relationship because of the company's unethical behavior. Conversely, 36 percent have started or deepened a relationship because of organizational ethics.

The survey confirmed Millennials and Gen Zs will actually start and/ or stop their relationships with companies based on their personal belief systems, which often relate to a company's positive or negative societal impact. They want to see declarations of higher purpose and social justice missions *evolve into meaningful action* and confirmation that business leaders genuinely serve as agents for positive change. They are becoming aware that businesses can choose to adhere to principles of conscious capitalism, that they can provide not just a livelihood, but they can improve the community and enrich the lives of their employees; however, "they don't see enough businesses standing up and filling the void."

Deloitte concludes that as global citizens with a powerful ability to make a difference, businesses should:

- Balance profit with protecting the planet and help solve society's most challenging problems
- Create a culture that encourages diversity, inclusion, and social mobility
- Educate people throughout their organization to encourage behaviors and attitudes that support their business's priorities
- Collaborate with other businesses, government, and educators to transform learning and enable individuals to access the skills they need to meet future job demands
- Take a lead on safeguarding their operations and data from physical and digital threats
- Examine their ethics and behavior and ask whether they're intruding too far into people's lives
- Demonstrate internally and externally what they are doing to make the world a better place

Additionally, the younger generations' economic, social, and political optimism and their belief in the dependability of traditional societal institutions are at record lows. It will be interesting to see how much their faith in government, society, and business continue to plummet in the 2020s with the advent of COVID-19 and the calls for racial equity.

They are also highly skeptical of their leaders' positive influence on society and commitment to improving the world. Most notably, they don't trust their leaders or corporate America. Why? *Because most businesses continue to care more about the bottom line than their employees.*

Larrissa Faw, a journalist and Forbes contributing author who studies Millennial workplace trends, coined the term "cause-sumption"—a philanthropic marketing trend, such as "buy one from us and we'll give one to a person in need." Tom's shoes and Paul Newman's products are examples of this type of consumerism. It's a purchasing habit driver that is hardly new. For decades, stakeholder capitalism and philanthropic efforts have been shifting from being "a nice thing to do" to mandatory. According to Horizon Media's Finger on the Pulse study, 81 percent of Millennials expect companies to make a public commitment to responsible corporate citizenship.[63] Faw quotes Kirk Olson, VP of Trend Sights at Horizon Media, as stating, "It used to be that companies would align with charities that shared their same values. "Now brands are taking these do-good values and baking them into their corporate identities." She also quotes Jamie Gutfreund, Chief Strategy Officer of the Intelligence Group, who says, "Marketers need to shift their mindset from the traditional ROI model to one based on 'ROR,' or Return on Relationship. In other words, what are you doing to fuel that expression and how are you partnering with each customer or prospect to help them establish their own personal brand?"

> *Apparently, nothing motivates or inspires this generation more than this concept of business doing well and doing good!*

Directing a resilient organization now requires appreciating this fundamental desire that drives Millennials, especially as they increasingly move into positions of authority and management. The shift toward valuing relational, societal, and environmental capital is just beginning. Spurred by social media, it will likely never end due to the increased awareness that we're all global citizens. According to the 2019 Deloitte Millennial Global Survey:

"The impact of myriad, radical changes to our daily lives has hit younger generations hard—economically, socially, and perhaps psychologically. Through this survey, this 'generation disrupted' is telling us that continuous change and upheaval have created a population that is different at its core. But young people are also providing valuable clues about how society's institutions can respond to those differences in mutually beneficial ways that could increase trust, generate positive societal impact, and meet their high expectations."[64]

Mind the Gap

When I visited England several years ago, I was highly amused by the announcement every few minutes at the subway system to "mind the gap" as you leave or enter a train. A gap exists that can trip you up as you step off a train. A gap also exists between all the carefully gathered data about what motivates Millennials and how much work or effort they'll put into something to actuate change.

When considering the results of the Deloitte Millennial Survey, a gap exists in comparison to actual field experiences. This gap exists between the belief system of the Millennials and their active participation in support of their belief system. Surveys might capture more of what Millennials *think* they want than what they're actually *willing to do* or, more precisely, *to sacrifice for*. At ICE, we haven't always experienced high volunteer turnout at the many charitable and philanthropic events we participate in. For example, I had hoped to receive more office drop-offs at our blanket and towel drives for the homeless or clothing drives for battered women reentering the workforce or more volunteers at the food bank when we helped out.

We endeavor to foster awareness and communal pride within ICE and being part of "something greater than their own work," even if they can't or don't actively engage in the activities. An organization that engages policies to create societal change might not galvanize all Millennials; however, even those who don't participate appear to be proud of the charitable work we do and our very vocal corporate commitment to improve the lives of those less fortunate in our community.

The good news is I've seen a narrowing of this gap in social impact activities. Employees have often enlisted participation to include their older children. People have very busy and demanding lives, but as their awareness increases, their engagement increases because of the impact they're making in the community.

It all starts with modeling positive behavior—again, it's as much about the striving as the succeeding!

How Do We Improve Our Community?

Since ICE began, we have actively engaged in numerous activities that have built our reputation and brand as a civic-minded company. Here are just a few examples:

- As part of the annual Solana Beach Presbyterian Church Community Serve Day, we maintained a home that houses individuals with disabilities. These homes are owned by the TERI organization (Training, Education, Resource Institute). Over eight years, we've painted and landscaped the property, and we're proud to know they consider this their "best maintained home"!

- Since 2017, we have had a Christmas "Giving Tree" where each employee picks an ornament that benefits a non-profit organization and we cover the cost of this donation.

- We have volunteered and packed food at the San Diego Food Bank.

- We have volunteered and assembled furniture at Father Joe's Villages.

- We have sponsored, attended, and volunteered at countless industry functions, such as golf tournaments, conferences, awards events, and fundraisers.

- We've donated to organizations that support our youth and our most vulnerable citizens, including Reality Changers, Casa de Amistad, Generate Hope, Military Outreach Ministry, San Diego Association of Legal Administrators, TERI, Compassion in Action, Plant with Purpose, transcenDANCE, and San Diego Economic Development Corporation (SDEDC), giving in significant and minor ways.
- We've served on non-profit boards, including the Urban Land Institute, SDEDC Foundation, National Association of International Office Providers (NAIOP), International Interior Design Association (IIDA), Athena, Athena Pinnacle Awards, and transcenDANCE.

We've worked hard to *build* community! We joke that ICE doesn't just stand for Innovative Commercial Environments but Inspiring Community Excellence. We regularly place effort in making our community better in the smallest and largest of ways. All efforts generate significant impact—it all matters and it all makes a difference.

Everything an Organization Does Can Inspire Societal Impact

Our awareness of the critical nature of giving has grown over the years. In 2019, we realized our holiday giving should reflect our values, so in lieu of a more traditional holiday client gift, such as a bottle of wine, we decided to invest in the future sustainability of our planet through Plant with Purpose. This local non-profit invests in global communities by planting trees in some of the world's most forsaken areas.

Our holiday gift to Plant with Purpose reflected the evolution of our values and a realization that *everything* we do must reflect our societal impact goals, our higher purpose, and our desire to be a missional organization. Our philanthropic efforts have become part of the reason for our existence—*to consistently raise awareness within our internal organization as well as our community as a whole.*

We purchased more than 200 trees from this organization to be planted by farmers across the world and included a note that provided an overview of the Plant with Purpose mission because we wanted to raise awareness of their work. We also gave out more than 200 beautifully wrapped tiny sapling trees to be planted in San Diego to reinforce this global effort. Plant with Purpose's mission is to break the cycle of poverty, make a positive impact on the environment, and spiritually and emotionally elevate communities around the world. The insert we included noted these details and statistics:

- Globally 800 million people live in poverty.
- 85 percent rely on agriculture and live in rural areas affected by an environmental crisis.
- When environmental systems are deforested, all forms of life suffer.
- People living in these areas have smaller crop yields, have unhealthy land, and are vulnerable to famine and disaster.
- Living in poverty is a daily struggle for survival with no opportunity to save and plan for the future.
- The stress of poverty strains relationships, decreases motivation, and robs people of their dignity. Their spiritual growth is stifled by desperation—they live without hope.

The gifts and sentiments were well-received and honored our conscious movement toward improving the planet and reflecting our corporate ethos.

Racism in America

Leadership is not limited to the management layer at ICE. We encourage everyone to think, behave, and lead as if they are in management. Our corporate culture of trust, autonomous thinking, and leadership can be captured in this one story.

In 2020, the unnecessary killing of George Floyd and the resulting mass protests shined a glaring light on the continuation of racist policies and belief systems that proliferate our society. As with COVID, there was no playbook for CEOs to access to make intelligent and empathetic decisions in regards to racism. A full week or more went by as I read statements from for-profit and non-profit organizations, small and mega-giant corporations with huge PR budgets; none resonated with me in the slightest. They generally did not offer words of substance or a way forward, but felt reactive and perfunctory.

This made me pause and reflect as I waited for my authentic response; I knew full well a performative statement would not reveal a thoughtful answer. As the CEO, I realized our response truly had to come from my heart, and although I was asked to respond quickly, I did not.

As a leader who guides with action as well as words, I pondered if our policies, culture, and past actions would suffice. When I received an email from Project Coordinator Sharriea Williams, I realized I was wrong to think our past actions would be sufficient to address our stance on racial equality. Sharriea heads up our culture committee and has become our most enthusiastic voice in reinforcing our empowering culture. I often call her our #1 Culture Warrior! She regularly sends updates on birthdays, work anniversaries, and notable holidays such as National Hugging Day or National Roof Over Your Head Day. We all appreciate her thoughtful, company-wide emails.

At that point, Sharriea had been with ICE for two years, so she knew who we were; she knew with conviction what we stand for, and she has often expressed pride to work at ICE. As a biracial woman, she wanted to know what our racial injustice position was and made the decision to bravely and notably raise my awareness of what it's like to be Black in America.

This is part of the email I received from Sharriea:

> "Being half-Black, this movement directly affects myself and my family and if I don't speak up, then I'm contributing to the silence that has allowed history to repeat itself. Knowing how powerfully driven ICE's voice

can be, it's a little bit disheartening to know that we, as a company, choose to stand by in silence . . . There is no unity or agreement in silence on this issue, and our individual voices do not carry more weight WITHOUT the additional support of our businesses/employers. History has never been changed by staying quiet on the sidelines. We, ICE, had a voice when it came to COVID and protecting the human race and saving lives. Why is saving Black Lives not as important to speak out about or support?

I do not mean this in an offensive way at all. You all are very aware of how much respect and love I have for ICE, and I know and believe that ICE does not support racism in any way. Which is why it's so important to me to hear your view/stance on this issue and why ICE chooses to stay silent. Whether it's voiced publicly or not.

I wanted to bring awareness of the humanitarian cultural and ethnic crises, as scary as it was and specifically to the Black Lives that have been affected. As our newly appointed culture committee leader, I plan on implementing ideas that increase racial awareness that expand our already diverse and inclusive culture at ICE. I want to promote education and understanding of the enormous impact this crisis is having on the Black community and to use that knowledge to help support not only the Black community but all minorities who have had to endure racism.

Having experienced racism as a child by a few family members, I know that education and knowledge alone go a long way. You're not born to be racist; you were taught. And just the same, it can be untaught.

ICE has already created a culture of safe space and openness where your voice can be heard, and had it not been for this culture, I might not have had the courage to voice my opinion on this matter. I'm grateful to work for a company that not only provides that space, but listens, and responds genuinely."

In this dearth of information, as a White woman lacking personal experience with racism, I asked Sharriea to help me craft a substantive message that offers all of us at ICE understanding, healing, and a plan to move forward. I let her know how grateful we were that she had the courage to send this email; then we went to work. We started by both attending Daymond John's *Real Talk Business Reboot* webinar hosted by *Inc. Magazine*. We watched a panel discussion hosted by a friend of Sharriea's, Dr. Antipas Harris, titled *A Dialogue on Racism in America*.

Referencing our motto of "first seek to understand, then be understood," I understood Sharriea's heart in wanting to be part of an organization that values JEDI because of the work I'd done within myself and the extensive research required to write *Inspiring Generational Leadership*. As a woman, I also understood what it felt like to be marginalized as a valuable employee simply because of my gender. Similar to Saundra's story in Chapter 2, I had to put in more than double the effort of my male counterparts, battle sexual harassment, and not have the administrative support I needed that men were easily given.

Sharriea was surprised but eager to assist in crafting our message. I reached out to both Black and White San Diego leaders and spent hours every day reading books and leadership newsletters to seek guidance in directing our stance. Sharriea also connected with her network and increased her reading. It took us a week to fine-tune the heartfelt internal letter that went to our teammates. We also issued an abbreviated version on social media and subsequently decided to include this letter in its entirety on our website.

THE WAY FORWARD

June 11, 2020

By: Sharriea Williams Project Coordinator & DeLinda Forsythe Founder/CEO

On June 5, I received a note from Sharriea Williams. She inquired what ICE would do or say in response to the recent protests against racism. I had been struggling with this question myself, reading superficial posts issued by various CEOs and organizations; all performative, none of which resonated any substance at all.

Sharriea has always been thoughtfully engaged at ICE through her group emails that raise awareness and celebrate a variety of organizations. Though a more internal person, you know where Sharriea's heart is and I appreciate that. Together, we drafted the ICE Statement on Inclusiveness.

In the last three months, non-business-related issues have taken the forefront in corporate America from COVID, to political partisan divisiveness, and now racism—first against Chinese people and now Black Americans. There is a titanic absence of thought leadership and training to prepare America's corporate leaders on how to respond authentically.

I have reached out to Black and White leaders alike for insight into how they are approaching this situation within their own companies. Considering that CEOs have not experienced a social justice climate such as this in sixty years, it is not surprising that none have suggestions for a clear path in which to move forward.

We have entered new, uncharted territory.

Then we talked, deeply, about what we learned. Together—we crafted the following:

1. Our goal is to take racism out of obscurity and shine a light on its destructive nature.
2. As an organization, we do not tolerate racism, as is clearly noted in our employee handbook.
3. We encourage internal sharing of our stories at ICE about our personal and our family's racist experiences, seeking to offer perspective and clarity on racism.
4. We seek to increase awareness and education in regards to the humanitarian crisis on race, utilizing the safe open platform we have at ICE to encourage our employees to have the hard conversations about race and any other social concerns.

5. We continue to offer employment and leadership positions at ICE that attract and empower minorities, adding that to our website so our position on these issues is vibrant and well-defined.

6. We encourage each other to participate in a weekly Toastmasters program to help them find and learn to use their voice to make an impact in society.

7. Children are not born identifying race, gender, or ethnicity in a negative way; they are taught racism. Kids are very aware of ways we differ, and exposure to books that promote diversity is something we encourage through our ICE book club to include children's books for our parents about racism, inclusion, and kindness.

As limited and imperfect a list as this is, it's a start as we all attempt to find a way forward in all this brokenness that deadens our spirits and attempts to steal our joy.

No one can change the past, but we can learn from it to shape a more inclusive future.

Let me end with this observation. Sharriea notably raised my awareness of my accountability when she referenced a quote from Archbishop Desmond Tutu: If you are neutral in situations of injustice, you have chosen the side of the oppressor. I'd like to add this gentle reminder from the honorable Dr. Martin Luther King, Jr: In the end, we will remember not the words of our enemies, but the silence of our friends.

Thank you,

Sharriea and DeLinda

What really helped me in this effort was the perspective I had gained from being part of the conscious capitalism movement. They are fierce supporters of JEDI and their credo from their www.consciouscapitalism.org website captures some of this ideal:

> We believe that business is good because it creates value, it is ethical because it is based on voluntary exchange, it is noble because it can elevate our existence and it is heroic because it lifts people out of poverty and creates prosperity.
>
> Free enterprise capitalism is the most powerful system for social cooperation and human progress ever conceived. It is one of the most compelling ideas we humans have ever had.
>
> **But we can aspire to do even more.**

Crafting this statement was completely out of both of our comfort zones, but that's okay; sticky and enduring change demands leaving the comfort of the known for the discomfort of the unknown.

Brand Reinforced

Our projects continue to become more creative, attracting the engagement of San Diego's most imaginative developers, architects, and interior designers. All of this has attracted top local and national talent to join ICE. Our ability to attract talent is more than just the creative work we do; it's what we do as an organization and as leaders in both our business and personal lives.

We know that our brand—reinforced through loyal relationships, authentic results, and charitable work—has created the ICE reputation.

> *We visibly live the ideals we profess. Leaders need to lead in deeds more than words.*

The response from our team was instantly positive; the pride they had in our "way forward" message was surprising, and it remains an effort I am proud of because it honored Sharriea and the millions of African Americans adversely affected in our country.

Simply raising awareness of organizations in your community that are Black-owned and then making the decision to support those organizations is a significant way we can individually bolster our local Black-owned businesses. An example of such support is when I received a thank you holiday gift of vegan cookies made by Maya's Cookies from the San Diego Economic Development Corporation. Maya's Cookies is a local Black-owned bakery. The SDEDC modeled their intention to live this belief.

Consistency in the smallest ways helps define your reputation. Our simple letter vigorously reinforced who we say we are as an organization. With their access to technology, Millennials know who you are and what you stand for by what you actually do, both during and after business hours—there is no distinction between your professional and personal lives.

Civic-Minded Generation

Millennials have a natural aptitude toward larger societal needs, civic engagement, and inclusive societal equality. They embrace high levels of compassion, but they need mentors and visionary philanthropists to emulate. Authentic mentors are critical in nurturing their innate dispositions to live out their caring temperaments. That is why this generation so desperately needs mentorship and authentic leaders.

The Lucky Attitude website,[65] quoting a *USA Today* article, notes that Millennials are the most civic-minded cohort since the 1940s. They "believe in the value of political engagement and are convinced that government can be a powerful force for good." (I would be curious to know if after 2020, they still hold this belief!) It also states that:

"Civic generations tend to bring about times of greater economic equality and more inclusive racial and ethnic concerns. It isn't surprising that a Civic generation like Millennials shows high levels of compassion—a characteristic instrumental in helping us build a powerful legacy.

The majority of Millennials say that the rising inequality gap is a serious problem in this country. A 2004 National Election Survey found that 84% of 18-to-26-year-olds felt that the gap between rich and poor had grown in the last twenty years and 94% said that this was a bad thing, a higher percentage than all other generations.

Millennials are likely to support a progressive tax system, to want an increase in the minimum wage, to support free trade, and to believe that government regulations on businesses are necessary in order to keep them in check and to protect consumers."

The 2014 Deloitte Millennial survey also noted that they "consider government to have the greatest potential to address society's biggest issues."[66]

Government certainly can be a factor in moving the needle toward equality, but the free-market system has a proven track record of elevating people out of poverty and creating prosperity. When businesses incorporate the tenets of conscious capitalism, which are in alignment with the values of Millennials, it enhances opportunity for all. It takes leadership awareness, an open mindset, and a committed community.

The Rainforest Book

I first learned about the importance of making business connections that unite the community through Greg Horowitt's 2012 book *The Rainforest: The Secret to Building the Next Silicon Valley.* I learned what I intuitively knew: Connecting like-minded people with daring ideas is one of the most powerful ways to initiate community change. Greg introduced me to the concept of business ecosystems and keystones. Let me explain both.

Rainforests are environments that encourage disconnected people to self-organize into greater forms of biological life, human ecosystems. Trust and increased communication improve effectiveness. Business rainforests are built from the bottom up through diverse and highly connected human interactions that enable the development of clusters. These human ecosystems reach across boundaries, bringing people together for the greater good, with a "pay it forward mentality."

Greg coined the term "keystones"—they are highly networked "deal-makers," community activists, and social connectors who provide unification of like-minded people within a geographical regional network. They have the ability to convince people to do things they otherwise would never do. They are leaders who drive innovation. Greg states:

> "Leaders—from CEOs and Prime Ministers on down—should focus more on the recipe, not just the ingredients, of innovation. We call upon *a new generation of leaders* to develop initiatives that nurture the growth of entire Rainforests. *Leaders must evolve as well.* It is not enough to encourage innovation among a small cluster of people who live close together, and who think and act alike. Globalization has destroyed that notion. Innovators today must engage with the world. *We are proposing a new active capitalism.* Capitalism is about decentralizing decision-making empowering individuals to connect, collaborate, experiment, and create . . . *The Rainforest* is not mere business theory, it provides a new paradigm for policies and strategies that transcend the left and right divides of the political spectrum. The mechanisms of the rainforest touch the heart of capitalism—making markets more efficient . . . And they validate our faith in innovation as a way to elevate the welfare of humankind."

Greg's concepts have stuck with me for years and shaped how I think and behave, striving to be more of a keystone, a connector of people. This philosophy has certainly galvanized the ICE brand and our ability to develop meaningful, long-term relationships that support the goals of others. It reinforces, once again, my higher purpose of "Doing well and doing good," which led to the idea of our "One Woman" group.

One Woman Can Change Anything—Many Women Can Change Everything

Most of us believe there is nothing we can do to influence change so we do nothing. Or we wait to discover a "huge" thing that never appears, again doing nothing to impact societal change. Let me share with you a story that illustrates how simple it can be to become a force for good. Though our story is just beginning with results still to be determined, it is worth sharing in keeping with my belief that the journey, the striving, is as critical as the final outcome.

It started with a conversation among friends, Kori Joneson, Lee Wills, Laura Hall, and Rashmi Char. All of these women are keystones in our community. We all agreed that business' purpose had shifted toward mutuality, a lifting of all boats equally. We discussed how capitalism could better live its potential to elevate humanity through teaching our children these principles and engaging in awareness building by simply talking to other business leaders in our community. We know the conscious capitalism movement seeks racial equality, and we trusted our collaboration would lead to the sharing of its values.

We anticipated a positive outcome of raised national awareness for racial and social justice as a result of the COVID-19 pandemic. We believed that government had shown its limitations in achieving equality. Perhaps the time to discuss conscious capitalism's ability to reduce inequality by providing business opportunities for minority-owned businesses was drawing near? We discussed how this might be the opportunity for civic-minded leaders to educate the community about the benefits of these principles and the increased financial success documented in *Firms of*

Endearment—that FoE's outperform the S&P 500 by fourteen times, leading to long-term increased business resiliency. Talent attraction and retention is one of the greatest challenges corporations face, and firms that embrace conscious capitalism's principles are more successful in winning the talent war.

We wondered if a spark lit by women in the business ecosystem could ignite the infinite influence of many women and be a force for good that inspires sincere change. We decided we wanted to "be the change" in our community.

The name of our group was inspired by the words on a necklace given to me by my husband. The sentiments seemed to capture our desire to find ways to make a difference in our community, to share our belief that the principles enforced through the conscious capitalism movement will unite diverse people.

one woman CAN CHANGE ANYTHING, *many women* CAN CHANGE EVERYTHING

Our group identified two actionable items and the purpose for our association.

Purpose: To raise awareness of this emerging redefinition of business as a modality to elevate humanity and encourage a more inclusive, diverse San Diego business ecosystem by connecting the San Diego community.

> *Awareness is like the sun. When it shines on things, they are transformed.*
> **—Thich Nhat Hanh**

Yes, it all starts with building awareness, so we committed to these two initiatives:

1. Girl Scouts—Teach the fundamentals of Conscious Capitalism to the Girl Scout organization with an end result of earning a Girl Scout Conscious Capitalist badge or patch. We were motivated that 53 percent of Girl Scout alums are business leaders; we see the opportunity to facilitate meaningful change by teaching these values to young girls.

2. Black Business Community—We became aware of the efforts of the Central San Diego Black Chamber of Commerce (CSD-BCC), to support Black entrepreneurs. Our second initiative was to introduce their organization to the principles of Conscious Capitalism. Our long-term goal would be to connect with their members and share success stories of local organizations leading with these principles, create free educational content that defined the benefits of stakeholder capitalism, and provide local mentors for Black entrepreneurs who lead with these business practices. We wanted to facilitate keystone connections.

As we move forward, we will find additional options to increase awareness—utilizing mentorship, hosting events, webinars, and speaking engagements are all areas of opportunity. Upon experiencing success with the Girl Scouts and CSDBCC, we would then engage our local San Diego Regional Economic Development Corporation (EDC) to disseminate the message. The EDC mission is to maximize economic prosperity and global competitiveness for the San Diego region. In 2016, the EDC began to strategize on an inclusive growth strategy and further raise the region's global profile. EDC Chief Operating Officer Lauree Sahba advised, "the 'right recovery' was advancing an inclusive growth initiative. We know the innovation economy will lead us out of this recession. These companies are EDC's core investment base. If we can influence the business community to be thoughtful, strategic, and collaborative, we can ensure a more resilient San Diego. The building blocks are: talent, jobs, and households."

Our local EDC is considered by many to be one of San Diego's crown jewels. It is always ahead of the curve and leading the community effort to foster a conscious business ecosystem. Its members are supportive of social justice, gender parity, and economic equality through entrepreneurism.

Keystone Associations and Life-Time Friendships

To understand the value of keystone relationships, let me share how friendships have influenced my life and career and how I met the wonderful women who comprise the One-Woman group.

It's critical to your personal development to align with like-minded associates who support your beliefs and see your potential, even when you don't; they encourage you to become your "best you." Through Holly Smithson, CEO of Athena, I was introduced to Lee Wills. The first time I heard Lee speak was at an Athena event in 2018 regarding diversity and inclusion. As the first in her family to graduate from college, Lee understands the critical nature of providing the best education possible for our children. Her son is currently working toward his PhD at Stanford. Her story resonated with me because I, too, feel education is the greatest gift we can give to our children.

Lee worked as the Global Director of Inclusion and Diversity at Intel and in similar roles at Qualcomm. When we met, she held the position of Head of Talent and Acquisition for Sony. Lee also serves on the board of the Central San Diego Black Chamber of Commerce. It was her suggestion to connect with the CSDBCC to elevate Black San Diego entrepreneurs through mentorship and training programs.

Joining Lee on the Athena speakers panel was the seventy-seven-year-old CEO of the Girl Scouts of the USA, Sylvia Acevedo. Sylvia's career as a storied engineer and businesswoman before joining the Girl Scouts was as impressive as the overview of her efforts to infuse her passion for STEM within the organization.

Sylvia started her career at NASA's Jet Propulsion Laboratory where she was on the Voyager 2 team. There were no bathrooms for females at the time, so she had to ride a bike to access a bathroom she could use. She noted the critical link between architecture and what and who is valued by a society. She drove inclusion, never giving up, demanding that all voices be heard. She went on to hold executive roles at Apple, Dell, and Autodesk, and in 2018, she was recognized in Forbes as one of America's Top 50 Women in Tech. Within her first three years as CEO of Girl Scouts, she supported the creation of over 100 badges in STEM! This event elevated my awareness of the critical nature of the Girl Scouts and women in the STEM workforce.

Also, through the Athena organization I met Rashmi Char. Rashmi is one of the most gracious women I've ever known. She grew up in India in a broad-minded family that offered her tremendous encouragement to strive to become whatever she wanted to be. Education was critical to her family so they provided the best schooling possible. Rashmi currently serves as the Vice President, Engineering for Qualcomm as well as on the Athena and the Girl Scout boards. She too deeply cares about gender parity and saw the potential to teach young girls these values and encourage ethical entrepreneurism with a focus on careers in STEM.

Kori Joneson, Board President of the Conscious Capitalism San Diego chapter, is a Millennial multiracial entrepreneur and the co-founder and principal of women-owned Symbio Strategies. Symbio is a firm that partners with business leaders to create a culture of connection over perfection in the workplace. Their Employee Experience System creates structure to support all voices being heard, team building, emotional well-being, and connection. Symbio's research and work shows that when we invite employees to candidly express how they are feeling, they engage in more meaningful dialogue, build trust, and evolve to have more autonomy. Her team is hoping to validate that their "human emotions matter" approach actually creates more engaged employees.

Kori and I met virtually every few weeks to ideate a roadmap to raise awareness and encourage organizations in San Diego to adopt the life-affirming and business-propelling principles of the Conscious Capitalism movement. We share the same values and passion of creating a more equitable workplace. Kori embodies the definition of a keystone; she dedicates time weekly, creating business connections that promote the principles of the Conscious Capitalism movement. When Kori introduced us to Laura Hall, a door cracked open for our ideas to potentially spread nationwide.

Laura Hall is the published author of *The ABCs of Conscious Capitalism for KIDs*, a former highly successful fashion executive from New York, and a co-founder of WHYZ Partners—a female-owned retail consumer goods consulting firm. Laura is also a new San Diego resident. She immediately became engaged with our idea to create a Girl Scout Conscious Capitalist patch for our San Diego Girl Scouts.

At the core of our One-Woman group was our desire to provide keystone connections. We wanted to better connect highly influential San Diego women and men who support an inclusive business climate and who seek to redefine the purpose of business as a means to elevate humanity for the benefit of all. Similar to the EDC, we are striving to raise awareness in support of social justice, gender parity, and economic equality issues by facilitating business connections and sharing these principles with entrepreneurs.

Since Millennials have an affinity to end societal disparity, perhaps now is the time to embrace strategies never tried before.

Reimagining Capitalism in a World on Fire

It took ten years for Harvard professor Rebecca Henderson to write *Reimagining Capitalism in a World on Fire*. It launched perfectly in April 2020 amid the COVID-19 pandemic and the civil unrest throughout America. I thoroughly enjoyed reading this book, which details how critical capitalism is to global stability but also how it is in desperate need of a makeover, and a little nip and tuck will not suffice. Ms. Henderson has titled this "the world's most important conversation." I highly recommend you read it for a deeper understanding of how some of our largest organizations have successfully engaged these principles with enormous financial and human capital success.

Henderson stresses that we must recalibrate how we lead corporations. She shares many success stories and their resulting financial achievement when business better reflects where we are in the human journey and the state of our world today. She heralds that now is the time to fast-track the reimagination of capitalism started years ago by John Mackey and Raj Sisodia.

Part of this perfect storm is the rapid increase of Millennials in the workforce. Their emergence as the largest business demographic in conjunction with a desire to align with the values of conscious capitalism offer the potential to advance this movement.

Corporate America and business leaders need to implement profound structural change. Many of the solutions Henderson is suggesting formulate the foundation of ICE—that business has the moral imperative to implement resonating and meaningful modifications. Our political system and our American way of life appear to be at risk if we don't transform the definition of capitalism and begin to rebuild our institutions, creating shared value for all individuals.

I had countless conversations with local and national business, governmental, and religious leaders in 2020 as the gravitas of the situation continued to escalate. I realized it all begins with our leaders shifting to a more inclusive mindset, valuing not only financial capital but human, societal, and environmental capital. Henderson lays out the steps necessary to achieve mutual equity that will sustain the American Dream for *all people* and certainly reinforces our belief that "Doing Well and Doing Good Need Not and *Should* Not Be Mutually Exclusive."

CHAPTER 11

Become an Authentically Magnetic Leader!

My passion for ethical leadership defines me. Ethics were not the bedrock for most of the dealerships I had previously worked for. Dealerships are not subject to rules and regulations; therefore, if desired, they were able to behave irresponsibly without consequences.

Ethical Leadership

One of my big drivers in starting ICE was to establish an elevated standard of ethical behavior. One of my aspirations was to establish a level of ethical accountability that just might encourage competitors to follow suit.

As ICE developed a reputation for ethical behavior, it progressed into real success by being less about profitability and more about relational longevity. All of us to a degree build relationships with our clients. Some turn into lifelong friendships, some are simply project oriented, but most of our staff respects and honors the relationships we are building. They understand how valuable our reputation is—it becomes personal for them. They understand that ethics is always top of mind for us. That's authentic employee engagement!

As Millennials continue to emerge as the majority workforce, this focus on ethics will continue to gain traction. According to the Clutch 2018 Workplace Values survey, 68 percent of respondents felt "maintaining high ethical standards" was very important to them.[67] It is so gratifying to see this growing awareness in the mindset of employees, which should shift corporate America to view integrity as the most critical value for a company.

It's About Others

To become an authentic leader, it's more effective to lead with a focus on others. The most respected and memorable leaders focus on serving others—it is not as much about the leader as it is about those who choose to follow. Leaders remain at an organization for a finite period of time, leaving their remarkable or unremarkable imprint. The focus of an authentic leader needs to be on the development of individuals and encouraging the development of future leaders.

We all have an ego; it's inherent in the human condition. It might be one of the largest contributors to discord and disconnection with others. Egos can build impenetrable walls and prevent the formation of connection, trust, and communication. When you lead with an unhealthy ego, it can create a wedge in relationships. As noted previously, relationships are central to successful human interaction and corporate environments.

The ego can be controlled and redirected with self-awareness, a great coach, mentor, or therapist. The sooner you get your ego out of the way, the better. Remember, your ego is not your amigo!

Attracting Talent

What are the ultimate benefits of being an authentically magnetic leader? While they are numerous, let me start with the incredible talent we attract. In a service industry such as ours, our workforce is our differentiator.

After we began our partnership with Teknion in 2017, we started to attract individuals with extensive industry experience. They started coming to us whether we posted a job position or not, specifically because of our industry reputation.

As employee Jim Lambert stated, "I watched your growth for years, following your industry accomplishments and your brand develop as an ethical company. I knew that one day the opportunity to join ICE would emerge; ICE was exactly the type of company I wanted to work for and be personally associated with. I waited patiently until you finally represented a major furniture manufacturer." I understood the hesitation in joining a furniture dealership not aligned with a major brand because unaligned dealerships can be unstable. Our dealership was strengthened once we aligned with Teknion.

By 2019, we were attracting not just the best local talent but nationwide talent! It was thirteen years in the making, but doing the right thing finally was paying off!

Leadership Skills for Today's Workforce

When I started ICE my "leadership skills" were limited to parenting skills, but I also had well-honed aggressive sales skills. They were all about tenacity, strength, and survival. I learned my skills from the street, and I eventually learned they did not resonate with our young employees.

Millennials respond best to patience, asking a lot of questions, and harmony. They blossom with encouragement and freedom. They want flexible work hours, and they thrive in safe emotional space where they're encouraged to find their own solutions and make their own mistakes.

I learned this through my relationship with Alysse. I had not experienced a leader model these traits, but Alysse exhibited them daily, and others responded positively to them. When I attempted to model and embrace her behaviors, I changed almost organically and naturally, not because I had to, but because her skills were definitely effective. I learned equally from watching her as she learned by watching me. Alysse got results, the staff positively responded to her leadership style, and they bloomed under her guidance.

I was not emotionally attached to my old ways—I was eager to evolve.

> *I was willing to change my ineffective choices when more effective options presented themselves.*

Learning to be a malleable leader is a process that starts with your heart, moves to your head, and then results in healthier behavior. The persona of being an infallible leader who has all the answers does not serve anyone well. For some leaders, being malleable can feel like you are giving up your power, which can result in a perception of being incapable. I believe now, more than ever, leaders need to demonstrate humanitarian leadership. When leaders focus on a more humanitarian approach, they can potentially learn new ways of leading.

The following checklist was presented at the 2018 annual Journey to Conscious Capitalism conference. It offers steps to help become a more conscious leader by propelling you through your comfort zone. Many of these practices I've effectively incorporated as a leader. Not all options will resonate with you, but I encourage you to explore those that may despite your discomfort.

CONSCIOUS LEADERSHIP "PRACTICES" CHECKLIST
Meditate/Quiet Contemplation Time
Personal Development (reading, seminars)
Emotional Healing (therapy, group work)
In Touch with Your Feelings/Emotions
Conscious Breakthroughs in Thinking
Making Intentional/Positive Changes in Your Life
Letting Go of Limiting Beliefs (can't, shouldn't, couldn't)
Dark Side/Shadow Awareness
Know & Live Your Values
Know & Live Your Passions

Know & Live by Your Innate Strengths
Have a Vision for Your Life
Live Your Life with a Known Purpose
Live from an Authentic-Self Mindset
Trust Others
Have a Spiritual Growth Process
Develop a Capacity for Love and Care (self, others)

Based on work by: Kevin Rafferty - The Conscious Leaders Coach

Developing Softer Leadership Skills

How do you develop softer leadership skills? Here are some suggestions:

- Gain awareness of your current skills or lack of skills—be honest with yourself.
- Create a written plan of what you want to change and share it with at least one person.
- Engage the assistance of another person to maintain accountability.
- Be honest with your progress and desire to change.
- Keep a journal of your thoughts, successes, and failures. This will create a lifetime record of your progress.
- Make positive change a habit.
- Surround yourself with like-minded individuals who reinforce your desire to transform yourself.

For example, if you lack empathy, you can make the decision to develop it. Similar to how exercise develops muscles or improves flexibility, you can change yourself into becoming a more empathetic person. In Joel Osteen's book, *Become a Better You*, I was exposed to the idea of generational change; often it takes multiple generations to produce significant and sustainable change. Over a decade ago, I shared this concept with Alysse, neither of us knowing how this lesson would manifest at ICE. Now I understand why it can take decades for real change to happen; it's just another reinforcement for why generational mentorship is so critical.

What Characteristics in a Leader Attract Talent?

I consistently receive positive feedback regarding my optimism. It is a trait anyone can choose to embrace. Offering words of encouragement and seeing the *possibilities* in that half-empty or half-full glass mentality has become my differentiator. At times, however, it was not always easy to maintain.

I believe the number-one talent a leader needs to embrace is optimism because people are naturally attracted to the positive energy that is hope. Lord John Grey's character in the Netflix series *Outlander* describes America as not actually a New World as they called it. "It is as old as the rest of the world, but what makes it new is that it offers hope." That's what optimism does—it offers hope. Optimistic leaders can foster the possibility of unlimited hope. It's what makes them magnetic.

It can be difficult to maintain a positive attitude during stressful times. Being positive is an "other-focused" perspective that doesn't let business or life circumstances cloud your desire to generate enthusiasm and hope in others. When instability hits an organization, leaders can let overwhelming responsibilities such as lost clients or a national crisis deter their ability to project optimism. I learned at a young age to foster an attitude that reflects a mindset of abundance by choosing to see the reality of a situation while still focusing my attention on the possibilities in the situation. I *chose* to see endless possibilities even when I wasn't *experiencing* them in my life.

Finding joy in the most difficult of situations is a choice, and it is what makes some people so memorable, so unusual, so magnetic.

> *Choosing joy is a choice not a circumstance.*

Character is forged in the fires of life. My diaries from years past often remind me of some of my difficult challenges, but I also often noted in them, "This is an opportunity for my character to grow." That was the healthy choice I made, and by making that choice, I inadvertently influenced others who watched me make that choice.

Let me share an example of a time when we all struggled to remain optimistic. Thursday, March 12, 2020 was the most disconcerting day of my career. It was the day I realized we were in a dire situation with the COVID-19 pandemic and we needed to issue decisive statements both internally to our staff and externally to our customers. I've managed ICE through many challenges, including the Great Recession, but since the last pandemic was 1918, I, as well as everyone in America, did not possess expertise to navigate anything as complex as a global pandemic. This was a challenge that profoundly affected every single person in America.

We worked feverishly to craft the most appropriate message. Let me stress the word *we* as our executive leadership team worked together fluidly and intelligently. The generational influence was tangible, seamlessly integrating my thirty-five years of business wisdom with Millennial perspective and technology acumen.

The information was coming at us so quickly we had to rethink the message multiple times to keep it relevant. As the CEO, it was my responsibility to convey the odd sense of calm I was feeling, not because I knew the outcome of COVID-19, but because it was out of our control.

Our first company-wide email went out that day. We shared a news story that explained what COVID-19 was and that experts in infectious disease prevention believed people under fifteen possess antibodies that provide protection against COVID-19 and they thought their immune systems were better able to fight off the virus. Because we have so many employees with young children, I knew their children's well-being had to be a huge concern for them. Our focus was first on our families as we attempted to provide calming and encouraging insight.

The following day, Friday the 13th, I went into the office to ascertain how everyone was feeling about this pandemic. Most were not concerned;

no one was panicking. We held a quick fifteen-minute remote as well as in-person meeting. This meeting conveyed assurance that ICE was closely following this situation, even though we didn't have the answers.

Our optimistic and transparent leadership style and our normal willingness to clearly project that "We don't have all the answers, but together, as a family, we'll get through this" communiqué set the stage for us to seamlessly weather this. We had built such a rock-solid culture of trust and transparency, but never had it seemed so critical as now. More than ever, we needed to embrace our core value of Embrace Workplace Family. This day set the stage for our new definition of success in 2020, which was "zero layoffs." Every decision moving forward took into account this perspective.

Since we had already implemented a work-from-home policy, we were seamlessly set up for house quarantine and extremely grateful that we had embraced this Millennial-centric structure years prior to the outbreak.

Our messaging throughout this time remained consistently positive. Perhaps our most important message was: "Take a lunch break, go for a walk in your neighborhood—working from home every day is going to be an adjustment! It's important to create a routine for yourself."

When business is abundant and easy, weak leadership isn't evident; only during times of crisis are strong and effective leaders evident. Who knew a crisis could shine such a bright light on leadership or lack of leadership? This was an extraordinary opportunity to cultivate leadership skills, fully integrating multi-generational perspectives. Could there be a more challenging incident? Our Millennial leaders were nimble and unswerving through this crisis, especially Alysse, who became even more focused, more tenacious.

As I've said before, tough times bring out the best or the worst in us, making us learn who we truly are, fundamentally—what our core values and personal character are. Throughout this entire crisis, we never lost our focus on conveying a positive message and the worth of each employee. I have no doubt that the positivity we felt and conveyed brought comfort to our team.

Martin Luther King, Jr., one of our country's most courageous and heroic leaders, says it far better than I ever could: "The ultimate measure of a man is not where he stands in moments of comfort and convenience but where he stands at times of challenge and controversy."

Spiritual Beings Having a Human Experience

Think of your behavior at work, your behavior in front of your children, at your place of worship, with your spouse; is it all the same behavior? Or do you shift how you speak, how you think, and how you behave from one situation to the next?

Leadership coaches are popularizing the idea that we need to "show up as our full, authentic selves," but what does this mean? Does it include our spiritual or religious selves? Recently, I was made aware of this thought leadership initiative within the conscious capitalism movement. The conscious leadership checklist noted previously mentions the need to have a spiritual growth process; this is not something I had heard of previously, and I find it intriguing.

In Chapter 7 I described the monthly conscious capitalism mastermind meeting I attend hosted by Ron Hill, retired Chief Enrichment Officer and Founder of Redemption Plus. During one of our first sessions, we broadly addressed the process of engaging spirituality within the workplace and what that meant to each of us. Some members discussed religion's inadvertent and unintentional ability to be exclusive and potentially divisive by seeing people as part of a particular religion or not. Most agreed that spirituality seeks to find commonality; it seeks inclusivity in seeing the likeness of ourselves in others. All saw spirituality as a potential great connector.

The idea of having spiritual or religious conversations at work has not been an acceptable practice, but I question that position. If we're to bring our whole selves to work, how do we leave out one of the most meaningful aspects of our lives? Seeking to find our higher purpose often evolves into finding the meaning of life, which is often at the center of the purpose of religion or spirituality. Leaving our spiritual selves at home is leaving a major part of ourselves out of the office environment, and I feel this does a great disservice to ourselves and others.

In my interview with Ron, he broke down how his firm learned to include spiritual practices at work that were designed to create inclusivity. They designed a voluntary daily meditation practice to help people discover and become more grounded in their spirituality. This often led to natural conversations about spirituality and religion. Many people, including Ron, led this daily practice. Ron advised, "If leaders aren't participating, then it makes others question if the practice is sincere and safe. It's all about making a safe container that fosters experiences that draw people closer in community and allows people to share who they truly are. The question isn't 'Are we human beings having a spiritual experience?' but 'Are we spiritual beings having a human experience?' That is the question we should be asking ourselves." This meditation practice emerged as a great connector for his employees because it was genuine.

Most importantly, we need to set an example for our children. Who and what do you want them to model? If your behavior is contradictory, do you not think your children will see this disingenuousness?

The concept of Spiritual Intelligence was surprisingly often discussed during Conscious Capitalism Inc. mastermind and Senior Leader Network meetings. I became aware of this effort because of our conversations, but I believe this emerging leadership initiative is gaining momentum because of employees' increased awareness. Since it is now the conscious employer's responsibility to model positive behavior, encourage introspection, and expand their employees' perspectives, will that now begin to include the development of their spiritual lives? If knowledge is the greatest gift we'll ever give to our children, and conscious leaders are striving to view everyone equally and as family, shouldn't leaders extend the pursuit of inclusive, respectful spiritual expression to their employees? Helping my son achieve the best education possible motivated me to start my company, and helping my coworkers reach their potential as fully evolved and happy human beings continues to motivate me. Why have I not encouraged spiritual growth within my coworkers? And why are so many leaders, including myself, fearful of spiritual conversations?

> *Courageous leaders don't avoid courageous conversations—*
> *they embolden them!*

Leadership is a 24/7 Job

Being a leader isn't just about leading during business hours. Real leadership affects the people you lead in every aspect of their lives. If you're not affecting that kind of real change, you're thinking and acting small.

Social media makes our lives highly visible. If you're making poor choices in your personal life and that is captured in a post, it is likely to impair how you're viewed as a leader. People want leaders who inspire and motivate them, who are positive influencers who affect positive behavior in others. No longer is there a separation between a business leader and their personal life. Here is where authenticity comes into play even more.

Let me share this example: Tom and I attended a church in Solana Beach for ten years. While we were members, we participated in a weekly small group meeting. As people moved or left the church, our group would change, so in the time we were members, we connected with more than fifty unique individuals through our weekly fellowship meeting. We were highly influenced by these individuals, both personally and in business, and our investment of time in this group positively and fundamentally changed every aspect of our lives, especially our responsibility to the planet and future generations. It also strengthened our marriage and reinforced the value of individual integrity.

The church concentrated on missional work, so we learned about the challenges of many in our community to include our Hispanic population, especially high school students focused on becoming first-generation college students through Reality Changers and Casa de Amistad. We learned about and soon invested monthly in Compassion in Action, a global non-profit with a mission to advance education for children living in poverty. It also has significantly reduced human trafficking.

Several years ago, we decided to expose our staff to the missional work of our church by allowing each employee to choose one of the many charities our church supports. We created a Christmas tree ornament representing each charity and their mission. Employees then selected an ornament that touched their hearts and we made a donation in their name. As leaders, we demonstrated to the staff our commitment to make a difference in the global community.

One of my commercial real estate broker friends started a non-profit to collect blankets and towels for the homeless in San Diego. This effort really tugged at my heart strings so I encouraged staff to participate. We displayed these generous gifts under our ICE "Giving Tree."

As my awareness grew, I realized I had to change how I give in every aspect of my life, leading to the Plant with Purpose partnership. ICE purchased one hundred trees to be planted in eight countries. Plant with Purpose is working to reverse deforestation in the world and has planted more than *28 million trees*. What a powerful mission, and what a gift to support this life-affirming organization that ultimately helps us all.

Leadership is a journey, not a destination. My point is: What my husband and I do in our personal lives spills over into every area of our lives. We are trying to make a difference. None of this goes unnoticed because someone is always watching us.

CHAPTER 12

Fostering Community

Nothing connects facts and statistics better than a personal narrative. Dan Ryan's paradigm shift in constructing a world-class gathering place designed to connect human networks that foster community, creativity, and output is more than a good story; it's a *great* story!

A Great Story

Dan has been the San Diego Senior Vice President of Alexandria Real Estate Equities, Inc. (ARE) since 2010. ARE is an urban office Real Estate Investment Trust started in 1994 in a basement in Pasadena, California. It was the first real estate organization to focus solely on the life science industry. From inception, ARE was driven to a higher calling, as defined in its mission statement:

> *To create clusters that ignite and accelerate the world's leading innovators in their noble pursuit to advance human health by curing disease and improving nutrition—*
> *THAT'S WHAT'S IN OUR DNA*™

The company was named after Alexandria, Egypt, the scientific capital of the ancient world, renowned for its noble pursuit of scientific advancement and revolutionary discoveries. From that humble basement, ARE has exploded into an investment-grade-rated S&P 500 REIT (real estate investment trust) with a 2019 market cap of $22.2 billion. It owns more than 34 million square feet of lab and office space across more than 250 buildings in seven US innovation clusters, including San Diego.

When I reached out to Dan to request an interview, it was on a hunch that his business philosophies were in alignment with both the tenets of conscious capitalism and ICE. Dan is responsible for all San Diego corporate development strategies; he establishes the vision and then provides "lots of room to execute the vision." I've gotten to know Dan from a professional distance. Many of my impressions were simply intuitive, but our lunch meeting confirmed all of my intuition!

When Dan joined ARE, it represented 1.3 million square feet of real estate in the San Diego region. As of August 2020, it owns 6.2 million square feet of commercial real estate with 4 million in the pipeline to develop.

I first became aware of ARE in 2013 when I toured The Alexandria in the Torrey Pines area of San Diego, a building they had recently renovated. As I walked the property, I was shocked at how much open space there was and how little leasable laboratory or office space the property offered—a contrast to every commercial real estate project I'd ever seen. I wondered why they had developed this property almost exclusively as an amenity property, which is an area dedicated to socialization such as dining, exercising, hosting community events, etc. and as Dan calls it "a respite to allow neurons to trigger, increase creativity, and visualize new possibilities." Such a property had never been developed in San Diego before. I suspected the idea was a gamble that would not pencil out financially.

Dan confirmed my initial impression: "It offered a high risk for failure. How do you make the revenue work? Every real estate transaction must maximize revenue. The Alexandria wasn't just a concept, it was a new business plan, a strategy that I formulated, and I had to work very hard to sell the potential for profitability to ARE executive management—a concept that hadn't been tried in the life sector industry prior to The Alexandria project." Dan presented the concept of The Alexandria as a new opportunity to nurture the local biotech ecosystem and "cultivate a playful spirit, encourage discovery and inspire collaboration."[68]

To Dan's advantage, Alexandria has a storied history of being the first. The founders were inspired with a vision to create a real estate company focused solely on providing laboratory and office space for the life science industry. Initial investors were highly skeptical; they felt it could not be profitable because of the high costs to build out laboratory spaces, extremely high barriers to entry for other developers, high barriers to exit for tenants, and dramatically limited Class A space availability. Investors were concerned with the dangerous risk of working with potentially unsafe or explosive chemical and biological materials. Leveraging their collective biotech and real estate experience, ARE proceeded to create and develop this niche market, despite investors' initial rejection.

Ironically, despite aforementioned concerns, they have become the most *in-demand real estate product today*. They have also become the most stable real estate investment throughout the COVID-19 crisis!

Creating this niche was just the company's first big idea. ARE was also instrumental in developing the "urban innovation cluster" concept in the early 2000s, which refocused individual asset development to a cluster campus strategy as a means to create and leverage interconnected business ecosystems and world-class academic institutions.

Developing Business Ecosystems

In Chapter 10, I detailed how *The Rainforest: The Secret to Building the Next Silicon Valley* was such an influential book in my life because it reinforced my belief in the importance of highly connected deal-makers called keystones. This book also redefined how business ecosystems are similar to rainforests in how they are dependent on other life forces. Startup companies can grow and economies can thrive when they nurture each other's growth. The authors, Victor Hwang and Greg Horowitt, argue that business rainforests thrive when certain cultural behaviors are enabled, unlocking enormous human potential that builds collaboration and "tribes of trust." Their theory of "the rainforest" was influenced amid breakthrough ideas in academia, insights on sociobiology from Harvard, economic transactions from the University of Chicago, design theory from Stanford, and new research in neuroscience and social network theory. Rainforests grow "wildly and abundantly, what might resemble a weed could be in actuality a new species. Rainforests are environments that encourage disconnected people to self-organize into greater forms of biological life, human ecosystems."[69]

Rainforests further the value of innovation clusters defined by Hwang and Horowitt as "a region of individuals or companies working together to lower transaction costs by working together. Trust and increased communication improve effectiveness. Rainforests are built from the bottom up, where irrational behavior reigns. We must retain the underlying human interactions that enable the development of clusters."[70]

Greg noted how clusters of innovation develop when you have an abundance of resources and cooperation between business, local government, and world-class educational facilities. All stakeholders need to connect in cultivating an innovation ecology—entrepreneurs, scientists, investors, research institutions, real estate developers, government representatives—*all* need to be committed to being part of this ecosystem. As students graduate from local universities, they tend to provide a steady stream of future talent; however, retaining talent remains one of the biggest challenges across all industries.

San Diego has effectively linked diverse industries through social networks such as CONNECT, Springboard, Athena, San Diego Economic Development Corporation, San Diego Venture Group, Urban Land Institute, NAIOP, and Biocom—all of these organizations were designed to connect individuals with diverse talent and skills and to *create community*. These associations break social barriers, allowing trust to develop so collaboration can be more free flowing. San Diego is often called "the biggest small town in America" because we are such a tight community—which is largely due to these highly engaged and connected organizations.

These "keystone" connections are precisely what ARE and Dan had envisioned. The Alexandria became the much-needed and world-class infrastructure featuring creative amenities that enabled people in the life sciences sector to connect in a social setting. This thereby *encouraged creativity to flourish*. ARE didn't just want to build a meeting place but an experience that created industry engagement, resulting in scientific and technological breakthroughs for the benefit of humankind.

ARE has had tremendous success in creating and improving clusters of innovation due to the scale of their properties. Dan noted the escalating increase in life science REITs in recent years as a good thing: "I'm happy others are replicating our model for success because it improves the ecosystem for everyone. To date, no one has been able to outscale our deliveries, but if they did, I'd welcome that." Whenever I've seen this "abundance mindset," I'm always surprised because it tends to be rare in leaders driven by a competitive spirit. It is truly an admirable trait—one we should all aspire to—because it is focused on the greater good, not individual success. When the entire region succeeds, everyone succeeds. Dan lives the values of "a rising tide lifts all boats."

It Was a Long Journey

Initially, San Diego did not offer an ideal climate for a biotech cluster to thrive due to an absence of political access to state and federal government and an absence of partnering resources between business, academia, and government. The San Diego biotech cluster has taken forty years to develop, but the groundwork needed to cultivate this innovation ecosystem was laid when the University of California San Diego (UCSD) campus was built in the 1950s, a collaboration between business and local government. It was built in the Torrey Pines Mesa area, the same area where The Alexandria is located. As UCSD expanded its biology and scientific departments, it began to emerge as an academic scientific leader, providing the foundation required for a cluster to emerge and an attractive draw to scientists and engineers outside of San Diego.[71]

Hybritech, started in 1978 and considered the first successful San Diego biotech firm, was sold to Eli Lilly in 1986. This emerged as the San Diego pattern—when small to mid-sized biotechs were acquired by large firms, they left the community. To truly become a cluster, the area had to attract and retain large scale companies, spreading deep roots in the community. However, as these companies left, they also left behind the talent that made them attractive to investors. These experienced biotechnology executives had no desire to leave the beauty and tight collegial spirit of San Diego.

The Voice of San Diego, an online news publication, noted in 2008 that due to the financial success of Hybritech and academic achievement of UCSD, San Diego had become the third largest life science cluster in the world; however, the proliferation of world-class research institutes along the Torrey Pines Mesa remained stubbornly minimal. San Diego continued to lack inspirational physical space, laboratories, and offices that would enable further collaboration.

> "Some in the industry are growing increasingly worried about the ability of San Diego to remain a viable biotech stronghold if the area can't provide the infrastructure needed once research leaves the university laboratories and is ready to be commercialized. Lucrative companies could decide to move or open spin-offs elsewhere, they say, in one of the many regions worldwide vying for their own biotech cluster."[72]

That's why the emergence of ARE in 2010 became the differentiating factor for San Diego; it built campuses not for quick profit but as a long-term investment strategy. ARE is a company that always thinks long-term; nothing is for quick profit.

The Built Environment Builds Community

ARE and ICE share the same belief regarding the critical nature of the built environment in creating physical spaces that foster safe emotional spaces. Physical environments can and should be designed to generate highly cooperative engagement that fosters a spirit of play, which often leads to innovative productivity. Kilroy Realty is another developer transforming the built environment of San Diego by fostering ecosystems of innovation. Kilroy's One Paseo project is considered by many to be the crown jewel of all of San Diego's mixed-use properties because it includes retail, restaurants, commercial offices, residential facilities and also plenty of outdoor open space with a community park; everything about One Paseo is designed to build community!

Alexandria, Kilroy Realty, and emerging life science real estate developer IQHQ are just some of the many San Diego developers working hard to build physical spaces that create community and connection. In the last ten years, San Diego has seen an extraordinary 82 percent increase in life science employees. The demand for Class A office and lab space that offers work-live-play campuses continues to evolve.

The Art of Placemaking and Making Purpose Tangible

Furniture is a critical piece in placemaking. The quality of construction and materials used, interior and landscape design, and the building's architectural features are all part of the furniture design inextricably linked to generating a memorable experience.

Prior to my meeting with Dan, I had not linked what we do as an organization to how ICE has created such a positive influence within the built environment. I hadn't realized the impact we made as an organization to our intricate local ecosystem in creating placemaking or how it blended so seamlessly with our purpose: *Creating Space to Transcend the Ordinary.*

I shared this realization and appreciation for our work with our team during a staff meeting. As I explained our part in developing this framework for San Diego to develop into an aspiring ecosystem of innovation, their sense of pride was visible, with comments such as "My work contributes to making an impact in the development of our business community? Wow, that brings tears to my eyes!", "We are helping build a more desirable city for the relocation of organizations?" and "I had no idea how much we contribute to making workplaces that attract and retain talent."

As I mentioned in Chapter 7 on higher purpose, it is becoming the CEO's responsibility to identify and provide a sense of purpose for their team. The genuine positive impact to our team, especially during such a stressful year, was definitely welcomed by all!

Values of Conscious Capitalism

During my meeting with Dan, my belief was confirmed that ARE is a conscious business enterprise, though it does not define itself as such. NAIOP, the commercial real estate development association that provides advocacy, education, and business opportunities in the commercial real estate development and investment industries, named ARE the NAIOP Developer of the Year in 2019 for the following reasons:[73]

- They were one of the first developers in the world to focus on environmental issues and "green" development, incorporating performance criteria for certified sustainable design and construction.

- ARE's portfolio includes more than sixty-five projects that are pursuing or have achieved LEED (environmental) sustainable certification.

- ARE's philanthropic activities focus on contributing to local organizations that enrich the communities in which ARE operates.

- They promote STEM education that cultivates the next generation of leaders and thinkers.

- Much of their philanthropic efforts provide support to our military and their families; they care about the health and safety of the brave individuals who defend our nation. They built and donated The Honor Foundation headquarters in San Diego, an organization that supports the transition for Navy SEALs into civilian life.

- Other philanthropic and volunteer programs include Operation CARE, Project Angel Food, CS4ALL, and the Navy SEAL Foundation.
- They provide early-stage companies with everything they need to be successful, including move-in-ready office and lab space, support resources, shared equipment, and creative amenities. ARE provides access to capital through the Alexandria Seed Capital platform.
- Capital investment and activity are integral components of their business strategy, providing strategic insights and extensive knowledge of cutting-edge science that strengthen keystone relationships within the life science community.
- Their success in placemaking draws the most engaged and exceptional tenant base, benefiting regional life science real estate competitors and the ecosystem as a whole.

From its inception, ARE established its sense of purpose—a commitment to being part of and building community—and a desire to elevate humanity through capitalism. This is a key definition of a conscious capitalist! Though they might not use the conscious capitalist term, their behavior exemplifies the tenets of conscious capitalism.

And what have been some of the financial rewards? They have close to a 0 percent vacancy rate. They have a full pipeline of work—about eight million square feet—of mostly pre-leased space extending out for two years!

They genuinely value all stakeholders: tenants, stockholders, employees, the local life science ecosystem, and their global and local communities. The values of ARE and ICE are in complete alignment. ARE is a large corporation unconsciously living the values of conscious capitalism. ICE is a small business that is thriving because we now consciously live into these values. Regardless of an organization's scale, all can employ these concepts with tremendous success.

"Doing well and doing good need not and should not be mutually exclusive." Many organizations do not understand the enormous success that can be achieved when organizations and communities are in alignment—Alexandria Real Estate does.

CHAPTER 13

Begin with the End in Mind: Succession Planning

ICE began as a scrappy startup with a focus more on survival than long-term vision—I suspect this describes most startups. But what if an organization started with equal parts inspiration and survival? That question led to a series of questions.

- What if a startup implemented long-term foresight that infused the company with purpose and a more enduring vision?
- What if the lessons and values we learned at ICE over fifteen years were always conscious efforts?
- Just as mentoring condenses the cycle to achieve more in your career, wouldn't intentional leadership also have the ability to positively impact an organization's profitability and stability?

For at least ten years, I planted seeds of entrepreneurship in Alysse. I didn't realize it initially, but seven years ago, I started to water and fertilize those seeds. Five years ago, we started conversations about the transition of ownership. It was a completely organic process, but what if it were more intentional, and as I noted in Chapter 2, what if we incorporated Stephen Covey's principle to "begin with the end in mind"?

How would a company develop if it was designed from the beginning with the end in mind? What if current ownership not only focused on present-day circumstances but also was keenly concerned with legacy and future ownership? What would you do differently if your values and corporate foundation had a more eternal perspective—not as focused on simply profit? To explore this, let's start at the beginning.

In the Beginning

ICE has continually evolved through the informal partnership I forged early on with Alysse. Her structural organizational skills and ability to adopt changing technology complemented my creative branding style and vision and my twenty years of furniture industry knowledge. We were able to work in concert because we offered skill sets that perfectly complemented each other. Of course, we've had uncomfortable interactions throughout the years, but we've always had mutual respect. We've established healthy boundaries that allowed for honest communication.

Alysse and I have become very close over the years, so close that Tom and I call her our "workplace daughter." I leaned heavily on my parenting skill set to lead everyone at ICE, but especially to mentor Alysse because she was there from the beginning while I was still understanding the intricacies of entrepreneurship. She has been more loyal than anyone in my business life, yet I've always maintained a professional and personal distance. It can be difficult to establish and maintain boundaries while simultaneously encouraging unfettered feedback. It requires a tremendous amount of trust and respect, which is earned over time, so starting this process early and consciously is an enormous advantage.

At ICE, we work very closely with our CPA, Thor Eakes, and we all value him as one of our most trusted advisors. I originally met Thor in my Vistage group in 2013, many years before he became our CPA. I got to know Thor well during our monthly meetings, and I always admired his integrity and level-headed approach to leadership. He has mentioned several times to me that most of his clients have not developed a succession plan, nor are they engaging mentorship or succession training. He was eager to learn how we intuitively designed our succession plan in order to share this knowledge with his clients. Thor has worked with hundreds of entrepreneurs over the years as their CPA, learning their most pressing and intimate concerns. He sent me this note, which offered a perspective I had not identified.

"I've found that most of my clients who are small business owners weren't necessarily entrepreneurs but usually they were individuals who had a specific technical expertise. In other words, people who were good at their job. At some point in their life, these people got the itch to start a company and be their own boss. Unfortunately, technical expertise does not necessitate entrepreneurial expertise. They were generally unprepared to become entrepreneurs. Over time, small business owners acquire ideas and tips that help them become somewhat of an entrepreneur. Their success in learning to become an entrepreneur will dictate the success of their business. This is where I see the owner creating his 'ceiling' for growth and success.

I love the concept of beginning with the end in mind. Many owners who desire better outcomes—such as higher growth, better work life balance, or a successful exit—fall short because they do not have a process in place for creating future leaders for their Company. They especially do not think of developing future leaders that can take over some of the entrepreneurial duties of the Company, scale their business, or mentor toward succession.

You were lucky to find Alysse. The two of you met at the same time when you were a willing teacher and she was a willing student. This is rare in business, even today, when we're all reading leadership books, attending training sessions, and working hard to become more informed and sentient entrepreneurs. Fortunately, Alysse was eager to learn and put in the time necessary to become a leader of your Company. Most people are not willing to invest that kind of time and sacrifice in order to make it."

Thor

Thor J. Eakes, CPA

EAKES & COMPANY

Thor really knows our company, and he's heard in detail the challenges we've experienced. It's gratifying to share your journey with peers and advisors who know how hard it was and how far you've come. Alysse and I were indeed lucky to find each other, but it was far more than luck that cultivated our relationship. I'm certainly not the only one who has influenced Alysse. Early on, she understood the value in modeling my behavior of community engagement in the San Diego real estate, construction, interior design, and architectural networks, and she also made the decision to actively seek the guidance of prominent industry leaders. Alysse had a mindset that could be molded—she wanted to change, to reach her untapped potential.

Although informal mentoring can be impactful, it is not as effective as formal mentorship. Had our mentorship been more systematic and I had been more mindful of seeing her potential, we may have achieved more in a shorter time frame. In hindsight, it could have been more effective to establish a formal plan that included short-term and long-term goals and a strategic career plan that included succession planning.

She clearly had the motivation to be an entrepreneur and has worked ceaselessly to earn the opportunity to take over ICE's reins. She not only saw ICE's potential, but she visualized herself as the company's future. She had a clear vision of the future and her role in it. What if I had been more involved in shaping this long-term prophecy? I would encourage leaders and business owners to start with this end in mind.

I love this question: "If I could do it over, what would I change?" I would thoughtfully hire, mentor, and inspire a successor to acquire my business—what I did informally I would execute formally.

You Can't Always Accomplish Your Goals Within One Lifetime

I've previously referenced Joel Osteen's *Become a Better You: 7 Keys to Improving Your Life Every Day*. I read this book in 2005 before I started ICE and prior to working with Alysse. I recalled Osteen mentioning the concept "Nothing truly great can ever be accomplished in just one lifetime." Let me share from Chapter 5 "Generational Blessing" of his book:

> "We need to understand that the generations are connected. You are sowing seeds for future generations. Whether you realize it or not, everything you do counts. Every time you persevere, every time you are faithful, every time you serve others, you are making a difference; you're storing up equity in your 'generational account.' You've got to learn to think more generationally.
>
> Any time you see somebody who's successful or has accomplished something great, you can be sure they didn't do it all by themselves.
>
> My grandmother never really enjoyed the blessings and the favor that her descendants did. Had she not been willing to pay the price, my father may never have escaped poverty, and I might not be enjoying the season of usefulness that I am experiencing today. These days, Victoria and I tend to get a lot of credit for the successful lives we are leading, but we have learned to look back and give credit to whom credit is due: our forefathers and foremothers.
>
> Remember, every lap we run is one less lap for those who come after us. You're making it easier on your children,

and on your grandchildren. Your dreams may not come to pass exactly as you would hope, but the seeds you sow may be harvested by your sons and your daughters."

These sentiments confirmed my long-held belief on the profound significance of generational influence.

Don and Jim Clifton

Another great example of generational impact can be found with Don Clifton and his son Jim. Don developed the CliftonStrengths program, which earned him a presidential commendation for his lifetime achievement as "the father of strengths-based psychology." He was an influencer and thought leader sixty years before the terms existed, and he is best remembered for his ability to bring out the best in people and in organizations.

His son Jim has continued his father's legacy as the CEO Chairman of the global analytics firm Gallup and is a best-selling author of several leadership books. Jim recalls this about his father:

> "As a child, I remember Dad had an interesting angle on everything: He would see someone selling rocks and say, 'Let's go see what is on this guy's mind.' I would say, 'He's just selling rocks,' but Dad was interested in the individual.
>
> He was always doing experiments with groups. Fifty-five years ago, he was working with mentors and poor people. He was ahead of his time. He would start a group with high school kids, dead-enders, high achievers, and others, then put us into those groups. I thought everybody was doing that. I had no idea that I was one of his lab rats!
>
> Dad spent his whole life figuring out people's strengths. He taught his entire life. He said weaknesses never really develop, and strengths develop your whole life. Yet most

institutions have us trying to fix our weaknesses. That is why humankind is not developing as fast as it should."[74]

In 1988, Don Clifton's firm purchased Gallup Inc., a firm founded in 1935 by George Gallup; Jim took over the management and transformed this US-based company into a worldwide organization with forty offices in thirty countries. Jim's most recent innovation is the Gallup World Poll, which polls over seven billion citizens globally in 160 countries. Jim's life confirms Joel's premise that the most significant impact might require generations of influence.

In a 2019 interview with *Authority Magazine*, Jim Clifton discussed this transformation:[75]

> "Our big breakthrough—one of Gallup's biggest ever—is that what the whole world wants is a good job. Our World Poll discovered the great global dream! People all over the world want a good job with mission, purpose— and one that they're really good at—with a living wage. This finding gets you pretty close to the meaning of life in the new millennium.
>
> Millennials are now the largest generation in the workforce. Build a culture for them where purpose trumps paycheck. They need meaning in their job that baby boomers like me didn't. This is a good thing. Great leaders have a higher purpose than just profit. Increasing profit should be assumed, but it is not the mission.
>
> Today's employees don't really want free lunch, toys in the office, volleyball courts or Bring Your Pet to Work Day. What they really want is career development. They want the same thing their team leader wants from them— they want to improve. They want someone to take a real interest in their development.

Maximizing an individual's potential begins with knowing their strengths and building their work and careers around those strengths. Organizations need to make a plan to develop the strengths versus fixing the weaknesses of every employee."

In addition to having a great mentor in his father, Jim discusses in the interview how he was "super-mentored" by Alec Gallup. Alec was twenty-three years older than Jim, and also the son of an extraordinarily accomplished man, George Gallup, the founder of Gallup Inc. This is what Jim had to say about Alec:

"Alec was born with a very high IQ and tested at genius level since he was a little boy. He convinced me that I needed a deeper understanding of world history and global politics to do my job better at Gallup. He also convinced me I needed to greatly improve my writing.

It was easy for me to believe he was right because *I knew he loved me and deeply cared about my development.* He went on to spend literally hundreds of hours educating me in world history, writing and, of course, everything imaginable about US and world polling. It was highly individualized development that money can't buy.

It changed my life."

Words like "I knew he loved me and deeply cared about my development" and "It changed my life"—these are words said about someone who took a parental-like interest in shaping the heart and mind of a young person. Alec no doubt embraced this "begin with the end in mind" philosophy, with the desire to create generational change in an organization started by Alec's father. Jim wasn't Alec's child, but he certainly mentored him as if the generational legacy of two generations of the Gallup family was on the line.

Here are some more nuggets from this article regarding Jim's viewpoint of leadership:

> "My teams and I are working on ways to establish cultures that create organic growth for organizations. American organizations aren't as entrepreneurial as they were 20 years ago, and Millennials aren't starting enough new businesses. This is causing economic dynamism to slow and driving growing disparity in income. The best jobs with a living wage rise up out of growing startups and existing companies that have real organic growth instead of growth through acquisitions.
>
> The practice of management has not evolved with the changing workplace. Gallup has discovered that a staggering 70% of the variation between great workplace engagement and lousy workplace engagement can be explained just by the quality of the manager or team leader. Leaders everywhere in the world have a tendency to name the wrong person manager and then train them on administrative things—not on how to maximize human potential!
>
> Change your management and leadership culture from being bosses to being coaches!"

Jim confirms the principles we naturally embrace at ICE—lead as if you're a performance and life skills coach and a parent! He understands that how we lead Millennials is wholly different from how we were taught to lead as Boomers.

> "Lousy managers create miserable employees who create negative business outcomes. Miserable employees ruin customer relationships. They have significantly worse health. Their miserable life at work goes home with them

and is the single biggest contributor to overall low life satisfaction and all the other things that go wrong.

Maybe the biggest change is for Millennials. Their work really is their life and their identity. The workplace is their society. In many cases, the workplace has become their family and community.

My leadership style is *high purpose or nothing at all.*"

Jim Clifton is a truly gifted leader, a man whose perspective was shaped over time through intentional mentorship. What can a leader with this kind of influence produce? When asked, "If you could inspire a movement that would bring the most amount of good to the most amount of people, what would that be?" Jim responded:

"I would fix income inequality.

The movement would be directed at increasing the number of quality startups and organic growth in existing organizations. Everyone in the whole world would know their God-given strengths and then tie them to building something—building anything: a company, a nonprofit, a new business startup, a new division within an organization. Build anything that creates any kind of 'customer.' Build a new church, an extraordinary child development center, a charter school, or build the next Apple or Amazon. Maybe the greatest of all—build a great family!

That is the meaning of life. We build as much as we can, and then we die. The name of the movement would be, 'Shut up and build.'

That would change the course of humankind by reversing economic decline, which would reverse income disparity as well as the most important reversal of all— disparities in hopes and dreams for a great life on earth."

Shane Jackson, President of Jackson Healthcare, is also a second-generation business owner. His father, Richard Jackson, started from very humble beginnings with a limited education, but he always desired to become an entrepreneur. He attended business night school to learn business skills. Richard was so affected by one of his professors, Bill Franklin, that he convinced him to leave his teaching job and join his company as a consultant! Bill is still as engaged with the company, and he continues to meet monthly with Shane, continuing the mentorship started with Richard decades ago. Shane noted that Bill has a very special place in his heart; his respect for Bill continues to grow. Shane's father long ago noted that "Bill doesn't always have the best answers but he sure has the best questions!" which reinforces Tiffany English's belief that it's the questions asked that lead to the development of future thinking leaders.

We may or may not have biological children, but all of us have an opportunity to show up in every area of our lives with deep and sincere caring, to treat our employees and coworkers as if they were family, and to demonstrate a mindset that embraces this concept of generational impact. That is a choice we can consciously make, and there are impressive business reasons to do so.

The Future of Business Belongs to the Talent War's Winner

What if your well-known future governance vision encompassed a trail-blazing leader whose values were in alignment with the majority of the talent you wanted to hire? Would this clear-eyed focus on the future attract potential employees? It has for ICE. As our company matures, our solid brand built on a foundation of leadership integrity is well-positioned for continued success based on our 2021 succession plan. It is as much an internal employee motivator as it is a magnet to attract the most accomplished talent.

One reason to record our history was to detail this visualization of our future by documenting who we were, who we are today, and what we've always stood for. How do you know where you're going if you don't know where you've been? How do you encourage buy-in and attract like-minded talent? In the battle to attract talent, sharing this vision, cementing this brand, and knowing that leadership was *developed* to strengthen our goals is a very potent cocktail.

I recently shared our story of Millennial engagement, training, mentorship, and advancement with Lee Wills. You might recall I mentioned Lee in Chapter 9; she was the Head of Talent and Acquisition for Sony in San Diego. She is intimately aware of the importance of developing and increasing employee engagement among Millennials. Lee was surprised by our success in retaining employees within this age group. Our retention average is five years while the average length of employment for Millennials is eighteen months. Lee noted that ICE is doing something right because in an age when it's hard to attract and retain talented workers, ICE is winning the talent war.

Why Begin with the End in Mind?

Thinking about your succession plan early can enormously benefit the organization in nuanced ways. A succession plan is not limited to just finding a successor; it benefits the company as a whole. Here are some examples:

1. **Brand:** If the redefinition of the purpose of business is to elevate humanity, it's necessary to build a corporation that reinforces a long-term, purpose-driven brand.

2. **People:** Succession planning solidifies your reputation as an organization that values people. This includes honoring their quality of life, mental health, work-life balance, and individual growth.

3. **Upward Mobility:** When you promote from within, you send a clear message that you honor and recognize your team members' efforts.

4. **Stability:** You establish a reputation of stability both internally and externally with a visible commitment to continuity in management, workplace culture, client relationships, and with vendor and manufacturer partners.

5. **Exit Strategy:** Beginning your succession plan as soon as practical ensures a seamless transition for your organization.
6. **Legacy:** For conscious leaders, the concept and value of a corporate legacy is integral in the development of next-generation leadership and ownership.
7. **Mentorship:** Mentoring tomorrow's leaders can potentially create the basis for a fulfilling life.
8. **Talent Magnet:** A culture known for mentoring can attract capable talent that is eager to learn.
9. **Culture:** Employing softer leadership skills and establishing a culture of mentorship can increase engagement and loyalty.

How to Identify Your Successor

When looking for a successor to your business, first select an individual who has a passion for your industry and is in alignment with your vision for the company. If you adhere to the principles of conscious capitalism, this would include how you value all stakeholders and the community, and it would reflect ethical leadership.

You might identify this person through previous employment, volunteer engagements, or through personal referral. You get to know a person's character, how they handle stress and crisis, when you work closely together, and this process can take years. It should be a natural and organic process. You want someone who inspires *you* to be more than you think you can be. Adopting an attitude of a lifetime learner should be shared by both participants—*both* need to share this inquisitive mindset. A great successor will want to take the business to levels you might not have visualized.

Alysse and I have changed quite a bit over the fourteen years we've worked together. Who we are today is not who we were—we've both matured and changed in very positive ways. It took years for us to appreciate each other's talents and perspectives and adopting the attitude that "we are all works in progress" smoothed out this process. It's best to avoid a potential successor who has a self-limiting perspective. Many people do not have the "gift of possibilities"; they see life in a narrow framework. They see themselves as they are today and believe it is the only way they'll ever be. If someone has bad habits or constricted thinking and does not desire to do the work needed to grow and learn new habits, that's not an ideal successor.

Let me provide an example of how the right successor handles crisis. Three months into navigating the new COVID-19 world, Alysse and I discussed selling ICE to her and when this transition would occur. We had discussed succession planning over a course of five years with a target 2020 or 2021 date.

Our sales were down considerably, so Alysse needed to focus on sales strategies, crafting Request for Proposal (RFP) responses, the discovery and integration of virtual sales tools, and cultivating new project opportunities. She had to completely relearn how to be a successful sales expert in the COVID-19 era, and then she had to coach her sales team to understand and embrace her techniques. Her ability to adapt quickly and her high comfort level with technology allowed her to manage effectively through this crisis. She also made enormous efforts to broaden her understanding of the crisis and understand the leadership skills she needed to adopt, so she consulted with industry peers and mentors and read leadership books.

All her efforts resulted in her gaining a higher level of appreciation of our employees' value and that "together, as a strong team, we can overcome any obstacle." Her behavior reinforced our workplace family value and, ultimately, led to a successful, albeit stressful navigation through 2020.

When I asked whether she still wanted to move forward with the purchase, I anticipated she would be hesitant. I believed the pandemic would illustrate how treacherous business can be. She completely surprised me when she said, "It feels like my entire life I've been preparing to lead through crisis, to be a calming presence, a solid foundation when everything around us feels like it's crumbling. I know this crisis is preparing me to be a better leader, a humbler and more compassionate leader. I do not fear this; I'm not intimidated by it. I'm embracing and learning from it."

> *That's the mindset you want to see in your successor—*
> *one of quiet, relaxed confidence.*

This was not at all a false, ego-centric bravado. This was wisdom grounded in experience, research, and truth, a personality that sought-out advice and actually took it! Wisdom that I believe was *fostered* by intentional, consistent mentorship provided by several mentors in every area of her life.

Summary of Steps and Characteristics

If I had to do it over again, I would be more mindful of this process and start with these steps:

1. Seeking and hiring a successor or multiple successors to mentor is a long-term process. That's why it should be started 5-10 years before you want to initiate it. "Begin with the end in mind." It is best to verify the potential of your replacement before advising them of your intentions. If you change your mind after suggesting this option, your successor is likely to leave your company. If they were valuable enough to become a successor, this loss is something you want to avoid. Take your time working together.

2. Create a written plan for yourself that has specific benchmarks and accomplishments you want your successor to achieve. Work with a trusted business consultant or coach to vet your observations. It's important you scrutinize your evaluations thoroughly—again, it could take years.

3. When your intuition tells you it's the right time to share your blueprint for succession with your mentee, co-create next-step strategies. Having a professional coach assist in this process is invaluable! We hired many professional consultants along the way.

4. It's your and your successor's foundational values that must be in alignment, not your personality styles, religion, political beliefs, or family upbringing. Shared ethical, foundational values are non-negotiable.

5. This relationship is very much like raising a child. It's important to establish respect and set expectations. You should anticipate push back, which is why establishing and enforcing boundaries and procedures is so important. There is a difference between deep questioning to gain understanding and being disrespectful. Your relationship with your mentee establishes boundaries for all employees.

6. A mentor's greatest contribution is their wisdom. A mentee needs to be appreciative of your time and the gift of mentorship. They need to show up for all meetings on time, and be prepared and organized. They need to take responsibility for their actions or inactions, and be able to take advice with a receptive mind. Feelings of resentment and a lack of accountability are not acceptable responses.

7. If they lack integrity, know you might not be able to teach this.

8. Just as the mentee needs to be respectful of you and your boundaries, the same goes for the mentor. The mentor should model the highest degree of maturity and integrity possible, setting the bar high and establishing what excellence looks like.

9. There will be times when you don't get along; no one behaves appropriately all the time. Being your authentic self and having honest conversations about this is critical. It comes back to mutual respect. If your mentee is defensive, you might want to evaluate your role in this response.

10. Learn to control your emotions; wait until things calm down before addressing conflict. Journal your thoughts and share them with a trusted advisor when contentious issues arise. Seek to be a peacemaker.

11. Learn to be a very good listener. Mentoring isn't always about talking; it's as much about listening and analyzing ideas and solutions together. If you do this right, your mentee could become one of your closest advisors and the mentor will learn as much as the mentee.

12. This might be the most important concept of all—provide as much positive feedback and praise as you can to build their confidence. Help them to realize and bolster their gifts and believe in their abilities; self-confidence doesn't build itself; it requires repetition through positive, consistent reinforcement. If they make a mistake, correct them in private and frame it as an opportunity to make better decisions. Remember, we're all works in progress, including the mentor.

CONCLUSION

I f business' new purpose is to elevate humanity, how can we best accomplish this? Mentorship and succession planning certainly offer great hope. Businesses that offer life coaching skills that improve employees and their families' lives also offer optimistic potential. Imagine just how much more successful a company would be if they encouraged everyone, not just their star performers or "heir apparent," to commit to personal growth and helped their staff to discover their "why?"

How Can Business Best Elevate Humanity?

Simon Sinek's 2018 video, *Life Advice Will Change Your Future*, details several significant life-affirming recommendations. He notes the impact on future generations when parents do not feel valued at work. He notes that parents who are marginalized or bullied at work are likely to become parents who bully, leading to kids who bully. Sinek reinforced my belief that we must lead through enlightened leadership skills, which include kindness, empathy, and a generous spirit. I saw that an eternal perspective was likely to evolve from multi-generational workplace mentorship and friendships.

Sinek provides many examples of how coworkers and managers can work together to inspire loyalty, build community, teach confidence, and inspire each other to do good—when "we do good for others, we inspire them to do good too." It creates a virtuous circle!

I suspect the concepts promoted in this book and through the grassroots efforts of Conscious Capitalism Inc. will lead to the establishment of these principles as the norm in corporate America. Since talent is one of the main ingredients to corporate success, it just might prove to be the most powerful incentive to change! As awareness grows and more organizations learn about the numerous benefits generated from becoming a conscious business enterprise, organizations that fail to adapt may very well struggle even to survive.

> *Organizations that fail to adapt to generational drivers may very well struggle even to survive.*

As we emerge from the challenging societal situation caused by COVID-19, what if we took the time to genuinely help people fill their emotional tanks and create a more positive internal narrative?

In writing the ICE story, I came to realize my highest and best purpose in retirement was not limited to simply sharing ICE's mentorship journey and the gratification of establishing a successful succession plan. Instead, my increased understanding of leading with the principles of the conscious capitalism movement had helped me visualize the next evolution of "conscious leadership."

I am looking forward to the retirement stage of my life. It is the fruit of all my work. I have an opportunity to give back, to seek unity, and to elevate humanity. Being vulnerable is a gift, if for no other reason than to be an example that life isn't about societal success or failure; it's about being the most authentic you possible without the chains of fear of failure. I wish you a life-affirming, abundance-attaining, and life-rocking journey!

A FINAL NOTE

Thank you for making the time in your busy life to read the simple story of ICE. With all the demands in our lives, few people are dedicated enough to read a book to the end, so congratulations. But now, what will you do with these ideas and concepts?

ICE's success is not difficult to recreate, but as with anything in life, in addition to resolute passion and a bit of effort, buy-in is required from all participants, especially leadership, to design and implement a more productive and healthier workplace.

Regardless of whether you are your organization's leader, as long as your organization is forward-thinking, creative, and open to employee input, you can be the catalyst for change. If your organization and its leaders are not open to change and not in alignment with your values, you will never be fully engaged or committed to that company. To live your best life, you will want to find or create a company that reflects your principles.

To create buy-in from leadership, you first need to share your vision. If leadership is flexible and desires to better inspire and connect with staff, it might consider change. You will need to create answers to these questions before approaching leadership. Remember, "First seek to understand and then be understood." For buy-in to happen, you need to anticipate and understand leadership's concerns and anticipate the answers to these questions:

- *Understand leadership's pain points.* What's in it for leadership and the organization? Is it employee retention and attraction? Is it higher profitability? Are the organization's leaders looking to craft a succession plan, or do they desire to work less and delegate more with complete confidence that the organization will maintain profitability, resilience, and continuity? Do they need to attract more clients or a more diverse client base? Are they struggling with lack of, or poor, brand recognition? Ask appropriate questions to build confidence and earn a reputation as a thoughtful, other-focused, and committed employee.

- Once you understand the organization's short-term and long-term needs, write up a plan to achieve organizational objectives. Work with a mentor or coach to craft this plan. It needs to be as professional as possible. Learn to think and act like an owner and you will be treated as one if you are in an organization that is forward thinking and aligned with your principles.

- Be positive and receptive to honest feedback; make the decision to learn from it, not to be offended or intimidated. Leadership's job is to punch holes and question unproven or new theories, concepts, and belief systems. If the organization's leaders are very traditional, they may not have had the good fortune to experience working in an empowered workplace and need to understand (again) "What's in it for me? Why do we need to change?"

- Work with a coach or mentor to role-play the presentation of your strategy so you become comfortable with push-back, communicating your ideas, and creating consensus.

- If appropriate, and with respectful caution, organize others in the company to vet, craft, and even present your blueprint for success. If you think this effort might be misconstrued, present to management what you're working on, get their buy-in, and build excitement so that employees will want to make the workplace function even more robustly. Leaders are far more able and eager to "tone down" passion than they are to deal with apathy and poor attitudes. Just remember, this is not about making others wrong, minimalizing their work, or making people feel as if they're failing; it's about improving and lifting up the organization to a higher level of excellence. Use words judiciously, and again, role-play with others to fine-tune your message and delivery.

- Many heads are better than one because they are more likely to solve a problem, discover new solutions, design an exciting path forward, and help each other succeed. Create synergy and excitement, not competition and marginalization. Read body language and be sensitive to what others might be hearing.

- Give management a copy of this book or any other book that promotes conscious leadership and the workplace of the future, or download some of my tips, articles, or this book's overview from my website www.DeLindaForsythe.com. If leadership and the organization you work at are open to change and improvement, it really is about education and expanding understanding.

If you are the leader and you're eager to implement some of these ideas but you need more help organizing and galvanizing your team, hire an outside coach or consultant to come alongside you to develop your blueprint for success. It is easier than you think to develop a culture of excellence. The nurturing and maintaining of it is what presents the bigger challenge.

As with every healthy relationship, a thoughtful plan and consistent maintenance will be required to keep it robust, but the effort pays enormous, immeasurable dividends. The benefits include a built-in succession plan, legacy consistency, resiliency during crisis, and committed loyalty from employees and customers. Higher profitability often results with a more energized and committed employee base.

Knowledge Is Not Powerful—
Applied Knowledge Is Powerful!

Finally, I challenge you—if your heart is telling you that the story of ICE—how we created a business model for people to personally and emotionally thrive—resonates with you, do something with that passion! Figure out how you can promote conscious capitalism in your community, at your workplace, at your place of worship, and with your children—share it everywhere you can. Use this formula to really learn this content:

- READ: Educate yourself by reading as many books as possible about the principles of conscious capitalism and get engaged in your local chapter.
- WRITE: Capture your notes in a book report.
- SPEAK: Share the ideas and notes with others—teach the concepts.

If you want to become a change agent for good in your world, please go to my website for additional free information and suggestions: www. DeLindaForsythe.com. You can also request a free consultation with me at the website. I'd love to help you craft a roadmap to create your own success.

Equally, I would enjoy learning if this book was helpful or how it can be improved for the next printing. Feedback, positive or negative, is of benefit to everyone. Email your thoughtful and helpful ideas to delinda@ delindaforsythe.com.

I wish you tremendous success and prosperity in life.

Your Friend,

DeLinda Forsythe

ADDITIONAL RESOURCES

Books

Athena Rising by W. Brad Johnson and David G. Smith

Become a Better You by Joel Osteen

Bringing Meaning into Monday by Mark D. Sauter

Community Before Self by Malin Burnham

Conscious Capitalism by John Mackey and Raj Sisodia

Conscious Leadership by John Mackey, Steve McIntosh, and Carter Phipps

Dare to Lead and *Daring Greatly* by Brené Brown

Firms of Endearment by Raj Sisodia, David B. Wolfe and Jay Sheth

Fierce Conversations by Susan Scott

Gathering Around the Table by Kari Warberg Block

It's Not What You Sell, It's What You Stand for by Roy M. Spence Jr.

Leading Well from Within by Daniel Friedland

Mentoring 101 by John Maxwell

Nurturing Our Humanity by Riane Eisler and Douglas P. Fry

Raving Fans by Ken Blanchard and Sheldon Bowles

Rehumanizing the Workplace by Rosie Ward and Jon Robison

Reimagining Capitalism in a World on Fire by Rebecca Henderson

Start with Why by Simon Sinek

StrengthsFinder 2.0 by Tom Rath

The 7 Habits of Highly Effective People by Stephen R. Covey

The ABCs of Conscious Capitalism for KIDs by Laura Hall

The One Minute Manager and *Raving Fans* by Ken Blanchard

The Purpose Driven Life by Rick Warren

The Rainforest: The Secret to Building the Next Silicon Valley by Victor W. Hwang and Greg Horowitt
Unleash Your Rising by Christine Gail

Podcasts, TEDx Talks
Brené Brown – anything from Brené Brown
Simon Sinek – anything from Simon Sinek
Ravi Rai
Tim Ferris Tribe of Mentors

Websites
Please go to www.delindaforsythe.com for free tips, exercises, videos, articles and websites for additional information on:
- Conscious Capitalism
- John Assaraf
- Nick Unsworth Life on Fire
- Unleash Your Rising

ABOUT THE AUTHOR

DeLinda Forsythe has been an executive and entrepreneur in the contract furniture industry for more than three decades. By far the most rewarding portion of those years started in 2006 when she was able to realize her dream of creating a workplace that allowed employees to thrive and reach their potential not only at work but as individuals and parents.

DeLinda field-tested her intuitive leadership philosophies as CEO and Founder of Innovative Commercial Environments (ICE) for fifteen years and was able to actualize her highest purpose in life and business—serving others. DeLinda has found great success mentoring Millennial employees, discovering that she learned as much as they did. Along with Millennial coworkers and workplace consultants, she was able to design and craft the workplace she aspired to work at. She visualized an office that provided a distinctive culture and experience for employees, customers, and vendor and supplier partners, as well as the San Diego community she loves and calls home.

ICE continues to evolve and is considered to be San Diego's "most creative office furniture dealership." During 2013-2020, ICE experienced unprecedented revenue growth; in an industry that historically experiences single digit growth, ICE has been an *Inc. 5000 winner seven times*; only 1.5 percent of all US firms have experienced this kind of consistent revenue growth. This accomplishment sent DeLinda into an eighteen-month research mission to understand *why*. Her research introduced her to the Conscious Capitalism movement and inspired her first book, *Inspiring Generational Leadership: Your Guide to Design a Conscious Culture*.

DeLinda has contributed to numerous non-profit organizations, serving on many boards that support her local business community, including being Chair of the San Diego Economic Development Foundation. She serves the conscious capitalism movement as a Founding Member of the Senior Leadership Network, in a Mastermind Group, and in her local Conscious Capitalism San Diego chapter. *The San Diego Business Journal* has repeatedly acknowledged Ms. Forsythe as one of the Top 500 Most Influential People in San Diego.

DeLinda and her husband, Tom Forsythe, live a purpose-filled life, enjoying philanthropy, spiritual development, and exploring the great outdoors in their RV with each other, their children, and grandchildren. This quote captures DeLinda's heart:

> *I slept and dreamt that life was joy. I awoke and saw that life was service.*
> *I acted and behold, **service was joy**.*
> **—Rabindranath Tagore**

ENDNOTES

1   https://www.fortunebuilders.com/san-diego-real-estate-market-trends/. Accessed November 27, 2020.

2   https://sbecouncil.org/ and https://www.cbsnews.com/news/black-owned-busineses-close-thousands-coronavirus-pandemic/. Accessed August 20, 2020.

3   https://www2.deloitte.com/cn/en/pages/about-deloitte/articles/2019-millennial-survey.html. Accessed November 27, 2020.

4   https://en.wikipedia.org/wiki/Republicanism_in_the_United_States. Accessed August 12, 2020.

5   https://news.gallup.com/businessjournal/26068/four-drivers-innovation.aspx. Accessed August 4, 2020.

6   https://news.gallup.com/businessjournal/151499/business-good-friends.aspx. Accessed August 12, 2020.

7   https://www.thestandupphilosophers.co.uk/philosophical-virtues-humility/. Accessed August 4, 2020.

8   https://www2.deloitte.com/content/dam/Deloitte/global/Documents/About-Deloitte/gx-dttl-2014-millennial-survey-report.pdf. Accessed August 19, 2020.

9   https://www.brookings.edu/wp-content/uploads/2016/06/brookings_winogradfinal.pdf. Accessed December 9, 2020.

10   https://www2.deloitte.com/us/en/pages/about-deloitte/articles/millennial-survey.html. Accessed December 9, 2020.

11   https://www2.deloitte.com/tr/en/pages/about-deloitte/articles/millennialsurvey-2018.html. Accessed December 9, 2020.

12   https://www2.deloitte.com/cn/en/pages/about-deloitte/articles/2019-millennial-survey.html. Accessed December 9, 2020.

13   https://www2.deloitte.com/global/en/pages/about-deloitte/articles/millennial-

survey.html. Accessed December 9, 2020.

14   www.consciouscapitalism.com. Accessed August 12, 2020.

15   https://victimsofcommunism.org/annual-poll/2019-annual-poll/. Accessed August 4, 2020.

16   Ibid.

17   https://www.heritage.org/international-economies/commentary/social-ism-vs-capitalism-one-clear-winner

https://www.aei.org/economics/political-economy/dont-tell-bernie-sanders-but-capitalism-has-made-human-life-fantastically-better-heres-how/

https://www.aier.org/article/socialism-will-deprive-you-of-what-you-need-to-survive/

https://foreignpolicy.com/2020/01/15/socialism-wont-work-capitalism-still-best/. All accessed August 19, 2020.

18   https://www2.deloitte.com/content/dam/Deloitte/global/Documents/About-Deloitte/gx-millenial-survey-2016-exec-summary.pdf. Accessed December 9, 2020.

19   https://www.youtube.com/watch?v=5MC2X-LRbkE. Accessed February 25, 2021.

20   Personal interview. August 3, 2020.

21   *The 7 Habits of Highly Effective People (25th Anniversary Edition)*. New York: Simon & Schuster, 2013. p. 198.

22   Personal interview. Sept. 4, 2020.

23   https://www.forbes.com/sites/annapowers/2018/06/27/a-study-finds-that-diverse-companies-produce-19-more-revenue/#1ea22fdd506f. Accessed November 27, 2020.

24   http://www.leadershipexpert.co.uk/importance-ethics-leadership.html. Accessed November 27, 2020.

25   https://online.olivet.edu/research-statistics-on-professional-mentors. Accessed November 27, 2020.

26   https://www.forbes.com/sites/forbesbusinesscouncil/2020/02/10/the-power-of-female-mentors-why-we-need-more-women-leading-todays-workforce/#fba56492d896. Accessed November 25, 2020.

27   *Athena Rising*. New York: Bibliomotion, p. 140.

28   http://business360.fortefoundation.org/male-mentorship-is-key-ingredi-ent-in-womens-success/. Accessed November 25, 2020.

29   Personal interview October 2020.

30   https://www.nytimes.com/2021/06/10/style/what-is-phexxi.html?searchResult-Position=1. Accessed June 17, 2021.

31   Personal interview October 2020.

32   https://www.forbes.com/sites/susanadams/2013/07/01/leadership-lessons-a-career-protecting-women/#7c6258782cf4. Accessed November 25, 2020.

33   https://www.nytimes.com/2021/06/10/style/what-is-phexxi.html?searchResult-Position=1. Accessed June 17, 2021.

34   https://brenebrown.com/blog/2013/01/14/shame-v-guilt/. Accessed December 10, 2020.

35   https://ideas.ted.com/finding-our-way-to-true-belonging/. Accessed December 10, 2020.

36   https://www.workhuman.com/company/. Accessed November 23, 2020.

37   https://www.whartonhealthcare.org/the_neuroscience_of_gratitude. Accessed November 23, 2020.

38   https://positivepsychology.com/neuroscience-of-gratitude/. Accessed November 24, 2020.

39   https://aifs.gov.au/sites/default/files/publication-documents/WP21.pdf. Accessed November 27, 2020.

40   https://kilroyrealty.com/property/one-paseo. Accessed February 26, 2021.

41   https://www.cnbc.com/2019/10/07/billionaire-richard-branson-dyslexia-helped-me-to-become-successful.html. Accessed November 27, 2020.

42   https://resources.careerbuilder.com/small-business/does-emotional-intelligence-matter-when-hiring. Accessed November 27, 2020.

43   https://www.fastcompany.com/90272895/5-reasons-empathy-is-the-most-important-leadership-skill. Accessed November 27, 2020.

44   https://medschool.ucla.edu/body.cfm?id=1158&action=detail&ref=1494. Accessed November 27, 2020.

45   https://brenebrown.com/blog/2018/10/15/clear-is-kind-unclear-is-unkind/. Accessed November 28, 2020.

46   Personal Interview. February 3, 2021.

47   https://www.researchgate.net/publication/247717438_Petty_Tyranny_in_Organizations. Accessed November 27, 2020.

48   https://chiefexecutive.net/defining-the-entrepreneurial-spirit/. Accessed Febru-

ary 26, 2021.

49   Personal Interview. January 24, 2021.

50   https://www.gallup.com/cliftonstrengths/en/249602/learning-clifton-strengths-don-clifton.aspx. Accessed November 23, 2020.

51   https://www.gettysburg.edu/news/stories?id=79db7b34-630c-4f49-ad32-4ab9ea48e72b&pageTitle=1%2F3+of+your+life+is+spent+at+work. Accessed December 14, 2020.

52   https://papers.ssrn.com/sol3/papers.cfm?abstract_id=2840005. Accessed December 14, 2020.

53   https://www.newsweek.com/people-sense-purpose-live-longer-study-suggests-1433771. Accessed November 24, 2020.

54   https://www.forbes.com/sites/margiewarrell/2017/05/30/feeling-stuck-take-zuckerbergs-advice-and-commit-to-a-purpose-bigger-than-yourself/?sh=2b2552877462

55   Personal interview. January 18, 2021.

56   https://hbr.org/2018/10/if-humility-is-so-important-why-are-leaders-so-arrogant. Accessed November 25, 2020.

57   https://hbr.org/1992/05/the-new-boundaries-of-the-boundaryless-company. Accessed November 25, 2020.

58   https://www.forbes.com/sites/kimelsesser/2020/01/23/goldman-sachs-wont-take-companies-public-if-they-have-all-male-corporate-boards/#34b2e4ba9475. Accessed November 27, 2020.

59   Personal Interview. October 26, 2020.

60   https://www.goalcast.com/2018/06/18/5-lessons-brene-brown-the-power-of-vulnerability/. Accessed November 27, 2020.

61   www.myneurogym.com. Accessed February 20, 2021.

62   https://www2.deloitte.com/global/en/pages/about-deloitte/articles/millennial-survey.html. Accessed November 25, 2020.

63   https://www.forbes.com/sites/larissafaw/#371646834f9b. Accessed November 27, 2020.

64   https://hbr.org/1992/05/the-new-boundaries-of-the-boundaryless-company. Accessed November 25, 2020.

65   https://luckyattitude.co.uk/millennial-characteristics/. Accessed November 27, 2020.

66   https://www2.deloitte.com/content/dam/Deloitte/global/Documents/

About-Deloitte/gx-dttl-2014-millennial-survey-report.pdf. Accessed August 19, 2020.

67   www.clutch.com. Accessed November 27, 2020.

68   www.thealexandria.com. Accessed November 27, 2020.

69   Hwang, Victor W. and Greg Horowitt. *The Rainforest: The Secret to Building the Next Silicon Valley*. Los Altos Hills, CA: Regenwald, 2012. p. 16.

70   Ibid. p. 16.

71   https://united-states-studies-centre.s3.amazonaws.com/attache/28/b6/e2/b3/7c/fe/a4/32/3f/4f/f6/07/26/b4/11/1e/BT3.pdf. Accessed November 27, 2020.

72   https://www.voiceofsandiego.org/topics/news/how-san-diego-biotech-started-and-where-its-going/. Accessed November 27, 2020.

73   https://www.naiop.org/en/Research-and-Publications/Magazine/2019/Fall-2019/Development-Ownership/Alexandria-Real-Estate-Equities-People-Passion-Purpose. Accessed November 27, 2020.

74   https://www.managementmattersnetwork.com/notable-quotable/articles/don-clifton. Accessed November 27, 2020.

75   https://medium.com/authority-magazine/gallup-chairman-and-ceo-jim-clifton-great-leaders-have-a-higher-purpose-than-just-profit-9c5772388e4. Accessed November 27, 2020.

A free ebook edition is available with the purchase of this book.

To claim your free ebook edition:

1. Visit MorganJamesBOGO.com
2. Sign your name CLEARLY in the space
3. Complete the form and submit a photo of the entire copyright page
4. You or your friend can download the ebook to your preferred device

Print & Digital Together Forever.

Snap a photo

Free ebook

Read anywhere